PATHER PANCHALI

Bibhutibhushan Bandopadhyay was born in 1894 in Muratipur, a small village about hundred miles north of Calcutta. Bandopadhyay attended a local village school, and his education would have ended there but for the assistance of a local benefactor whose generosity made it possible for him to attend high school. In 1914 he passed the Matriculation examination and was admitted to Ripon College, Calcutta, from where he graduated in 1918. He took up teaching as his profession and, but for short intervals in which he worked as a cattle inspector and then as a clerk, he continued as a teacher for the greater part of his life. He died in November 1950.

His first publication was a short story which appeared in a Calcutta journal in 1922. From then on he wrote regularly. He is credited with fifty published works, seventeen of which are novels and twenty, collections of short stories. His greatest work, however, and that which brought him fame is *Pather Panchali*. It first appeared serially in the journal *Vichitra*, but was published in book form in November 1929. Since then six other editions have been published including two abridged versions for children.

T.W. Clark and Tarapada Mukherji are both teachers of Bengali at the School of Oriental and African Studies in the University of London.

PATHER PANCHALI

SONG OF THE ROAD

Bibhutibhushan Bandopadhyay

Translated into the English by
T.W. Clark and Tarapada Mukherji

HarperCollins *Publishers* India
a joint venture with

New Delhi

HarperCollins *Publishers* India
a joint venture with
The India Today Group

Copyright © Sahitya Akademi
English Translation Copyright © UNESCO

First published 1968
First published by HarperCollins *Publishers* India 1999

Eighth impression 2006

Cover photograph Copyright © Sandip Ray

ISBN 13: 978 81 7223 333 4
ISBN 10: 81 7223 333 7

HarperCollins *Publishers*
1A Hamilton House, Connaught Place, New Delhi 110 001, India
77-85 Fulham Palace Road, London W6 8JB, United Kingdom
Hazelton Lanes, 55 Avenue Road, Suite 2900, Toronto, Ontario M5R 3L2
and 1995 Markham Road, Scarborough, Ontario M1B 5M8, Canada
25 Ryde Road, Pymble, Sydney, NSW 2073, Australia
31 View Road, Glenfield, Auckland 10, New Zealand
10 East 53rd Street, New York NY 10022, USA

Printed and bound at
Thomson Press (India) Ltd.

CONTENTS

THE AUTHOR'S NAME

⋘◉⋙

Some Bengali Brahmins spell their family names in two ways. The author of this book is variously known as Bandyopadhyay or Banerji. The former is used on formal occasions, in documents, etc., the latter is used in speech, and consequently it has become the accepted anglicized version of the name. For this latter reason, and because Banerji is easier for a foreign reader to pronounce than Bandyopadhyay, we have adopted the spelling of Banerji.

INTRODUCTION

Bibhutibhushan Banerji, the author of *Pather Panchali*, was born on 12 September 1894, in Muratipur, a village north of Calcutta and not far from Kanchrapara. He died on 1 November 1950. His ancestors lived originally in Panita in the 24 Parganas; but his great grandfather, who was a village doctor, moved to Nangram in the Barrackpore district, which from then on remained the family home. Bibhutibhushan's father, Mahananda Banerji, earned a precarious living as a family priest and by singing traditional songs, for which, because he had a good voice, he won a considerable local reputation. Mrinalini Devi, the author's mother came from Muratipur. The family was very poor, because though Mahananda was a talented man, he was impractical and apparently incapable of earning enough to support them. Mrinalini Devi was often at her wits' end to provide even the barest subsistence for her household, which included an old widowed relative, Menaka Devi.

Banerji's education began at a local village school, but later with financial assistance from a benefactor he moved to a high school at Nangram, where in 1914 in spite of difficulties caused by his extreme indigence he was placed in the first class of the matriculation list. Thereupon he was admitted to Ripon College in Calcutta; and in 1916 he secured a first class pass in the intermediate examination, and two years later was awarded a B.A. degree. About this time he married but his wife died shortly afterwards. His career was varied. After graduation he became a teacher; then he was appointed inspector to the Society for the Protection of Cattle, and later he became a clerk in an estate office. Finally however, he returned to his first profession, and continued as a teacher for the rest of his working life. He married a second time in 1940 and had one son.

His first literary venture was a short story, *Upeksita,* which was published in 1922 by the Calcutta journal *Pravasi.* A list compiled by the Bengal Library credits him with fifty published works. Of these, seventeen were novels, twenty volumes of short stories, and the remainder a miscellaneous collection, including autobiographical writings, travel books, at least one of famous stories from other lands, a Bengali grammar, a translation of *Ivanhoe,* and some excursions into astrology and the occult, a subject which always fascinated him.

In assessing Banerji's stature as a writer, account must be taken of his popularity in Bengal. His fifty published works, of which over twelve ran to a second edition and three or four to a third, testify to the regard in which he was held by his own people. *Pather Panchali* however was without

question his greatest achievement. It was first issued serially
in the journal *Vichitra*, in 1928 and 1929; and in November
1929 it appeared in book form. Since then six other editions
have been printed, including two abridged versions for children,
one of which is now prescribed as a text book for schools.
A film version of the story was produced by Satyajit Ray. It
was enormously popular in Bengal, and won international
fame by being granted an award at the Cannes Film Festival,
since when it has toured successfully in many Western countries.
There is little doubt that Banerji's reputation was established
by *Pather Panchali,* his first major work, and it is probable that
much of the success of his later writings was due to its popularity.
None of them including *Aparajito,* the sequel to *Pather Panchali,*
was received with anything like the same enthusiasm; and I
suspect that some of them might have attracted little notice
apart from the glory reflected on them by that first great
masterpiece. Banerji ranks as one of the greatest of the twentieth
century prose writers in Bengali, a company which includes
Rabindranath Tagore and Saratchandra Chatterji; but his fame,
unlike theirs, rests in large measure on the high quality and
lasting appeal of this one work, *Pather Panchali.*

The immediate appeal of *Pather Panchali,* which the
passage of time has done nothing to weaken, can in the main
be attributed to two factors; first, its vivid, moving and
utterly authentic portrayal of village people and their day
to day life; secondly the fact that the subject was presented
through the minds, eyes and lips of a small boy and his sister.
Opu and Durga are real, live children. They think, behave
and talk at all times like children, and the Bengalis took them
to their hearts at once. Few authors in any literature can rival
Banerji in his understanding of, and sympathy for, the nature
of a child; and he writes without any trace of adult
condescension. Village life had been painted before by

Bengali writers; with convincing realism by Saratchandra, though he does not refrain from critical and sometimes searing comment, and romantically by Tagore, who presents village life nostalgically as an ideal condition which the modern age is fast losing. In *Pather Panchali* the village is not idealized; it is not explained or commented on; it is presented as it is, objectively at times, but more often subjectively, by the people who live in it, and in particular by the two children. There is little formal description. It is not necessary to describe the things one lives with every day; one knows them, as the reader comes to know the village of Nishchindipur, through familiarity.

The title is untranslatable. The first word *pather* is the genitive case of a noun which means *road;* but the second word has no equivalent in English. It is the name of a class of long narrative poems which form a large part of medieval Bengali literature, comprising the vernacular versions of the two great epics of Indian tradition and the corpus of poems, also of epic length, which are known as *mangalkavya*. These poems (*panchali*) were transmitted from generation to generation by singers who chanted them with musical accompaniment at the appropriate ceremonies, which often lasted for ten days or more, or by actors who produced them in popular form on the stage of the indigenous theatre. The heroes, and the episodes in which they figure, were part and parcel of the Bengali cultural inheritance, and still are. One thinks of the story of Karna, one of the warriors of the Mahabharat, which so deeply moved Opu, the boy hero of *Pather Panchali*, and of the incident from the jatra play of the banished king and his two children.

Song of the Road has been used as a subtitle to *Pather Panchali*, because the Bengalis who have been consulted tend to feel that, in spite of its manifest inadequacy, it is the nearest one can get by way of translation; but were I free to ignore the exigencies of translation and choose an English title more in keeping with the content and spirit of Banerji's novel, I should prefer *Bends in the Road,* a phrase which occurs in several places in the text. It retains, as the original does, the symbolism of a road broken into a series of stretches divided from one another by bends which conceal what lies ahead. This symbolism of a road viewed in segments conforms also with the episodic structure of the book. The characters walk along wondering what the road has in store for them round the next bend. Some of the stretches are lush with grass and fruit, gay with flowers and bird-song; but others are hard under foot and strewn with thorns, sometimes white-hot with the summer heat, sometimes lashed by storms and darkened by threatening clouds; though always there is hope that the air will be kinder and the going less arduous further on. There is frequently a discontinuity in the narrative from chapter units; but the road is one, in spite of changes of mood, scene and incident. The events in the story too are separated from one another in time, in places by only an hour or so, in others by a lapse of years; but Opu and Durga still walk on, growing continuously in character and experience and in the nature of their dreams and their hopes for the future. They encounter other travellers on their journey, some of whom go with them along several stretches of the road, others whom they meet only once; but all leave their marks on the lives of the principals and strengthen the emotional impulses which drive them on. These subsidiary characters are vividly portrayed. There is old Indir, Durga's auntie whom she can never forget, Opu's Vaisnava grandpa, Proshonno the schoolmaster, who wielded the cane so expertly and recited so beautifully, Ajoy the child actor, the desperately unhappy widow of Tomrej, the callous and selfish Onnoda Ray, and the pathetic little Gulki, to mention only some.

The principal characters are four, of whom Opu and Durga hold first place. The story is about them; and the reader lives and grows with them, feels with and for them, looks through their eyes, and knows the worlds and the people in it as they know them. The other principals are the parents of Opu and Durga, Shorbojoya and Horihor and their poor and dilapidated home, and the village Nishchindipur, with its galaxy of children, women and men on the one hand, and on the other, portrayed so often as personified beings, the trees, fruits and flowers; the paths through the village, past the houses, down to the bathing steps, through the jungle and across the open country; the birds, the sky, the clouds and Opu's constant friend, the evening sun.

Occasionally the scene is set outside Nishchindipur, as when Opu goes away with his father and meets Omola, or when Horihor is looking for work at Krishnagar; but in a very real sense they are still at home. Opu's mind at every turn harks back to Durga and Shorbojoya; and his family's plight is never out of Horihor's mind. Even when Opu in imagination soars into the far distances of the sky or follows the road of his dreams beyond the horizon, he rushes back and throws his arms around his mother. Herein lies the unity of the book. In spite of its episodic structure and its occasional abrupt transitions from one incident to another, it is emotionally coherent, and its narrative is integrated about the children in their village. Yet it would appear that the author achieved this coherence, this dramatic unity, without fully realizing that he had done so; for having brought the story to a point of climax he does not end, but continues with chapters which emotionally and dramatically belong to the sequel. The climax surely is reached when Opu and his parents leave Nishchindipur; and what follows, if the reader goes on with it, is something of an anticlimax. When the train journey to Benares begins, the cast has already broken up. For Opu the road goes on; but Durga, his home and his village, are now finally left behind. As the train draws away from the station the last chords of the symphony are struck, and the rest should be silence.

With these considerations in mind we have ended *Pather Panchali* with Opu looking out of the train window sobbing his goodbyes to his sister, his home and his village. This decision finds corroboration in a like decision by others who have in different ways been concerned with the presentation of our story. Satyajit Ray, who produced the filmed version, chose to end at this same point; as did Sajanikanta Das who abbreviated the book for children. We are informed also that the Sahitya Akademi, New Delhi, and the French translator of the text, concur with this placement of the conclusion and the reasons which have determined it. Why was the author of another mind? This question is difficult to answer; but the title *Pather Panchali* may provide a clue. The audience who listened to the chanting of the old panchalis, which went on from day to day, were so enthralled by the immediate present, by the incident which was being chanted to them at any one time, that few of them could have given any thought to the structure of the work as a whole. It had to run its course, episode by episode; and it was the episodes which were to them important. So I suggest it was with Banerji. His naïve genius could not have realized the dramatic quality of his creation. He could only see himself as the author of a panchali which had to go on from situation to situation without thought of a climax. It may also be that he had lived so long with Opu, as we shall see later, that he could not be parted from him.

The merits of Banerji's work rests on the ease with which it is written, with its naturally executed changes of style, and on the vivid and sympathetic realism of its portrayal of the day to day life of the two children, their parents and the other members of the village community. Its naturalness, its realism and its faithfulness in detail would seem in large measure to derive from the autobiographical foundations which underlie its conception. The author was able to live in Opu and make him so convincing, because in a very true sense he was Opu. Opu's childhood was a reflection of his own, and Opu's environment a reproduction of that in which he himself grew up, for Nishchindipur was no purely fictitious village. He tells us in one of his diaries that he modelled Shorbojoya on his own mother, both of whom bore throughout their lives the burden of crushing poverty. Mahananda Banerji, his father, was an unpractical scholar and dreamer, a man who in spite of his obvious talents was found wanting in the ordinary duties of a father and husband. This was the cloth Horihor was cut from. In his diaries too the author makes mention of an older sister, who was probably a cousin and not his own sister. The diary references however leave us in no doubt that his 'didi', as he calls her, had all those qualities which Opu loved so deeply in Durga, the same motherly kindness and capacity for happiness, and even the same dry hair. The old aunt was there too in Menaka Devi, the aged widowed relative, who lived with the Banerji family.

In one of his novels Bankimchandra Chatterji explains to his readers that it is an author's privilege to penetrate the minds of his characters and set forth their inmost thoughts; and how tedious, banal and predictable those thoughts so often are! In *Pather Panchali* too we know what Opu is thinking, but how differently Banerji handles those moments of introspection! Opu's thoughts and fancies, his games and impersonations, are projections of the author's own, as are his love of trees, roads and rivers, his hopes for the future, his love of stories and his interest in magic. In them all we sense the truth of actual experience, without which they could so easily have degenerated into unconvincing and mawkish sentiment. It should not be supposed that *Pather Panchali* is pure autobiography, but it is near enough to it to breathe a realism which pure fiction, even the greatest, can seldom achieve.

Once the reader is embarked upon the second section he will sense a marked difference between it and the former. Part II is based on the life itself; Part I on hearsay. Opu was born in Part I, but he was not old enough to participate consciously in the life of the world around him until the first chapter of Part II, and he learned the stories of the past piecemeal by report. Part I is casually organized and disjointed. There are abrupt transitions from the present to the past and back again to the present, and many of the episodes narrated are laconic in brevity. Even the paragraphs in places are isolated units, rather than items in an integrated and continuous whole. Banerji seldom explains. He tells what happened, and leaves the reader to integrate the different incidents as he reads on, to weave them for himself into the fabric of the whole. For the book has unity, and the contributions of Part I to that unity are significant though it is not always easy to see their immediate relevance. Two examples spring particularly to mind. Indir Thakrun dies her sad and cruel death, but the reader will later in the book be driven to reflect whether the 'way' she walked, and the happy consummation she failed to achieve for all her seventy years of searching, are not the same 'way' and the same failure we see in the life of Shorbojoya. Do we not feel sometimes that the 'unseen arbiter' may be visiting Shorbojoya's sins of inhumanity on her own head and those of her children? Secondly there is the curse of Biru Ray. Horihor was the first eldest son to survive the curse of God which brought Biru Ray's son and the sons of his brothers to a premature death. But had the curse completely worked itself out? Was the amulet fully successful in warding off disaster? Did not its power live on in Horihor's congenital inability to face up to the realities of life and make reasonable provisions for his wife and children? These questions are never answered; but they brood over the second section with a nagging persistence and imbue with deeper darkness the clouds of tragedy which so often sweep over the village sky.

In preparing a translation of *Pather Panchali* for the English reader three problems in particular had to be solved, two of a technical nature, the third cultural. First, personal names required transliteration, and the method adopted is deliberately inconsistent. The names of the principal characters, common objects and places are spelt in English in such a way that the reader in saying them can come as close as possible to the Bengali pronunciation. Thus we have *Opu, Horihor, Shorbojoya,* not *Apu, Harihar, Sarvajaya,* which forms, bating diacritics, the Royal Asiatic Society's transcription table would have required. Other words however, including many of Sanskrit origin, have forms which are now established in English orthography. These are kept, e.g. *Calcutta, Laksmi, Krishnagar.* Secondly, trees, flowers, etc., play a prominent part in the book and their names must be retained; but many of them have no popular equivalent in English. Furthermore not all of them have been botanically classified; though even if they had, Latin terms might have made awkward reading. In consequence, where a popular equivalent exists it is used; but in other cases the Bengali name in transliteration is employed, though care has been taken to ensure that the reader is made aware that the reference is to a tree, etc., and where possible what kind of tree, etc., it is.

The cultural problem has proved more difficult. The use of a particular word or phrase in Bengali is sufficient to invoke for a reader of that language a whole sequence of thoughts and related situations, many of which pertain to the prescriptions of his religion. The phrases 'Shrove Tuesday' and 'Christmas tree' would ordinarily require no explanation for the English reader; but they might have no meaning at all to a non-English, non-Christian reader if they were merely transliterated into his language; and a dictionary, if it helped at all, would not furnish the range of allusion an English-speaking Christian would have immediately at call. Similarly, to take a simple Bengali example, the word *ekadaßi,* which occurs in Chapter 1, needs no gloss for the Bengali reader, but the English reader for full comprehension must be told that the term is the name of the eleventh day of the lunar fortnight, when Hindu widows are required to observe a fast. Then too there is the complex business of ritual defilement, which the Hindu is taught from childhood and knows thereafter automatically, but of which the English reader will be ignorant. In a scholarly work explanations could be supplied in footnotes, but such a device would be troublesome in a book like this. Whatever therefore has been deemed necessary to bridge the divide between Bengali and English culture has been written into the text: I hope not obtrusively.

In bringing this work to its final form the translators are indebted to a number of individuals and organizations: to Dr Daniel L. Milton and UNESCO for their advice and encouragement; to the Sahitya Akademi for their continued and helpful interest in the work; to Mrs Bonnie R. Crown of the Asia Society, New York, for arranging simultaneous publication in the USA; and to Satyajit Ray, who lent his advice in the difficult problem of providing a title and a subtitle for the translated work. To all these and to others who have shown practical interest in our pleasing but exacting task, we are happy to record our gratitude.

131, Arthur Road   T. W. Clark
Wimbledon Park, London.

Part I

The Old Aunt

ONE

❦

Horihor Ray was a Brahmin. He lived in a small brick-built house in the village of Nishchindipur. It was the last house at the extreme northern end of the village. He was not well-to-do. All he had to live on was the meagre rent from a tiny plot of land he had inherited from his father and some fees paid to him by a few households he served as family priest.

Indir Thakrun, a distant widowed relative of Horihor's was sitting on the verandah. It was the day after her fast—this was the fast all widows are required to observe on the eleventh day of each fortnight—and she was eating her morning meal of baked rice. Horihor's six-year-old daughter was with her. The child did not say a word; but her eyes were wide open and expectant as she followed every movement of the old woman's hand from the bowl to her mouth. The

3

level of rice in the bowl however fell steadily lower and lower, and the little one became increasingly downcast. Once or twice she came near to asking for some, but could not bring herself to do so. When at last the rice was all gone, the old woman looked at her and exclaimed, 'Oh, my dear, and I haven't left any for you! How thoughtless of me.'

There was disappointment in the girl's eyes but all she said was, 'That's all right, Auntie. You go on with your meal.'

Indir had two large ripe bananas, and she broke one of them in two and gave half to the child. The little one's eyes brightened at once. She took the gift from her auntie's hand and began to munch the fruit slowly and with obvious enjoyment. But not for long. Her mother called out to her from inside the house, 'What are you hanging about there for? Come in here.'

Indir replied, 'Let her be, my dear. She's not doing any harm. She's only sitting here with me. Do let her stay.'

'No!' the mother said sternly. 'It's not right for her to stare at you while you're having your food. I don't like that sort of thing. Get up and come here at once.'

The child got up nervously and went inside.

Indir Thakrun was a very distant relative of Horihor's on his mother's side. Horihor's forbears had lived in the neighbouring village of Bishnupur. His father, Ramchand, lost his first wife at a very young age, and it soon became apparent to his mortification and distress that his father had no intention of arranging a second marriage for him. At first Ramchand was too shy to raise the subject, but after a year or so had elapsed without his father doing anything, he was driven in sheer desperation to employ a variety of weapons, some blunt and direct, others subtle and far from obvious. One day after his midday meal he began to toss about restlessly on his bed—there was nobody in sight, but somebody, he

4

thought, was bound to notice in time—and when somebody did come in and ask him what the matter was, he replied with a whine, 'I've nobody to look after me. Who is there who cares whether I've got a headache or not?' The result of this piece of play-acting was that he was soon married to a girl from Nishchindipur. Shortly afterwards his father died, and Ramchand shut up the house at Bishnupur and moved permanently to Nishchindipur. All this happened while he was still young. On his arrival in Nishchindipur he began to study Sanskrit in the local school—his father-in-law paid the fees and in time he became known as the foremost scholar in the district. He did not however attempt to take up any employment, and there is serious doubt whether he was capable of doing the sort of work that would have earned him a living. For nine months out of the twelve his wife and son stayed with his father-in-law Brojo Chokroborti, while he himself spent most of his days playing dice at Potiram Mukherji's. Nevertheless he never forgot to present himself twice a day at his father-in-law's house at meal times. When it was pointed out to him that he had a wife and a son, and that he ought to make provision for their future, he would reply, 'There's nothing to worry about. If they get no more to eat than the rice that is left on the floor of Brojo Chokroborti's barn, they'll not starve for at least two generations.' Whereupon he turned his attention back to the much more important problem of throwing that five and six which were necessary if he was to defeat his opponent.

After his father-in-law's death, it did not take Ramchand long to realize how wrong he had been to suppose that the rice store would last for ever. He owned practically no land and he had very little money. Being a Brahmin, he had a few religious clients whom he visited from time to time; but the fees they paid him were all the income he had, though somehow it sufficed to support his son. Some time previously a distant relative of Ramchand's had married into the Chokroborti household and come to live with them; and Ramchand contrived to get a little help from him. This relative's son, Nilmoni Ray, was in government service and his work very frequently took him away from home: so in the end he closed down the house in Nishchindipur, which was his now, and went with his old mother to live nearer his work. From then on his house, which was next door to Ramchand's remained empty and soon became derelict.

There is a story that Indir Thakrun had been married to a Kulin Brahmin. Kulins were notorious for multiple marriages, and Indir's husband who apparently had many wives, seldom came to visit her. On the few occasions he did come, he stayed no more than a night or two, and after collecting all the money which custom decreed to be his due, he ticked off the village in his book and went with his coolie to the next village he had married into. In consequence Indir Thakrun had very little memory of her husband. When her father and mother died she got a little food from her brother's house; but unfortunately her brother died too, and at an early age. Some time later Horihor's father Ramchand came and built a house on the site that had belonged to Indir's parents and from then on she became a member of his household. But all that is very old history.

Many years had passed since then. Many generations of water lilies had grown and died in the Shankhari pond. Sitanath Mukherji had planted some new mango trees in what had been the Chokrobortis' garden but they too had become old and died. New families had come to live in some of the houses in the village, but others had been abandoned and were now in ruins. Many Golok Chokrobortis and Brojo Chokrobortis had died and been forgotten: and the clear waters of the Ichamoti, in the endless tides of time, had swept away like a straw or a fleck of foam all the Johnsons and Thomsons of the indigo factory, and all the Mojumdars.

Only Indir Thakrun was still alive, no longer the slim, smiling-faced girl of the year 1833, but an old woman of seventy-five. Her cheeks were sunken; her body bent forward from her waist; and her eyes could not longer make out distant objects as they once did. When any one passed in front of the house, she used to raise her hand to her brow and peer out from under it, a gesture which was intended to convey that she was trying to shield her eyes from the glare of the sun. 'Who is that?' she would say. 'Nobin? Behari? Oh no, it's you Raju!'

How the place had changed within the sight of those eyes! The compound of Brojo Chokroborti was a forest of weeds, and one would never have thought looking at it now that there had ever been a time when the whole village gathered there to celebrate the Lakshmi Festival. What dice playing went on in that vast room every morning and evening! And the bamboo grove, how different it was then! And for the winter festival eighty to ninety pounds of rice used to be ground up for cakes and sweets. If she closed her eyes Indir Thakrun could see it all as before. She could see the wife of the Ray family, beautiful and pure as the goddess Jagaddhatri, grinding all that rice; and because it was part of the ceremony the neighbours gathered round to watch. She could hear the noise of the husker, and see her golden bangles sliding up and down her arms as she worked. Shortly after her own husband's death, that lovely woman used to feed Indir Thakrun with her own hands on the day after the widows' fast. But now she and all the others were gone, and no one was left with whom old Indir could talk and exchange memories.

In time Ramchand, who had taken her into his home, died too. His son Horihor was still only a child. He used to play and jump about on the road that led down to the water's edge. Then one day he climbed into a tamarind tree in the Mukherjis' garden to get at the unripe fruit, and fell and broke his arm. He was in bed for two or three months. That was more recent history. He had married young with great ceremony; but after his father's death he left his ten-year-old bride in her father's house and went away from the district. For eight to ten years they had no news of him, except for a line or two written very infrequently. Once in a while he used to send the old woman a small money order. Difficult though it was, she managed somehow to look after his house; but many a day she had nothing to eat and much of her time was spent begging at the doors of her neighbours.

Some six or seven years ago, after a long absence, Horihor came to Nishchindipur and set up house. He had a small daughter, now almost six, whose love and companionship made these years in Horihor's household seem to Indir like those long past days when she was a young woman and a mother. She wanted no other joys in her straitened existence. The road of her life was an old road. She had walked along it since childhood, and now even the slightest bend in it made her happy, and was an occasion for rejoicing.

She could not bear to let Horihor's little daughter out of her sight. She had once had a daughter of her own—her name was Bishveshvari—who had married young and died shortly afterwards. And now after forty years she had come back from the shores of death to the arms of that lonely mother as Horihor's daughter. In one moment, after forty years, the mother's love which had slept and almost guttered out, revived, with yearning fondness and the hunger of a life now almost at its close, awakened by the shy look in a child's face and the laugh in her innocent eyes.

8

But what she yearned for was not to be. Horihor's wife was very beautiful of face, but she had a most uncertain temper; and what is more, she could not bear the sight of the old woman. To her Indir was an outsider—for no one could say how she was related to the family—who just sat there eating up half their food.

Twice a day at least she quarrelled with the old woman over some trifle or other; and sometimes after they had had a particularly long bout of quarrelling, Indir would take her brass pot under her arm—it was all she had—and say, 'I'm off, young mistress, and if I ever set foot inside this house again … !' But there was sadness in her heart and she used to spend the whole day in the bamboo grove. Towards evening, as soon as she knew about it, the little daughter used to go after her, pull at her sari and say, 'Get up, Auntie, I'll tell Mummy not to scold you any more. Come back, Auntie'; and in the darkness of the evening she used to return to the house holding the child's hand. Shorbojoya, the wife, turned away from her. 'So the old wretch has come back, has she', she commented. 'I suppose she's nowhere else to go to. There's no kitchen fire for her except this one. And she knows it! Yet she had the cheek to say she was going away.' This sort of incident began within a year of Horihor's return to the house, and it was repeated very often.

In the eastern part of Horihor's compound there was a thatched hut, which had lain unrepaired for a long time. It was there that the old woman lived. On a bamboo peg hung two dirty garments, the torn ends of which she had knotted together. She did not sew nowadays because she could no longer see well enough to thread her needle; so when her clothes tore she tied knots in them. To one side of the room there was a frayed grass mat and a few torn baby quilts, crude patchwork affairs. Some torn clothes, which were all she had,

9

were tied up in a bundle. It may be that she was saving them to make into another baby's quilt. But she had no need for quilts now and even if she had her eyes were not strong enough to stitch the rags together. Yet she kept them with great care; and whenever there was a sunny day during the monsoon she took them out and aired them in the sun. In a wicker-work case, also tied up in a bundle, were a few torn red-bordered saris. They had been Bishveshvari's. The old woman had a jar too, made of sheet brass, an earthenware vessel for curds, and a few odd earthenware pots. The brass jar was full of baked rice, some of which she used to grind at night with pestle and mortar and eat a little at a time. In one of her earthenware pots she kept her oil, in another salt, and in a third some date molasses. Shorbojoya did not always give her such things when she asked for them, so she used to take them secretly when Shorbojoya was not looking and hide them in a wicker basket she had got at the time of her marriage.

Shorbojoya hardly ever set foot in the old woman's room, but almost every evening her daughter used to go there and sit on a quilt on the floor of the verandah for hours listening to her auntie's fairy tales. After a while, when she had heard a number of stories, the girl would say, 'Auntie, please tell me that story about the robbers, the one about the robbery at the house in the village fifty years ago!' She had heard it many times before, but every few days it had to be repeated. She was most insistent. She liked to listen to her auntie's ballads as well. Indir Thakrun knew a number of old ballads by heart, and in her young days she had been an object of much admiration with her playmates because she knew so many. She had not had such a good listener for many a long year, and she used to refresh her memory now by reciting all her ballads to her young niece in the evening; and in this way she did not get rusty. She droned through them in a long sing-song chant.

'O Lolita and Chompo, I've a song to sing-o.
Radha's thief wore his ...'

At this point in the line she used to pause and look at
her niece with smiling expectancy. The child who was hanging
on to every word chimed in immediately.

' ... hair in a ring-o ...'

And as she said it she bobbed her head in time and
pronounced 'ring-o' with much more emphasis than necessary.
What fun it all was! The old woman often tried to catch her
out by stopping abruptly before she had got to the end of
a verse. But the child was not to be caught. She remembered
them all.

And when it was quite late her mother called her to
supper, and she got up and went away.

TWO

◦◎◦

Horihor's family had lived originally at Bishnupur. There too dwelt ancient family of the Choudhuris. The Choudhuris were very wealthy people who had induced a few Brahmins to settle in the village by making them grants of land free of all charges. Horihor's ancestor, Bihsnuram Ray, was one of these Brahmins.

At that time British power in the country was not firmly established, and it was dangerous to travel about because the roads were infested with bandits. There were river pirates too. The robber gangs consisted mostly of low-caste people, Goyalas, Bagdis and Bauris. They were tough, strong men, and well-practised in the use of staves and spears: They worshipped a goddess who was known as Kali of the Dacoits, and built temples in her honour. Even today you can see remains of some of these temples on the outskirts of remote villages. By day the bandits lived the lives of ordinary people, but at night they worshipped Kali and issued forth to plunder the home of some householder in a distant village. Many a wealthy family of those days built up its fortune by dacoity; indeed every student of ancient history knows that the wealth of most of the Bengali zamindars today is derived from the gold and jewels that their ancestors looted.

Bishnuram Ray's son, Biru Ray, had this sort of ill reputation. He was the leader of a gang of mercenary thugs whose den was on the bank of a stretch of water known as the Thakurjhi Lake. It lay in the middle of the vast Shonadanga plain not far from the road which ran to the north of Nishchindipur from Chuyadanga through Nawabganj to Taki. The gang used to hide under a huge banyan tree near the lake, and there they murdered unwary wayfarers and stole whatever they had on them. Their method of operation was brutally simple. They first stunned and then killed their victim, and when he was dead they searched his body. It sometimes happened that their dead victim had no money on him at all, in which case they tossed the body into the lake and went back quite unperturbed to their tree in the hope of making good their lost labour at the expense of the next traveller who chanced to come along. The banyan tree still stands in the vast plain to the north of the village, and near the road there is a shallow depression which even today is known as the Thakurjhi Lake. There is no trace of water there now because the lake has been almost completely filled in, but from time to time farmers, ploughing that lowlying piece of land before sowing their rice crop, have been known to turn up human skulls.

There is a story of an old Brahmin from east Bengal and his young son who were returning home from the Kaliganj district by way of Taki and Sripur. It was the month of November. The old man had left home to collect money to help pay for his daughter's marriage, and he had therefore a certain amount of cash on him. He also had some luggage. The two of them had their meal at Horidaspur and took to the road again just after midday, planning to spend the night in an inn at Nawabganj which was some ten miles further on. They were not unaware of the dangers of the highway, but they had miscalculated the time. Days in November are short, and long before they reached Nawabganj the sun had begun to set across the plain of Shonadanga. They hurried as fast as they could but when they came to the Thakurjhi Lake they fell into the hands of the footpads.

As the robbers first struck at him with their staves, the Brahmin screamed and ran away from the road across the open country. They boy ran after him. But he was an old man and his son was only a lad, so they had little chance of outdistancing their attackers, who soon caught up with them and surrounded them. The helpless Brahmin pleaded with them. 'It doesn't matter if you kill me,' he said, 'but spare my son. He is the only male left in the family, and we must have some one to serve our ancestors.' By chance Biru Ray himself was with the gang that night. Recognizing him to be a Brahmin, the terrified old man fell at his feet and prayed earnestly that he would spare the life of his son. The simple fellow did not understand that the thugs were not at all perturbed about his ancestors; what they were perturbed about was the danger that might befall them if they let any of their victims go. So in the darkness of that old autumn night Biru Ray had the bodies of the unfortunate father and son buried together in a winding sheet of weeds and dark grass under the waters of the Thakurjhi Lake; and then he returned home.

Not long after this incident—in fact it was in the following year, 1831 to be precise—at about the time of the autumn festival, Biru Ray and his family were returning home by boat from his father-in-law's house at Holudbere. Their route took them to the Modhumoti across the wide salt flats below Nokipur, and thence, after two days' sailing with the tide, to South Sripur. From there it was only a four-day journey home.

They sailed all of next day and in the evening their boat came to the landing steps at Taki. As they intended to spend the festival at home, they bought what was needed for it in Taki bazar, and spent the night there, setting sail for home next day at dawn. On the afternoon of the second day they beached the boat on a large uninhabited sandbank at the junction of the wide Dholchite canal and the Ichamoti river, to await the tide; and went ashore to prepare a meal. The sandbank was huge, but there was no vegetation on it beyond a few scattered clumps of coarse grass. They were all happy as they settled down to cook, the boatmen on one side of the boat and Biru Ray's family on the other; happy because they were going home, but more particularly so on this occasion because the autumn festival was near at hand, and that is always a time of jollity.

It was a moonlit night, and the water gleamed across the salt flats. There was a slight breeze, and everything seemed to ripple, the grass on the sandbank and the water, and even the sky and the moonlight. Suddenly there was an odd sound, and some of the boatmen stood up from their cooking to see what it was. What they had heard was a movement on the other side of the grass clumps and the indistinct sound of a frightened voice, followed by silence. They were curious and went round behind the long grass to investigate. As they approached the spot they heard a soft swooshing sound and something slithered into the water; but there was not a soul on that side of the sandbank and nothing else they could see either.

While they were trying to puzzle out what it was they had heard, some of the others joined them. Biru Ray heard the noise they were making, and he came too, his servant with him. Then what had happened suddenly dawned on them. Biru Ray's son had been in the boat with them, but where was he now? They recollected that a little while ago, while they were busy cooking, he had wandered off for a walk along the moonlit sand. The faces of the boatmen went pale. They had had experience of these salt marshes, and they knew that large crocodiles used to lurk on the sandbanks behind clumps of grass waiting for their prey. That must have been the noise they had heard. One of those crocodiles had pulled Biru Ray's son down the bank into the water.

They did what they could. They probed around with their punting poles. They cast off the boat and searched the main channel until far into the night. There was weeping and deep lamentation. A year ago at this same evening hour an incident had occurred in the open country near the Thakurjhi Lake. Biru Ray had been a fool; but he knew now by bitter experience that the unseen arbiter of right and wrong is not cheated of his retribution because the deed lies buried under the dark grass of a lake. His way is light even in darkness.

Biru Ray went home, but he did not live long. The consequences of his wicked deed as far as his family was concerned were extraordinary. His only son was dead, but his brothers had sons. The eldest of them however did not live long. They all died of some disease or other before they reached manhood. People said that the curse of Brahma had fallen on the family. When Horihor Ray was born his mother went to worship at the shrine of Tarakeshvar. There with many tears she told her story to a holy man. He gave her a charm. Whether it was because of the power of this charm or because the curse of God, like camphor which evaporates, had lost its potency after two generations, Horihor survived and after all these years was still alive today.

THREE

Some time had elapsed. It was dark and Durga was in bed. Her auntie was not with them, because just over two months ago she had had a quarrel with Shorbojoya and gone off in a huff to stay in the house of a relative who lived in a distant village. Shorbojoya had not been very well and yesterday they had moved her into an outside shed they used as a confinement room. In consequence Durga was left to look after herself. There was nobody to see whether she had anything to eat or when she went to bed, and night after night, when she did get to bed, she cried herself to sleep. Tonight fairly late, she was awakened by the sound of voices outside. Kuruni's mother, the midwife, was standing under the eaves of the roof talking to Nera's grandmother and some other people were with her. They all seemed busy and anxious. Durga lay awake for a while and then tried to get to sleep again.

A breeze had sprung up and was whispering among the bamboos; a light was burning in the confinement room, and somebody was talking. The moonlight shone on the porch verandah, a cool wind blew through the house, and after a few minutes she fell asleep. Later on she was wakened again from her sleep by a noise she could not immediately place. Some one was moving about. Her father came out of his room and ran to the confinement shed talking excitedly. 'How is she? How is it going?' And then a most amazing sound came from the shed. It was her mother's voice. Durga did not know what was happening, and though it was late and she was very sleepy she remained sitting up for a while. She felt frightened. Why was her mother making that extraordinary noise? What were they doing to her mother?

The child remained sitting up a little longer, but as she could not make out what was happening she lay down again and was soon asleep. A few moments passed and she woke up once more. It was a kitten mewing, or something that sounded very like it. Then it came to her in a flash. Her cat had kittens and had hidden them in the broken hearth on the verandah of her auntie's room. Poor darling things! Their eyes were not open yet; and she thought with alarm that the tomcat from next door must have come and was eating them up. That is what the noise was. So heavy with sleep though she was she got up and went as fast as she could out in the dark to her auntie's verandah; but when she put her hand down into the hearth there was the soft fur of the kittens. They were sleeping peacefully, and the tomcat was nowhere to be seen. This left her completely at a loss to know what noise it was that she had heard, so she went back to bed and very soon she was asleep again. Yet even in her sleep she could still hear a kitten whimpering somewhere.

Next morning she sat up and was wiping her eyes when Kuruni's mother, the midwife, came in and said, 'Durga, you had a little brother last night. Do you want to see him? My goodness, what a to-do we had, and how your mother screamed! It was a near thing, I can tell you. I must go and make an offering at the shrine of that saint of ours in Kalipur. He certainly looked after us last night.'

Durga was off like a shot and peeped in at the door of the shed. It was only a lean-to affair, and the walls were made of palm leaves. Her mother was lying right up against the wall fast asleep, and in a quilt by her side lay a creature that was very little bigger than a big glass doll. It looked pink and incredibly tiny. It was asleep too. She could not see very well because of the nasty smoke from the charcoal fire; but she stood there for a while, and as she watched the little thing opened its eyes and blinked around. Then it moved its incredibly small hands and started to cry in a thin high-pitched voice, and she realized at once what it was she had heard last night when she thought there was a kitten crying. It was just like a kitten's cry. From a distance they sounded exactly the same. And as she looked at her brother, so helpless, so incredibly tiny, and very wizened, her young heart filled with love, sympathy and apprehension. She wanted to go in, but Nera's grandmother and Kuruni's mother, the midwife, both told her not to; so she stayed where she was.

As soon as Shorbojoya was able to get up she put Khoka—most baby boys are called Khoka—in a tiny cradle, and his little sister used to sit rocking him and singing him songs. In the evening she told him stories too, and these reminded her of the stories her auntie used to tell her, and her eyes filled with tears. She sang him many of her auntie's songs. From time to time the neighbours came in to have a look at him. They peered down at him and exclaimed, 'A little son is the light of a house! What lovely hair he has! And how fair he is!' And as they went away they would say to another, 'Did you notice his pretty little smile?'

Durga however had only one thought: she longed for her auntie to come and have a look at him. Everybody else came, but not their own auntie. Would she never come back? Child as she was she knew well enough that nobody in the house really loved her auntie, and that neither her father nor her mother would make any effort to get her back again. Often during the day she looked into her auntie's room, and it made her very sad. The door stood open. Bats squeaked in and out of the porch. The yard outside was never swept as it used to be, and weeds and worthless little plants were growing in it. Her auntie, she knew, would never have left them there; and her big eyes filled with tears. How could she ever forget her and her songs and stories!

One day Hori Palit's daughter came and said to Shorbojoya, 'I saw your old auntie near the bank of the pond. She was coming across the fields. She's got her water-pot and bundle with her. She had got as far as the Chokrobortis' house. She must be sitting there still. Why don't you let Durga go for her? If she takes her by the hand and brings her back she won't be angry any more.'

The old woman was sitting in Hori Palit's house, and the children of the neighbourhood were telling her all about Horihor's baby son.

'O Auntie!' The old woman looked up with a start. It was Durga. She was out of breath. She had been running so fast. Auntie stretched her arms out eagerly and the child jumped into her lap, her face wreathed in smiles and her eyes full of tears. All the others who were with them in the yard had tears in their eyes too, all of them, young and old alike. Hori

Palit's wife, a woman well on in years, said to her, 'What did I tell you, Granny? She was your daughter in a previous life, and now she's come back to you again.'

When at last they got to the house and the old woman saw the baby, she had a good cry. 'After all this time the new moon shines in the house,' she said. Next morning she got up and began to sweep the yard, and to pull up all the weeds; and Durga felt that there was happiness in the family now, as there had never been before.

After her midday meal the old lady was sitting at the back of the house near the path that ran through the grove. She was slicing bamboos for her fire. There were no houses between where she was and the river; and the river was not very near. It was about half a mile away. In between lay large mango orchards, groves of bamboos growing in clumps, and wild jungle trees. While Indir was working Durga came and sat beside her, and chattered continuously. As soon as a bundle of sticks was ready, the child carried it into the house and the old woman went on cutting some more, until slowly, as she sat there in the cool shade of the bamboos, there stole over her that comfortable laziness which often comes to one in the middle of the afternoon, and her mind slipped back into the past, that far far distant past which for her held so many memories; and she spoke her memories aloud.

'My husband only came to see me about three times. It all seems like a dream now. Once he brought some food in his bundle. Bishveshvari was two then. I wasn't sure what it was that he had brought, but everybody thought it looked like lumps of sugar; so I took one or two of them, dipped them in the water jar and ate them. Some time after that a man arrived at the house. It was beginning to get dark and I saw him standing under the old guava tree. He had come from my father-in-law's house, and he had a letter in his hand; but there was no one about who could read it for me. My brother Golok had died the year before. So I took it to the dice room in my Uncle Brojo's house. I can see it all clearly still. My two elder uncles, my uncle Brojo, Yodu Ray, the brother of Potit Ray who lived on the other side of the village, and Bhojohori, a relation of my brother Golok's by marriage—they were all there. One of my uncles read the letter. He sat in silence for a moment and then asked, "Who brought this letter, Indir?" After a while they took me into the house. They made me take the bangles off my arms, and the silver wristlets my father and mother had given me—I was so fond of them when I was a girl; and I had to rub the vermilion mark off my forehead and go and bathe in the river. I knew then I was a widow. It all happened so long ago. It seems like a dream now, yet it's as fresh in my mind as if it happened only the other day.'

Then she began to talk about Nibaron. 'Nibaron, Nibaron!' she said. 'He was my uncle Brojo's son. He was sixteen. What lovely hair he had, and what a fair skin! He was in a room on the ground floor of the house—it is no more than a bamboo grove now, and covered with weeds. He was in bed with a high fever, and on the point of death; but he lingered on for a few days more. The poor lad was constantly calling out for water, but Ishan, the village doctor, wouldn't let him have any. He gave us a bag of aniseed instead and told us to let him suck that when he was thirsty. He died on the fourth night, and as he lay dying all he could say was "Water, water!"; but not a drop dare we give him. For five days after his death his mother refused to let any water pass her lips and none of us could persuade her to. In the end, on the fifth day, Ramchand, her husband's elder brother went himself into her room and pleaded with her. "What'll happen to me if you die? I'm an old man and there's nobody but you I can

23

turn to." My aunt was the daughter of a rich and respectable family. She was as beautiful as the goddess Jagadhatri. She had been the most beautiful bride in our district. Yet she would not drink water until her husband had touched it with his foot. That will show you that she was a wife of the good old type. She did all the cooking herself, and then used to feed the whole family and anyone else who was in the house, but she had no food herself until late afternoon, and that too very simple food. She was as generous as Annapurna, the goddess of bounty herself. She loved preparing meals for people and waiting on them. Therefore, because she was this kind of a woman, her brother-in-law's plea touched her sensitive heart, and she got up and began to take water. But she didn't live long. Within eighteen months of her son's death she followed him.'

'Give me some water, Mummy. Just a drop.'

'No, darling. You mustn't drink water. The doctor says it's bad for you.'

'Just a little, Mummy. Only one sip.'

And the gentle swish swish of the bamboos and the songs of many birds came floating together across all those fifty years of the old woman's life.

'You're sleepy, Auntie. Go and lie down.'

Indir had let the knife slip out of her hand. 'Good gracious me!' she said. 'I've been dozing again. I mustn't do that any more at this time of the day. Bring me that big stick from over there, dear.'

FOUR

◦◦◦

The baby was now nearly ten-months old. He was a delicate-looking child, and his face was extraordinarily small. He had only two teeth, both in his lower gum, and when he laughed, which he did very often whether there was a reason for it or not, he showed his gums and the two milk teeth in them. Everybody said to his mother, 'Your baby's always laughing.' And they were right. Once anything set him off there was no stopping him, and he would go on and on, until his mother had to check him. 'That's enough for today,' she used to say. 'You've laughed a lot today. Save a little for tomorrow.' He had learned to say two words. When he was happy he said, 'Je, je, je,' and his laugh showed both his teeth. When he was angry he said, 'Na, na, na,' and cried; and it was not a pretty cry. When he got hold of anything no matter

25

what it was, a lump of clay, a piece of wood, or the end of his mother's sari, he put it into his mouth and bit at it with his teeth. Sometimes at feeding time, quite suddenly he would bite at the metal spoon. He loved doing it, and it made his mother laugh. 'My goodness, child!' she said. 'What are you biting the spoon for? Let go. What do you think you're doing? You've only got two teeth and what will you have to laugh with if you break them?' But he would not stop, so his mother put her finger into his mouth and gently prised the spoon loose.

Shorbojoya could not leave her baby son to Durga all the time, so when she wanted to work she fenced off a part of the verandah with slats of bamboo and put him inside. There he lay just like a prisoner in a cell. Sometimes he laughed to himself, sometimes he chattered away in a language no one could understand, to listeners no one could see; and at other times he caught hold of the bamboo slats and pulled himself on to his feet and stared out into the bamboo grove. One day when his mother came back after her bath in the tank and he heard the swish of her wet clothes, he stopped playing and turned his head this way and that to see where she was, and the moment he caught sight of her he laid hold of the woodwork and pulled himself up, his face covered with smiles. 'What on earth have you been doing to yourself?' she exclaimed. 'I put some kohl round your eyes, and you've gone and rubbed it all over your face. You look just like a magpie. Come here and let me see to you.' She rubbed his nose and mouth vigorously to get the black off, and when she had finished his pink face was quite red. He put up a great show of resistance and protested angrily, but his mother took no notice. Afterwards however whenever he saw his mother with a cloth in her hands, he climbed clumsily on to his knees and scrambled away from her to the other side of the pen.

Often when she got back from the tank she would say, 'What's that you're saying Baby? Are you saying tu-u-u? Let me see you do to-and-fro. To-and-fro, rock to-and-fro!' and straightaway he would sit up and begin to rock backwards and forwards as hard as he could, waving his hands and singing gleefully, 'Je-e-e-, je-je-e!' And he went on and on and on, until his mother had to say, 'All right, stop now. Don't rock any more. That's quite enough, more than enough.'

Now and then while she was working, Shorbojoya suddenly stopped to listen. There was no sound from the pen. He had become quiet. Her heart missed a beat. What if a jackal had taken him! She rushed off at once to see. He had fallen asleep just where he was, his tiny hands flopped out on the floor like champa flowers which had been tipped out of a bucket; and swarms of ants, red ones and black ones, and flies too, were making greedily towards him. His thin red lips were quivering slightly, and now and then he swallowed and breathed deeply. He looked as if he was going to wake up, but the next moment he was fast asleep and she could not hear him breathing at all. So it went on. From dawn till dusk and on into the night that lonely house by the bamboo grove echoed with the happy, meaningless songs and the laughter of a ten-month-old child.

A mother gives all her love to bringing up her son, and through the ages the wonder of a mother's love has been sung in all languages. But is what the child gives to his mother of no account? It is true that when he comes he seems to bring nothing with him, but who can set a price on the laugh that steals her heart, on his childish changes of mood, his face which looks as though it had been fashioned out of the moon, and the limping incoherence of his efforts to speak? These things are his wealth, and he barters them for his mother's loving care. He does not come to her empty-handed like a beggar.

Once when Horihor was doing his accounts and writing, Shorbojoya brought the child in to him. 'Look after him for a bit. Durga's out somewhere, and the old woman's gone down to the tank. It's time for my bath, and I can't possibly go while I've got the child on my hands. So you must have him for a short time.'

'No, I can't now. I'm very busy. You mustn't disturb me now.' Shorbojoya was angry. She dumped the child on the floor and went off. Horihor continued doing his accounts, but suddenly he noticed that the child had picked up one of his slippers and was chewing it. He snatched it away from him and said peevishly, 'I knew something like this would happen, and here I am with all this work to do!' Presently a sparrow came and perched on the ledge of the verandah. Khoka was electrified, and tried to attract his father's attention by waving his hands in the direction of the bird; but that failing he started to talk to it himself. 'Je-je-je-je-!' Horihor's irritation left him, and a feeling of deep tenderness took its place.

His mind went back to a night years ago. He had just returned from a visit to western India. The neighbours had advised him to go to his father-in-law's house and bring his wife back with him. So he went. His boat reached the village in the afternoon. He had been there only once since his marriage and had forgotten the way, but some people directed him and eventually he came to the house. He stood outside and called, and a slender, fair-faced young woman came out to see who it was, but as soon as their eyes met she disappeared inside the house. Horihor wondered who she was. Could it be his wife? Was it possible that she had grown up so much? His questions were answered when later in the evening Shorbojoya came into his room. She was wearing a red-bordered sari made of coarse silk. It was her mother's and had been kept in store, as the poor do store things. Horihor looked at her in amazement. He could see in this young woman no resemblance to the girl he had married ten years ago. It looked as if someone had fashioned an entirely new creature. The simplicity of the child's face had gone, it is true, but it did take Horihor long to realize that in its place had come a beauty that was very rare indeed. What shapely hands and feet she had! And there was grace in her step as she walked, a grace he had never known before.

To begin with Shorbojoya was tongue-tied. She was grown up now; but in a very real sense she had never met her husband before and was experiencing afresh the shyness of a new bride. It was Horihor who spoke first. 'Come and sit here,' he said. 'How are you?' She gave a little smile and some of her shyness left her. 'It's been such a long time. I thought you'd forgotten. Why did you stay away so long?' Then she laughed. 'Why? Was it because you didn't like me?' She had a marked country brogue, which Horihor found refreshing and very musical. He noticed too that she had no ornaments except one or two shellac and glass bangles on her arms. She was the daughter of a poor family and there was no one to give her presents. It had been very wrong of him not to keep in touch with them all these years. Shorbojoya too was having a good look at him, though earlier that evening she had peeped at him a number of times from the next room. He was youthful and healthy; his limbs were shapely and he had an elegance not common among Bengali villagers. She had learned from what her father and mother had been saying that her husband had come back from the west a very well-educated man, and he had probably made quite a bit of money too. At last her troubles were at an end. After all these years God had been kind to her. People had been saying that her husband had become a hermit and would never return. She did her best not to believe them and went on hoping that he would come back, though as the years went by her hopes became more and more forlorn. Many a night she lay awake worrying. She avoided weddings and other ceremonies in the village. People were kind, but their sympathy did not console her and she did not want it. Night after night she lay alone and lonely in her room, and the golden dreams of childhood slowly turned to tears and ebbed away. There was no one she could open her heart to. And she sat and thought, 'Is this really to be my life? If my husband doesn't come back at all what'll happen to me when my father and mother die? Who'll give me a home?' But now it was all right.

Horihor laughed. 'Did you know who I was when you saw me standing at the gate? I want the truth now.'

'What a question to ask! Of course I did. At first I wasn't quite sure, but then—'

'You guessed.'

'No, it wasn't a guess. I promise you it wasn't. Didn't you notice that I pulled my sari over my face and went inside?'

A moment of silence fell on them and then she began to question him. 'What about you! Did you know me when you saw me? Don't tell me a story now. I want the truth too.'

So they talked on into the night, sometimes seriously sometimes in jest. Tears welled up into her eyes when the conversation turned to her brother who was dead; whereupon Horihor changed the subject and asked her who Bina was married to. Bina was Shobojoya's sister. He had not known her name until he heard his father-in-law mention it earlier in the evening.

'Her husband lives at Kurule Binodpur. There's a big river there. What's its name? Modhumoti! Yes, that's it. It's on the bank of the Modhumoti.'

One question came into Shorbojoya's mind time and time again. Would her husband take her with him? Or would he

stay with her a little while and then go back to Benares or
Gaya? It was on the tip of her tongue to ask him, but she
could not force the words out. There was something inside
her which told her not to. 'If he wants to go and leave me
he can,' she thought. 'Why should I plead with him? I have
too much pride for that.'

Horihor solved the problem himself. 'I'm going to take
you home tomorrow, to Nishchindipur.'

Shorbojoya was startled, and it took her some time to get
control of herself. 'Tomorrow?' she cried. 'Why tomorrow?
You've been away for so long, why can't you stay for a few
days at least. Father and mother won't want you to go as soon
as that. Besides, I've got a friend, my best friend, and they
want you to go to their house the day after tomorrow.'

'Who is this best friend of yours?'

'Her home's not far from here; but since her marriage
she's been living on the other side of the village.' Then she
laughed.

'She says she's going to come and have a look at you
tomorrow morning.'

So the conversation flowed on. The night was late; and
in a tree outside a nightjar was calling. Horihor could see
it all again so clearly. There in that remote village, under the
shade of the bamboo grove, was home; there was love. Yet
month after month, year after year, his wife prayed for him
to come and made all ready to welcome him, but she had
waited in vain; while he, a lonely homeless creature, without
a place to call his own, had been wearing himself out wandering
among arid, unfriendly hills in the west; and to what end?
Outside the nightjar still cried its monotonous cry, and the
moonlight was becoming paler and paler. Horihor became
conscious of the deep mystery that lies at the heart of life.
Before them was the road of a new life, stretching out into

31

the future which that night had ushered in. What that new life would be, who could tell? What had the goddess of life in store for them? What was she packing in their hamper for the uncharted years that lay ahead? Both of them seemed to be pondering the same thoughts as they sat together silently staring out of the window into the moonlit night.

It was all so far in the past now; and this child of theirs, they had not even thought of him then.

FIVE

Indir Thakrun had been back six or seven months, and during the whole of that time Shorbojoya had not spoken a single kind word to her. She called her an old witch, and a vampire, because she was convinced that Durga was fonder of the old woman than she was of her mother. She was jealous and very angry to think that the child of her womb was being estranged from her; and she dropped hints at every meal that it would be a good thing if Indir made her way somewhere else while she was still able to go. But what way was there? For the last seventy years, as long as she could remember, she had been searching for that way in vain. Where was she likely to find it now in her old age? She had thought about it often enough, but thinking had brought no answer.

Then, as the rains were coming to an end, an idea

suddenly occurred to her. Her son-in-law, Chondro Mojumdar, was still alive. He lived in Bhandarhati, some twelve miles away; and he was well-off too and kept a good home. She had completely lost touch with him since her daughter's death, which was some thirty-five or thirty-six years ago; that she knew; but after all she told herself he was her son-in-law, and if she went to him he could hardly refuse to take her in.

Her cart reached Bhandarhati village just before dark and stopped in front of a large house. The driver called out at once to announce their arrival, and a young man of about twenty-four or twenty-five came down the steps and asked where they had come from. Behind him, inside the house, stood an old man. 'Who is it, Radhu?' he asked. 'Find out where they've come from.' Indir recognized him at once. It was her son-in-law Chondro; and for a moment she was utterly tongue-tied. He was an old man with white hair, very different from the strong, sturdy and handsome young man she had known forty years ago. She could feel her heart thumping in her breast, and she was overcome with emotion, a confused emotion which was neither happiness nor sorrow but a mixture of both; and then in her bewilderment she heard herself crying out a name, a name which had not passed her lips for many years, her daughter's.

Chondro Mojumdar gaped with astonishment, and for a minute or two he seemed to be groping in space like a blind man. Then it came back to him and he bent down respectfully to touch his mother-in-law's feet. Indir managed to control herself in time to pull her sari over her face, but she found it hard to speak. 'After these many years, my son, I've come to you. All I want is a corner to live in. I've not many days of life left, and I've no one else in the world. Only a little rice and some clothes.'

Mojumdar told his son to take her things out of the cart and show her the way into the house.

The house itself, apart from the kitchen, a variety of sheds and other auxiliary structures, consisted of two main buildings which were quite separate from one another. The pillars and crossbeams of these buildings were of tal palm wood, a timber which only a fairly rich man could afford, and the roofs of both had been laid in eight sections. Inside there was so much furniture and so many chests and boxes that in spite of the size of the rooms there was little space to move about in. The household was in the joint charge of the widowed daughter of Mojumdar's second marriage and his eldest son's wife. The wives of his other three sons lived there too, and he had three or four grandchildren. The widowed daughter of the house received Indir very kindly. She made her sit beside her and placed a glass of water in front of her. Then she cut up some fruit for her and fed her tenderly with her own hands, asking her about herself as she did so.

'You've never seen me before, Granny, have you? No, I thought you hadn't. What a pity you didn't think of coming to us earlier! We should have loved to have you with us .... Here's some sugar cane. Would you like me to cut some of it up for you? But, oh! I forgot! How thoughtless of me! What about your teeth? Can you chew sugar cane?'

There was a lot of noise in the kitchen outside where the children were having their evening meal. One of them shouted out to her mother. 'Look what Umi's done, Mummy! She's spilled the pulse all over my plate.' One of the son's wives shouted back. 'Why did you have to sit next to her? I tell you every day to sit further away. And you Umi, you're going too far. Stop it.'

Ten or twelve days passed. Everything was new to the old woman, and she did not feel at home. The house was different, and so were the ways of the household. It was not what she was used to and she did not fit in. She found the strangeness of it oppressive, and in the evening when she was alone she thought of the faces of the two children she had left behind in Nishchindipur. Within two or three weeks she was anxious to go back. She knew she could never be happy here. The eldest son's wife had been far from pleased when the old man's mother-in-law turned up and did not hesitate to show her displeasure when she heard that she might stay on indefinitely. So naturally she was delighted when there was talk of her going back. What Chondro Mojumdar thought, God only knows. He was afraid of his eldest son and his wife and consequently never said anything about it one way or the other.

So in time Indir Thakrun was home again, sitting on the verandah outside her own room. She had both the children with her, and as she watched the leaves of the coconut tree quivering in the moonlight she dozed off happily.

At first Durga had been very cross with her, and for a while would not talk to her or go anywhere near her; but it did not take the old woman long to win her round and now they were friends again. 'How pretty you'd look in a pair of those red flower-shaped earrings!' she was saying as she caressed the child's head. 'But no, they're out of fashion nowadays. They're wearing something else now. What on earth do they call them?'

It was winter time, and the old woman went to call on Ramnath Ganguli who lived at the other side of the village.

'It's very cold nowadays, Ram,' she said, 'and I've nothing warm to wrap round me. If only you could give me a ...'

'Yes, yes, of course; but come later on. I can't give you a wrap this month. I might be able to manage it next month.'

Day after day she came and went, until at last one day he produced a piece of red cotton cloth from Kusthia.

'You can have this one, Didi,' he said. 'It's very warm. It cost me nine and a half annas. You can't get good cloth like this in Nawabganj nowadays. I got it on Wednesday. Open it up and have a look.'

Indir could hardly believe her eyes. She spluttered with joy as she unfolded it and wrapped it round herself. 'Oh, it's lovely!' she exclaimed. 'It'll be beautifully warm; it's so nice and thick. God grant you long life, and your sons too! Very few people worry about the poor nowadays. I've been asking that Onnoda for a piece of cloth for these last three years. He keeps on saying he'll give me one, but he never docs. I haven't much longer to live, and this will last me for the rest of my life.'

She had to share her delight with some one, so she rushed back home to show her new possession to Shorbojoya. Shorbojoya however was far from pleased. 'How often must I tell you, Auntie,' she said angrily, 'that I won't have you going around begging from door to door while you're staying in my house. If you must beg, then go somewhere else and do it.' The old woman was used to remarks like this. She had to swallow them at least ten times a day, and she swallowed this one too, comforting herself however, as she was frequently wont to do, by muttering an old rhyme:

'Canes and birches may hurt the feet
But a bowl of rice still tastes as sweet.'

Durga on the other hand was thrilled. 'How much did it cost, Auntie? It's a lovely red, isn't it?'

'I'll leave it to you when I die,' the old woman promised. 'You'll be able to wear it when you grow up.'

It was a new piece of cloth and the smell of the starch was still in it. Indir liked that. It was a complete luxury for her to have anything new. Next morning she put it on and went outside to do her sweeping; and from time to time she stopped to look at herself. There was no need for her to go beyond the compound; but go she did, and stood by the path that led to the bathing steps. The women of the village were going and coming that way all morning, and if anyone passed without noticing what she was wearing she called out to her, 'Who's that? Oh, it's you, Raji's mother! You're late this morning, aren't you?'

Having attracted attention she laughed and looked down at herself. 'Ramnath from over there gave it to me. It cost nine and a half annas.'

Some of the younger women teased her. 'That red cloth does suit you, Granny. You look just like a bride.'

SIX

One morning a woman named Dashi Thakrun, who kept a small stall in the village, walked into the yard and called to Shorbojoya from the foot of the steps. 'You owe me two pice, my dear,' she said with a grin, 'and I've come to collect them. Your Aunt Indir bought a custard apple from me yesterday; and she told me I could come and get the money from you.'

'A custard apple!' Shorbojoya echoed. She was busy at the time and it took a minute or two for the full meaning of what Dashi Thakrun had said to sink in. Do you mean to say that she went and bought a custard apple from you?'

Dashi Thakrun was a tradeswoman, and a hard-bitten one too. She gave nothing away. Whatever it was, a tamarind, a wild plum, or even a leaf or two of spinach, she wanted

39

money for it. The amiable grin vanished from her face at once. 'Are you suggesting that I would come all this way in the heat of the day and tell you a lie for two pice? Go and ask her yourself if you don't believe me. The trade price for custard apples is four pice; but she's an old woman, and as she wanted one to eat I let her have it for two pice.'

Shorbojoya was so angry that words failed her. A custard apple indeed! There were so many of them growing wild in the jungle that even the cattle got tired of eating them. Why on earth should anyone who lived in a village like theirs ever want to go and pay money for one!

Unfortunately for her Indir chose this very moment to walk in through the gate. Shorbojoya fairly jumped at her. 'You old hag!' she burst out. 'You're more than half in your grave already! Does it never occur to you to be careful with money, especially when it belongs to the people you live on? Dashi says you went and bought a custard apple from her. Today it's a custard apple. Yesterday it was a sweet. Where do you think I'm going to find the money to pay for all the things you want to eat? If you want to buy unnecessary luxuries for yourself why don't you spend your own money on them? You ought to be ashamed of yourself buying them at somebody else's expense!'

Indir went pale, her old face seemed to shrivel up; but she tried to force a smile. 'Do give it to her, please,' she said. 'Just this once. It was a ripe custard apple, and I couldn't resist it. You won't have me with you much longer. So please pay her the money.'

Shorbojoya screamed even more shrilly than before. 'It's money, money, money all the time! You think of nothing else. You've got pots and pans of your own, haven't you? Why don't you go and sell one of them and pay her yourself?' With that she snatched up a water pot and went out by the back door to get some water from the tank.

Dashi Thakrun stood still for a moment and then she called out after her. 'Where do I come in? Are you going to leave me to whistle for my money? I've never had so much trouble with a customer before.... But it was very wrong of you, Aunt Indir,' she said turning to the old woman. 'If you hadn't any money of your own you should never have asked me for that custard apple. You mustn't come to me for anything else unless you've the money to pay for it. It's all right for the two of you to quarrel, but I'm a poor woman. I'll come back again this evening. See that you have the money ready for me then, my dear.'

Durga followed Dashi out into the yard. 'Auntie's a very old woman. She got a custard apple from you, and that's what's got her into all this trouble. She only wanted something to eat, Aunt Dashi; and it was a lovely custard apple too. I know because she gave me half of it. Besides, you've got a whole tree of them at your house, haven't you, Auntie?' Dashi walked off, but Durga ran after her. 'I'll tell you what, Auntie. I've got a pice in my doll's box. You can have that; but I can't give it to you now because the room's locked and Mummy's gone off with the key. When she comes back, if you promise not to tell her, I'll get it without letting her see what I'm doing; and then I'll bring it to you.'

It was not noon yet, but old Indir was already leaving the house. In her left hand she had a little bundle wrapped round with a dirty piece of cloth, and her brass jar hung from her right arm. Under her arm she was clutching her old mat which was frayed at the edges and had long strands of grass hanging loose from it.

Durga called out to her. 'Please, Auntie, don't go away and leave us. No, Auntie, you mustn't. Where are you going to?' She ran after her and tugged at the mat. 'Don't go, Auntie. If you do I shall cry. You know I shall.'

Shorbojoya, who was home by now, called to her from the verandah. 'Go by all means if you want to. I don't want to stop you. But why must you choose to do it at an inauspicious time of the day and bring bad luck on all of us? There are the children to think of, and my husband too. You've lived off him all these years. Surely he's entitled to some consideration! You know quite well that if you go off in the middle of the day before having your meal, it will bring bad luck on the house. But perhaps that's what you want to happen. It must be, or you would not sneak off like this.'

The old woman did not turn back, even though Durga ran all the way down the path with her crying. She went right on through the village until she got to the Ghoshals' house. When Nobin Ghoshal's wife heard her story, she clasped her hands to her face. 'You poor thing!' she said. 'I've never heard anything like it. You'd better make your home with us.' Indir stayed with her for a month or so, and then she moved on to Tinkori Ghoshal's house; and after that to Purno Chokroborti's. They all showed her the utmost kindness to begin with, but as the weeks went past her welcome began to wear thin, and they showed in a variety of ways that they were getting tired of her. She went on to one or two other houses, all the time hoping that if nobody else came to call her home Horihor himself would come for her. Three months passed, and still nobody came; not even Durga. The old woman tried to comfort herself by saying that it was too far for a little girl to walk; and once or twice she wandered towards the house hoping to see the child; but she never so much as caught a glimpse of her.

An outsider cannot stay in other people's houses all the year round. There was a thatched cottage at the eastern end of the village. It had belonged to Chinte Goyalini, but was now empty. So after two months the Ghoshals and others all joined forces and did it up for her, promising that they would help her with food and with whatever else she needed. It was a very small place. Its walls were made of split bamboos, and it stood in a grove away from the rest of the houses. News of what was going on was regularly reported to Shorbojoya. 'Let other people have a taste of her,' she commented. 'I'm not going to have her back here again whatever happens. She didn't hesitate to cast her evil eye on my children; so I'll see that she does not darken my doors again. She can go and die on a dunghill, for all I care.' For the first few days the families who had promised to help Indir brought her all she could want and more; but slowly their interest waned, and she began to be in want. 'Why did I have to lose my temper and come away as I did? Shorbojoya didn't want me to leave, and Durga cried and tried to pull me back,' she thought to herself, and the tears trickled down her shrunken cheeks. 'I must have lived a very sinful life in my previous birth for all this sorrow to come upon me now. Oh, that my daughter were still alive!'

It was April, and the last day of the Bengali year. It was like a furnace outside and though towards evening a breeze sprang up it did little to dispel the heat. The end-of-the-year festivities were still going on, and the sound of drums could be heard from the distant fair-ground.

Indir had been out in the sun, wandering desperately from house to house in spite of the heat, and when she got back in the evening she had fever. She spread her mat on the verandah and lay there in silence. Near her head was an earthenware pot with some water in it—she had pawned her brass jar some time ago for four annas, to buy rice with— and as the fever made her thirsty, she turned over occasionally and sipped from it.

'Auntie!' The old woman threw off her coverlet and

43

raised her head. It was Durga. She was coming up the steps on to the verandah, and behind her came Behari Chokroborti's daughter Raji, whose home was in the same part of the village as Durga's. ·Durga was wearing a clean sari, and she had something wrapped up in it. Indir could not speak, but she stretched out her thin arms towards the child and clasped her eagerly to her bosom, which was now hot with fever.

'You won't tell anybody, Auntie, will you?' Durga whispered. 'The fair's on, you know; and as soon as it got dark I slipped away while nobody was looking. Raji came with me. Look what I got at the fair; and it's all for you, Auntie.'

She opened her little bundle.

'It's baked rice, Auntie. Two pice worth, and I've brought you two sweets too. And look at this. It's a wooden doll for Opu.'

The old woman sat straight up, and began to finger the presents. 'Let me have a look at them, darling,' she said. 'What a lot you've brought me. May you live to be a queen for being so kind to your old auntie. Let me see Opu's doll too. It is pretty, isn't it? How much did you have to pay for it?'

When the first burst of conversation was over Durga said, 'Auntie, your body's very hot.'

'Yes, it is, I've been walking round all day. That's why I'm hot. So I thought I'd lie down for a bit.'

Durga was only a child, but she knew fully well why her auntie had been out in the sun. The old body, which she now stroked so lovingly, was shrivelled up with misery and hunger. 'You simply must come home, Auntie,' she said. 'There's nobody to tell me stories in the evening. So you will come, won't you? Come tomorrow. Say that you will.'

The old woman could not contain her joy. 'Your mother has sent for me then?' she said.

'No, Auntie,' said Raji. 'Her mother has not sent for you. She told Durga that she wasn't to come and see you; and if we so much as suggest coming she gets angry with us. But do come all the same, Auntie. She'll forget what's happened if you just speak to her about it.'

'Yes, yes!' Durga chimed in. 'Promise you'll come tomorrow, Auntie. Mummy won't say anything I'm sure…. But I'd better be going now. You won't tell anybody I've been to see you, will you, Auntie? And you'll come tomorrow morning, won't you?'

Indir felt a little better when she got up next morning. As soon as it was light she wrapped her two torn saris and a few dirty scraps of cloth in a bundle, and set off. On the way she met Gopi Bostom's wife.

'So you're going home, are you, Granny? I suppose Opu's mother is not angry with you any more now?'

The old woman gave a little laugh. 'Durga came to see me last night to ask me to go back. How the poor thing cried. She told me her mother had sent her to say, "Come back, Auntie. Come home again." So I said to the child, "All right, but wait till morning. I'll come then, as soon as it's light." How the poor darling cried and begged of me to go back. It's morning now, and I'm going.'

There was nobody in the house when she arrived, so she put her bundle down and sat on the verandah steps. What with having fever all night and dragging her feeble body such a long way in the hot sun, she was utterly exhausted. Presently Shorbojoya came in through the back door. She had been down to the river for her bath. When she saw the old woman sitting there she stood stock still, as if she could not believe her eyes. Indir laughed. 'Hello, my dear,' she said. 'It's been a long time; but I've come back at last. I'm too old to go away and live somewhere else. So I thought …'

45

Shorbojoya moved towards her. 'What do you mean by coming into this house?' she hissed. Her manner and the tone of voice in which she spoke dried up the smile on Indir's lips. She did not say anything though Shorbojoya did not give her a chance to. 'There's no place for you here,' she said. 'I told you that the day you went away. I don't know where you've come from, but wherever it was, go back.'

The old woman went cold in spite of the heat. For a while not a sound came from her, then suddenly she broke down and sobbed violently. 'No, no, my dear! Don't say that. Just a cornerr … that's all I want … just a corner. I'm an old dying woman. Where is there for me to go? Besides, this piece of land….'

'Stop,' Shorbojoya shouted. 'Don't you dare to mention this piece of land. I suppose you haven't been able to sleep for thinking of all the luck you've brought upon this piece of land, as you call it. Get out. Go away this very minute. I'll create a frightful scene if you don't.'

Indir had never for a moment thought that her return would provoke such an outburst as this. She looked about her blindly with eyes which saw nothing and then she began to grope round with her hands for something to hold on to like a drowning man. The one thing in her life which she had felt sure of was being dragged away from under her feet for ever, and she was powerless to prevent it.

'Go away,' repeated Shorbojoya. 'I won't have you sitting here a minute longer. It's getting late and I've got work to do. There's no room for you here now.'

The old woman took hold of her bundle and with a great effort struggled to her feet. She walked across the yard. Her eyes fell on the broom she used to sweep the yard with. It was leaning against the corner of the wall. Nobody had touched it for months. She saw the grass growing in the yard, and the lemon tree she had planted with such care; and then she looked at the broom again—she had been so fond of it. She thought of Durga and Opu, and of this piece of land, which had been her uncle Brojo's. She was seventy years old, and these were all she had, all she had ever known or loved; and now they were being taken away from her.

As she was passing under the sojne tree, her bundle under her arm, one of the women from the Ray's house saw her and called out, 'Where are you going to, Granny? Aren't you going back home?' There was no reply to the question, so the woman, thought to herself, 'The poor dear's gone quite deaf nowadays.'

That evening someone came from the other side of the village with a message for Shorbojoya: 'Ma, I think your old auntie's dying. She's been lying near the Palits' rice barn since midday. She wandered about in the sun until she couldn't go any further. I think you ought to come and see her. Where's your husband? Isn't he at home? Tell him to come too if he's in.'

Indir Thakrun was lying under the plinth of the Palit's rice barn; and there could be no doubt that she was dying. She began to feel ill as soon as she got to her feet and staggered away from Horihor's house. She went as far as she could and then lay down in the nearest shade she could find. The Palits took her indoors, and fanned her and rubbed oil on her chest and her back; but after they had done all they could they realized that she was sinking fast, and they carried her outside. One of them said, 'Why did she ever have to go out in the sun today?' Another said, 'It's only a faint I think. She'll come round in a bit.'

Bishu Palit said, 'This is not faint. She's not going to come round. Horihor hasn't come. I suppose he's not at home. I sent word to them, but who would come all this way on a day like this?'

Phoni, the eldest son of Dinu Chokroborti, heard them talking as he was going by, and he came in to see what was happening. 'How very fortunate that you've come!' they all exclaimed as soon as they saw him. 'Pour some Ganges water into her mouth. You can see what a fix we're in. There aren't any Brahmins in this part of the village, and we were at our wits' end to know who would give her Ganges water.' Phoni had a thorn stick in his hand. He gave it to Bishu Palit and squatted down near the old woman's head. He took some water in a copper ladle and called to her, 'Auntie!'

Indir opened her eyes, but there was no sight in them as she turned her head towards him. She did not reply. He spoke to her again, 'Auntie! How are you? Aren't you feeling very well?' He poured a little water over her mouth, but none of it passed her lips. 'Try again,' Bishu Palit said.

After a few minutes Phoni closed her eyelids, and from the sunken sockets tears welled out and flowed down her wasted cheeks.

The death of Indir Thakrun brought the old days to an end in Nishchindipur village.

Part II

Children Make Their Own Toys

SEVEN

Indir Thakrun had been dead for four or five years. It was January, and the day of the festival of the goddess Sarasvati; and it was still quite cold. A few people from Nishchindipur were going to look at the blue-throated jay in the open country outside the village, and their way lay along a narrow path which was hemmed in on both sides by undergrowth.

One of them said, 'Hori, have you leased your banana orchard to Bhushno Goyala again?'

The man addressed was Horihor Ray, but he looked very different from the Horihor of ten or so years ago. You would never have thought he was the same man. He was now middle-aged, the father of two children, and very much weighed down by his family responsibilities. He collected his rent and went round from village to village to make sure he received all the fees which were due to him as a Brahmin. He haggled in the country markets over the price of vegetables just like any peasant. He bore no resemblance to the uninhibited, care-free young man of earlier days who wandered wherever he would. The years he once spent in the west had slowly become a thing of the past. Then, he had sat on the broad battlements of the Chunar fort and watched the sun set over the distant mountains; he had spent many a night under the bay trees on the road to Kedar, and had plucked bitter oranges in the grove near the shrine of Shah Kasim Sulemani. And there was that stream of paradise, the Alokananda, clear as pure silver and ice-cold; and the steps that led down to it at Dasasvamedh Ghat. Sometimes he thought of these things, but only as a dream from a past long since dead.

Horihor was on the point of saying 'yes' to the question his companion had asked him when his attention was distracted and he turned and looked behind him instead. 'Where's the lad got to now?' he said. 'Khoka, oh, Khoka-a-a!' Round a bend in the road a boy of six or seven came running after him, a bright-faced delicate-looking child. 'Don't lag behind, Khoka, run along in front of us,' Horihor said to him.

'Something went into the forest, Daddy. What was it? It had big ears.'

Horihor ignored the question and started to talk to Nobin Palit about fishing. The boy asked again, insistently.

'Something ran into the forest. It had big ears. What was it?'

'I don't know, child. I can't go on answering all your questions. You've been asking what this was and what that was ever since we came out. In any case I didn't see what it was that went into the forest. Come along now. Keep in front of us.'

The boy went ahead as his father told him.

Nobin Palit took up the conversation. 'One thing, Hori,' he said, 'if ever you feel like going fishing you'd better come with me to the Boinsha beel. Nepal Parui—you know him of course; he lives in the east part of the village—well, he's got a dam built there. He gets round about a hundred pounds of fish every day without any trouble; and not a fish weighs less than ten pounds. I heard that late one night, out in the deep water in the middle of the beel, there were so many big fish jumping about that it sounded for all the world like cows lashing their tails at milking time, if you know what I mean.' They all crowded in upon Nobin Palit and stared at him in amazement. 'It's an old beel,' he went on. 'Goodness knows how long it's been there, and it's very deep too. You must have seen it. Out in the middle there's a black patch of water, with lots of lotuses growing in it. That's where the fish were. Some of them said they were boyal fish, but others said they were evil spirits. The fishermen themselves weren't sure, so they sat there in the boat trembling with fear until there was enough light to see by.'

He was warming up to his story, when Horihor's small son screamed with excitement and pointed with his finger towards a clump of grass near the roadside. 'There it goes. Look Daddy! It's gone now. Such big ears! It's ...'

His father called out from behind. 'No! Don't go in there, it's full of thorns.' And he came up quickly and grabbed hold of the boy's hand. 'What a nuisance you are child! I've told you a hundred times to be quiet, but you take no notice. That's why I didn't want to bring you with me.'

The lad looked up at his father, his face shining with excitement and joy, 'What was it, Daddy?'

'How can I tell what it was? I didn't see it. It was probably a pig or something. Run along now, and keep in the middle of the road.'

'It wasn't a pig, Daddy. It was too small.' And he bent down and showed him how high it was from the ground.

'Yes, yes! I understand. You don't need to show me. Run along.'

'It was a hare, Khoka, a hare,' said Nobin Palit. 'They live in the thatch grass.' Opu had seen a picture of a hare under the letter H in his spelling reader, but he had not realized till now that a hare was a living thing that could jump and run away, and that you could see it with your eyes.

A hare! a real live hare that actually jumps up before your very eyes and then runs away! It was not a picture, or even a glass doll, but a real live hare with its ears standing up. And it lives in clumps of grass and among the bushes. Things like that do not happen in everyday life. He could not believe his eyes.

They had come to the end of the jungle path now and passed out into the open country. The river lay ahead of them, and on the bank, partly hidden by some thorn bushes, they noticed some mounds which on closer inspection turned out to be heaps of bricks. They were the ruins of the firehouse of an old indigo factory. At one time, in the days of the indigo trade, Nishchindipur had been the headquarters of the Bengal Indigo Concern. There had been fourteen factories in the area, and John Lermor, the manager of the Nishchindipur factory, held sway over them all like an emperor; but now his factory and its buildings, the vats, the firehouse, the manager's bungalow and the office, were not more than heaps of rubble overgrown with jungle. There was a time when the name of the mighty John Lermor had such power that at the mere mention of it tigers and cows went down to the same watering place to drink. Yet today, except for a few extremely old people, nobody remembered him.

Between the jungle thickets in the open country grew clumps of tall grass, yellow-flowering bushes and wild plum trees; and over all this tangle of luxuriant growth the kolmi creeper had spread its large green leaves completely engulfing it, and in the cool shade beneath its leafy roof a few fully-open wild flowers thrust up their heads towards the sky in an attempt to catch the sunlight, while in that lovely forest green which deepened as the sun set, the birds began to sing. Nature had scattered its riches with a prodigal hand, like a king whose bounty knows no end. She knew not poverty, or even that virtue of the middle classes, thrift. The day waned, and field, river and forest began to be enshrouded in the magic curtain of the dusk.

The party went on walking across the open plain, and Nobin Palit went on talking. He was telling them in great detail of the money he had made some years ago by growing sweet potatoes in the fields to the north of the village. On and on he went, until another who was panting for an opportunity to have his say, interrupted him to impart the startling tidings that the bricks from the factory field were going to be sold and that Moti Dan of Nawabganj was already haggling over the price. Moti Dan, just fancy! He had been a nobody once but now he was a very rich man. So they talked on, regaling one another with information of great importance, the high cost of living, the fire in Kundu's storehouse in Asharhu bazar, the date fixed for the marriage of Dinu Ganguli's daughter, and much else.

'Daddy, when are we going to see the blue-throated jay?'

'Keep your eyes skinned. It will come and sit on that thorn bush any time now.'

The boy looked up and stared hard at the tops of all the thorn bushes they came across; but not for long. There were some wild plum trees dotted about here and there, and they were not very high. The plums were ripe too; so from then on he had eyes only for plums. Once or twice he tried to

55

pluck some, but his father scolded him and told him to leave them alone. How could fruit grow on such small trees? They had plum trees at home but they were very high, and he had never been able to reach the branches. One day he tried to knock some fruit down with a pole, but it was too heavy for him, and he could not lift it high enough even though he used both hands. Moreover he had learned that it was impossible to eat forbidden fruit without being found out. His mother always seemed to hear about it and came and took him home. 'What will you be up to next, you naughty boy?' she used to say. 'You know you've only just got over your fever and here you are wandering about under the plum trees. The moment my back is turned you're off somewhere. How many plums have you eaten? Let me have a look at your mouth.'

'I haven't eaten any. There wasn't a single one lying on the ground, and you know I can't reach high enough to get them off the trees, don't you?' So saying, he lifted up his pretty little face and opened his mouth. His mother looked inside carefully. It smelt as sweet as fresh butter, and she kissed him.

'You must never eat wild plums, Khoka, never! When you're a bit stronger I'll pickle some for you and keep them in a jar, and you can have them in the hot weather. But you must never eat them without asking me first. Do you understand?'

At this point Horihor interrupted his concentration on plums. 'Khoka, you're always asking about factories. Well, there's one over there. It belonged to some sahibs. Can you see it?'

The old factory sprawled over a large tract of land by the river like the skeleton of some ferocious prehistoric monster; and the still winter afternoon, like the hand of passing time, was gradually spreading its dusky mantle over it. Not far from the factory compound Opu saw the grave of a little boy, Manager Lermor's only son. It was quite deserted and overgrown with weeds, yet of all that remained to mark the vast headquarters of the Bengal Indigo Concern the grave alone remained whole. If you went near enough you could still make out the inscription on its old black slab.

Here lies Edwin Lermor
The only son of John and Mrs Lermor,
Born May 13, 1853. Died April 27, 1860.

There were many trees round the grave, but nearest to it, with leafy branches spread wide to give it shade, was a wild shondal tree; and in the hot weather by day or by night, whenever the wind blew up hard from the delta, it let its clusters of yellow flowers fall on the time-stained tomb of that forgotten foreign child. Everyone else might have forgotten him, but the trees of the forest still remembered.

The boy's eyes drank it all in and he was speechless with wonder. He was six-years-old and this was the first time he had come so far from home. Until today the boundaries of his world had been Nera's house on the one side and the land in front of his own home as far as Ranu's place on the other. Once or twice his mother had taken him to the tank for a bath, and from the steps down to the water he had caught sight of the ruined firehouse of a factory faintly visible in the distance. He had pointed to it with his finger and asked, 'Is that the factory there, Mummy?' He had heard his father, his sister and the neighbours talk about the open country where the factory was, but this was the first time he had been to it. Anything further away than this, he imagined, could only be the land of the fairy tales his mother used to tell him, the country called Black Lanka, where the exiled prince slept with his sword by his side, alone under the tree where the bengama and bengami birds lived. No man lived further away than that. The factory was the world's last frontier, and beyond it lay only the realm of the unknown where nothing was impossible.

On the way back he saw a bunch of brightly coloured fruit on a squat bush by the roadside and he stretched out his hand to pluck it. His father shouted out to him at once, 'Don't touch it, don't touch it. It's the cow-itch flower. What will you be up to next, child? You're always up to some mischief. I shan't bring you out with me again, that's certain. Now you'll have blisters all over your hand. I've told you time and time again to walk in the middle of the path, but you take not the slightest notice.'

'Why should I have blisters on my hand, Daddy?'

'Because it's poisonous. It's bound to give you blisters. It'll itch first and then start to burn, and that'll make you cry.'

Horihor went through the village and brought the lad home by the back door. Shorbojoya heard the door open and came out to meet them. 'You're very late. Why did you take him so far, and without anything warm on either?'

'What a trial it is taking him anywhere!' replied his father. 'He runs here, there and everywhere. I never know where he is. And he went and grabbed hold of some cow-itch flowers too.' Then he turned to the boy again. 'Well, my lad,' he said, 'you've been clamouring to see the place where the factory is, and now you've seen it. I hope you're satisfied.'

EIGHT

It was between eight and nine in the morning. Horihor's son was sitting on the verandah playing by himself. By his side he had a small tin box with a broken lid, and the contents of the box were tipped out on to the floor. They consisted of a wooden horse, faded and discoloured, a dented tin whistle which had cost four pice, a few cowrie shells—these he kept hidden away for fear anybody should know they were there, because he had, unbeknown to his mother, pulled them from the basket she used when she was saying her prayers to Lakshmi—a pistol worth two pice, and some grey seeds they called natas. They were dry and round like marbles. His sister had got them from somewhere because she liked the look of them. She had given him a few and kept the rest in her doll's box. He also had a few pieces of broken earthenware tiles. These he kept most carefully in his box. He intended to use them for their Ganges and Jamuna game. He felt sure that they would go dead straight when he pitched them. This was the sum total of all his possessions and very precious they were. He had just finished playing with the tin whistle, having lost interest in it after he had blown it a time or two. That is why it was lying on the floor by his side. The wooden horse had also had its turn, and it too was lying on the floor by his side rather like a prisoner in a cell. Now it was time for a game of Ganges and Jamuna, so he took up the tiles and drew imaginary squares for the court. Then closing his eyes he began to throw the tiles to find out whether they would go straight or not.

While he was playing with the tiles his sister Durga called out to him from under the jackfruit tree in the yard. 'Opu, Opu!' and there was a hint of caution in her voice. She had not been in the house for some time and had obviously just come back from somewhere. Opu's reaction to the sound of her voice was automatic. He quickly snatched up the cowrie shells he had stolen from the Lashkmi basket and put them away out of sight. Not till he had done this did he reply:

'What it is, Didi?'

She beckoned to him. 'Come here. I want to tell you something.'

Durga was then between ten and eleven. She was a thin child, and not nearly as fair as Opu; in fact she was rather dark. She was wearing glass bangles. Her clothes were dirty, and her hair was so dry that it blew about in whatever wind there was. Her face was not badly shaped, and she had very big eyes like Opu's. Opu went down from the verandah to where she was standing.

'What is it?'

She had a coconut shell in her hand, and she held it out

for him to see. There were some slices of green mango in it. Then lowering her voice Durga said, 'Mummy hasn't got back from her bath yet, has she?'

Opu shook his head, 'No.'

Then she said in a whisper, 'Do you think you could get some oil and salt? I want to make a mango pickle.'

Opu was delighted. 'Where did you get them from, Didi?'

'They had fallen from the shindurkoto tree in the Palits' orchard. Go and get the oil and salt.'

Opu looked hard at her. 'But won't Mummy beat me if I touch the oil jar before I've had my clothes washed? You know how strict she is about it.'

'Go on. Hurry up. Mummy won't be back for some time yet. She's gone to do some washing. Hurry up and be quick about it.'

'Give me the coconut bowl,' Opu said. 'I can put the oil straight into it and you can go and watch the back door in case she comes.'

Durga said in a low voice, 'Mind how you pour it out. Don't spill any on the floor. If you do Mummy will find out. You're so clumsy with your hands.'

When he came back Durga took the shell from him and began to stir the mangoes in the oil. Then she said, 'Hold out your hand. Here's one for you.'

'Are you going to eat all the rest yourself, Didi?'

'There are not all that many. But all right then; here you are. You can have these two as well. That's a lot. Don't they look nice. Do you think you could get a chilli? If you can I'll give you one more.'

'How can I get a chilli, Didi? Mummy keeps them on the shelf, and I can't reach it.'

'All right then, don't bother. I'll get some more mangoes this afternoon. There are quite a lot on the tree at the side

61

of the Palits' tank. They'll fall as soon the heat of the sun gets on them.'

Horihor's house was surrounded on all sides by jungle. His cousin, Nilmoni Ray, had died the year before, and his widow was living in her father's house; and their compound which was next door to Horihor's was now overgrown with weeds and bushes. There was no other house nearby. Bhubon Mukherji's which was the nearest was five minutes' walk away. Horihor's house had not been repaired for a long time. The verandah in front was very dilapidated and quite a forest of weeds had taken root in the cracks. The doors and a windows had broken away from their hinges and were only held in place by coconut ropes.

The back door opened with a creak and a moment later the children heard Shorbojoya's voice. 'Durga! Durga!'

Durga said to Opu, 'Mummy's calling. Go and see what she wants. But swallow that mango first. But stop; you've got some salt on your mouth. Wipe it off before you go.'

Durga could not answer her mother's call herself. Her mouth was full. She swallowed as fast as she could, but there were a number of pieces left, so she went and hid behind the trunk of the juckfruit tree and began to gulp them down like a cow. Opu stood by her doing his best to get his bit down. There was no time to chew it, and he looked at his sister and smiled guiltily. As soon as the bowl was empty Durga hurled it over the castor-oil tree fence into the weeds in Nilmoni Ray's compound. Then she looked at her brother.

'Wipe your face, you little monkey. You've still got some salt on it;' and having seen to that she went into the house with a look of utter innocence on her face. 'What is it, Mummy?'

'Where have you been? You seem to think that I can do everything single-handed. I've been washing the whole morning and my body aches all over. Don't you think I've a right to expect some help from you? You're a big girl now, but you don't do a hand's turn in the house; you spend all your time wandering round the village. And as for that little monkey. Where's he got to?'

Opu came in. 'I'm hungry, Mummy.'

'Oh, you are, are you? Well, you'll have to wait until I get my breath back. You're both hungry all the time. You're always clamouring for something or the other. Oh, Durga! Go and see why the calf is crying.'

A little later Shorbojoya was sitting on the kitchen verandah slicing a cucumber for them with the cooking knife. Opu was sitting by her.

'Do take out the sticky part, Mummy. It makes my mouth feel funny.'

Durga took the piece that was handed to her and said timidly, 'Is there any of that baked rice left, Mummy?'

Opu started to chew his piece. 'Ugh, I can't chew it! That mango has set my teeth ...' The look in Durga's eyes made him stop and he left the sentence unfinished, but his mother had heard.

'Mango? Where did you get a mango from?'

Opu was too frightened to say anything about it, so he looked appealingly at his sister. Shorbojoya followed his glance and said to Durga, 'You've been out again, I suppose?'

Durga's face showed that she was trapped. 'Why don't you make him tell you.' she said. 'I ... I was only standing under the jackfruit tree. When you called I....'

At this moment Shorno the milkwoman came to milk the cow and the subject was dropped. Shorbojoya said to Durga, 'Go and hold the calf. It's been crying so long it must be exhausted. It's a weak little thing too. Shorno, if you come as late as this it'll die of hunger. We've had to keep it tied up all morning because you didn't come in time.'

63

Opu followed Durga out to watch the cow being milked. As soon as he came down into the yard Durga gave him a hard slap on the back. 'You little monkey!' Then she wrinkled up her face as he had done and mimicked him, 'That mango has set my teeth on edge! I suppose you'll be expecting me to give you some more mangoes to eat! Well, I shan't. I'm going to get some from the Potlis' tree this afternoon and I shall pickle them. There are some big ones on their trees and they're as sweet as sugar. But don't think I shall give you any, 'because I shan't, you little silly! You've no brains at all.'

Horihor came home early in the afternoon. He had finished his work. For the past few weeks he had been doing some clerical work for Onnoda Ray in the village.

'I don't see Opu anywhere,' he said.

'Oh, he's asleep in his room.'

'And Durga?'

'She went out after she'd finished her meal. But when is she ever at home? Food is the only thing that'll bring her back. She'll come in all right when she's hungry. She's probably wandering round under the fruit trees in somebody's orchard. And it's the hot weather now and the middle of the day too. I tell her she'll get fever again. Moreover she's grown up now. I keep trying to make her understand. But do you think she takes any notice? Not the slightest.'

Horihor sat down to his meal and talked as he ate.

'I went to Dasghara today to collect a debt that's been outstanding for some time. You know about that, don't you? There's a man there, an influential man, and very wealthy too—he has five or six rice barns. When he saw me he saluted most respectfully, and said, "Do you recognize me, revered sir?" I said, "No, my dear man, I don't. Where did I ...?" He said, "It was when you father was alive. He did me the honour of coming to our house regularly to conduct our festivals. Your family were like spiritual advisers to us. Now we are thinking of being initiated, of taking a sacred text, all of us, and if you approve, I wonder if I might ask you to perform the ceremony for us." I said, "I'm afraid I can't give you an answer at once; but in a day or two when I come back.... You understand, don't you?" '

Shorbojoya was standing with a bowl of soup in her hands. She put it on the floor by his side and sat down facing him. 'There's no harm in it, is there? Why not do it for them? What caste are they?' Horihor replied in a whisper, 'You mustn't tell anybody. They're low-caste people, Shodgops. You're inclined to go round gossiping, you know ...'

'Who am I likely to go and talk to? What does it matter if they are Shodgops? Why not do it for them? Things are very difficult just now. All we have is the eight rupees you get from the Rays' house, and you only get that every two or three months. I met Shejbou yesterday on the way to the tank and she said, "I don't usually lend money except on security, but you pleaded so hard I let you have some. It's over five months ago now, and I can't afford to wait any longer." Radha Bostom's wife is nagging at me too. She duns me for payment at least twice a day. And here at home, Opu has scarcely anything to wear. The few clothes he has are stitched together in several places. The little darling doesn't seem to mind; he dances around happily enough in his rags; but I'm so ashamed. I feel sometimes as if I could willingly drop through the ground.'

'And he said something else too, you know,' Horihor went on ignoring his wife's interruption. He said that there were no Brahmins in their village, and that if we went to live there he would set us up with a house and some land. He's very anxious to have a family of Brahmins permanently settled in the village. He would be prepared to give us some rice fields, and there's no shortage of money. It looks to me as though the goddess of wealth has taken up her abode with the farming people nowadays, while folks of good families have to live from hand to mouth.'

Shorbojoya was so excited she could not speak for a minute. 'At once, at once!' she spluttered. 'Why didn't you agree at once? You should have said, "All right, we'll come." To think that we might be living under the patronage of a rich man like that! What have you got to keep you here? Only this old family house and a pittance we have to scrape and scrounge for!'

Horihor laughed, 'You silly thing!' he said. 'It would never have done to consent at once. These are low-caste people. They would have thought the Brahmin's pot had indeed run dry. That's no way to handle the situation, to let them think that we are down and out, I mean. Just let me talk it over quietly with Mojumdar. And there's another thing. There's much more to getting away from this place than just saying we're going. What about these wretched people here? They would certainly say, "Pay up," and "If you don't pay we won't let you go." No, I must talk it over first and see what I can work out.'

At this point Durga came tiptoeing in. She stood for a moment behind the gate and peeped in furtively. When she saw that her father and mother were in and awake she went along the fence and got up to the balcony on the other side of the house. She pushed gently at the door there, but it was locked. Now she was in a quandary. She could not stay on the balcony; it was too hot for her feet, but on the other hand she did not want to be seen. So she got down and went and stood under the jackfruit tree in the yard. She had been out in the sun and her face was very red; and she had something tied up carefully in the end of her sari. If she had found the outside door open and her mother had been asleep, she would have crept in quietly and got into bed. That was why she had come home; but she had not the courage to go in by the front door and pass through the house in front of her father and mother, especially her mother. She stood for a while under the jackfruit tree, but she could not make up her mind what to do. She looked about listlessly, and then she sat down and untied the knot in her sari. It contained a number of dry fruit seeds. She took them out and looked at them and then started to count them, one, two three, four, and on up to twenty-six. She put two or three of them on the back of her hand, threw them up and caught them in her palm. Then she thought to herself, 'I'll give Opu these, and the rest I'll keep in my doll's box. They're very shiny ones. They only fell from the tree today. It was very lucky I got there as soon as I did or the cows would have eaten them up. That red cow next door is an absolute fiend; she'll go anywhere if she thinks there's anything to eat. I must have a lot of seeds now, what with these and those I had before.'

When she had had enough of playing with the seeds she tied them up again in her sari. Suddenly she had an idea. It must have been a good one for she shook her dry hair so hard that it blew out in the wind. Then she went straight out of the yard.

NINE

Not far from Opu's home there was a very large banyan tree, but only the top of it could be seen from the windows of the verandah. Opu used to stand and stare at it very often, and whenever he did so his mind went wandering to distant places, to a land which was a long, long, long way off. He had no idea what land it was, nor where it was or anything about it; except that he fancied it must be like the countries his mother used to tell him about, the countries where the princes of fairyland lived.

Mere awareness of distance was enough to fill his little mind with a feeling of wonder and make him happy. The blue sky was a long way off. So was the paper kite that flew in it. The field near the indigo factory was a a long way off too. He could not explain what he felt, but whenever he thought of things or places which were a long way off he seemed to be lifted out of himself and transported to another world. But, and this is the most amazing part of it, whenever this fascination of distance took possession of him, his thoughts suddenly turned to his mother who always seemed to be left behind when he went on his long journeys. He felt worried about her and was in a panic to get back to her as quickly as he could. It happened to him so often. A long way off, high up in the sky, a large hawk was flying. Slowly it became smaller and smaller and smaller until it passed beyond the high tips of the palm trees near Nila's house and gradually faded away into the distant sky. His eyes followed the circling bird until it finally vanished from his sight; then they came back to earth with a jerk and he bounded from the outer room, across the verandah into the kitchen, and threw his arms round his mother who was in the middle of her housework. 'Let me go!' she exclaimed. 'What a baby you are! You mustn't touch me now, you know you mustn't. I'm cooking; it's wrong to touch me before I've washed my hands. Let go of me, darling! I've got to finish frying these prawns for you. You like prawns, don't you? Well, don't be a naughty boy then. Let me go!'

One day, as she often did after their midday meal, Shorbojoya lay down by the window, spread her sari around her, and began to chant part of the Mahabharat from a tattered copy of the poem by Kasidas. A fish hawk called from the coconut tree at the side of the house, and Opu, who was seated by her side, was writing his a b c, and listening to her as she sang. Suddenly she broke off and called out to Durga. 'Durga, get me some betel.' Opu wanted her to go on. 'Mummy, what about the story of the girl who collected cow-dung?'

'The story of the girl and the cow-dung, you say? Oh,

you mean that story of Hari Hor's! It's not in this book; it's in the *Annadamangal.*'

By this time she had the betel in her mouth and went droning on.

'The king said, "Hear me while I tell
A wondrous tale, which mark you well,
Of King Somadutt who lived in Sind,
A foe alike of gods ..." '

At this point Opu interrupted her. He held his hand up to her mouth and asked for a bit of the betel she was chewing. She took some of it out of her mouth and put it into his outstretched hand. 'Be careful though,' she said, 'it's very bitter. It's the khoyer bark. I tell your father every day not to buy this kind of bark, but still ...'

Opu was not listening. His eyes were fixed on the bamboos outside the window and on the crisscross of light and shade they cast on the jungle bushes beneath. All he heard—he had ears for nothing else—was that story from the Mahabharat, the story of the battle of Kurukshetra, and in particular the part about Karna. Of all the characters in the Mahabharat he liked Karna best. He had a special sympathy for him: Karna with his chariot wheels stuck in the mud, making a superhuman effort to drag them clear; Karna, for the moment unarmed and alone, his hands busy with the chariot wheels, making his pathetic appeal to Arjun's chivalry. But alas, Arjun spurned his plea and struck him dead with a shaft from his bow. As he listened to his mother telling this part of the story Opu's young heart was stricken with grief, and there was no holding back the tears. They flooded out of his eyes and streamed down his soft delicate cheeks; but as he wept there was born in his mind a sympathetic insight he had not experienced before, and with it a feeling of happiness,

happiness that comes of weeping for another's sorrow. There is a road through life which leads to compassion, compassion for the tears of man, compassion for his poverty, compassion for his pain, his hopelessness, his sense of frustration and his death; and the signposts which pointed the way for Opu were the midday sun, the musty smell which spread through the air from the torn pages of that old book, and the gentle music of his mother's voice. Then as the day wore on, Shorbojoya returned to her housework and Opu went out and stood on the verandah, staring at the distant banyan tree. Sometimes the high branches were hazy in the shimmering heat of mid-summer; at other times they glowed red in the still light of the evening sun. More than anything else, it was the sight of the tree stained with the red colours of evening that filled his mind with grief; and in the far distance, beyond the banyan tree, where the sky leant down to the earth, he could see Karna, his hands labouring to drag the chariot wheels clear of the mud. Every day he laboured, every day, Karna, the mighty hero, the object of a pity which could never end. It was Arjun who won the kingdom; it was Arjun who won the fame; it was Arjun who slew his hapless foe with a bolt loosed from his chariot; but his was not the victory. Karna was the victor; Karna it was who lived on in the tears of countless generations, ever present where love is born of human pain.

Day after day Opu listened to the tales of the Mahabharat war, but there were not nearly enough battles for him. So to make good this deficiency he worked out a plan whereby he could revel in battles to his heart's content. He armed himself with a bamboo switch and a thin branch from a tree. Then he paced up and down the path, which led through the grove, or up and down the yard outside the house, and there he re-enacted the scenes for himself. First, Dron shot

71

ten arrows. It could not have been fewer. And what did Arjun do? He fired off at least two hundred arrows. Then—oh!— what a battle there was; what a battle! There were so many arrows that the sky became dark with them. (Yet, however many arrows his fancy launched, his imaginary battle did not outdo Kasidas's story of the Mahabharat war as he heard his mother sing it.) What did Arjun do next? He seized his shield and his sword and leapt down from the chariot. And how he fought! Duryodhan came, and then Bhim. Their arrows darkened the sky. You could not see a thing. But the battle in which the warriors of the Mahabharat won their fame lasted only eighteen days. If they had been alive today they would have realized that the path to glory had in the meantime become much more difficult. To satisfy the eager longings of a boy they would have had to ply their weapons for months on end without respite. Could even they have fought for so long?

It was a summer day at the beginning of May. The scene was the edge of the jungle near Nilmoni Ray's house. It was just before noon. The teacher Dron was in great trouble. Arjun's chariot, the one with the monkey banner, had run over his shoulder. There was Arjun's bow, the Gandiva, and in it the fatal arrow which the god Brahma had given him. In a second it would be fired. The hosts of the Kurus, Dron's troops, had already raised a cry of alarm, when an amused voice called out from the jungle thickets behind him, 'What on earth are you up to, Opu?' Opu started and released the bowstring which was at that moment drawn right back to his ear. Then he looked round and saw his sister standing among the bushes laughing at him. 'You silly boy!' she said. 'What are you doing muttering to yourself and waving your arms and legs about?' Then affectionately, 'Silly! What a silly boy you are! What were you talking to yourself for?'

72

Opu flushed with embarrassment. He made several efforts to speak, but the words would not come. 'Oh ... I ... I ... wasn't ... talking to myself ... you know ... I ... !'

Durga was very amused but presently she stopped laughing and taking Opu by the hand said, 'Come along with me,' and led him off into the wood. After they had gone a little way, she pointed ahead and said with a laugh, 'Can you see all those custard apples? Lots of them are ripe, you know. How do you think we can get them down?'

'Oh, yes! I can see them. There they are! Lots and lots of them. Couldn't we knock them off with a stick?'

'Yes, perhaps we could,' she said. 'Run back home and get me the fruit pole. It's inside the house. They'd fall for certain if we could shake them with the pole.'

'All right! You wait here. I'll get it.'

Opu came back with the pole, but try as they would they succeeded in knocking only four or five down. The tree was too high for them. Even with the pole Durga could not reach the top branches where most of the fruit was. She gave up trying after a while and said, 'These few will do for today. Let's take them home. I'll get Mummy to come with us tomorrow when we go down for our bath. She should be able to reach them with the pole. So come on; carry the pole and let me take the custard apples. But wait a minute; wouldn't you like me to make you a nosegay?'

Just down the slope there was a bush with a china-rose creeper growing over it. Durga had just spotted it and she noticed that there were lots of white buds on it. So putting down the fruit she went in close to the bush and began to pluck some of the buds. 'Come here,' she said to Opu, 'and let me make a nosegay for you.' She was very fond of making china-rose nosegays. Whenever she went into the forest she was on the lookout for flowers to make them with, and if

Opu was there she would make one for him too. If the truth were known Opu did not like wearing flowers, and he would have liked to tell her so, but he did not want to do that because he was afraid it might annoy her; and he did not want to do that because it was she who searched the jungle and collected all sorts of fruits which she gave to him when nobody was looking, jujube fruit, rose-apples, wild custard apples, hog-plums. All these and more she got for him, and they both ate them, though they knew quite well that their mother had told them that fruit like that was not good to eat and that they were not to eat it. Consequently though he did not in the least want to wear a flower on his nose he had not the courage to refuse when his sister made one for him.

When Durga broke off a flower bud a white gummy liquid oozed out, and she put some of it on Opu's nose to hold the flower on with. Then she put a flower on her own nose too; and when she had finished she lifted Opu's chin up and turned his face towards her, saying, 'Let me see what it looks like—oh, that's lovely! Let's go home and show Mummy.'

Opu protested and said he did not want to.

'Of course we must,' Durga said. 'It looks very nice. Mind you don't knock if off.'

When they reached home Durga put the fruit down on the kitchen verandah. Shorbojoya was cooking at the time, but when she saw what it was that Durga had brought she was very pleased.

'Where did you get them?' she asked.

'In the lichee jungle. There are lots of them. If you come with us tomorrow we can get lots more. They're ever so ripe, as red as vermilion powder.' Saying this Durga moved to one side so that her mother could have a better look at the fruit. 'Do have a look at them, Mummy.'

Opu was standing just behind his sister. He still had the flower on his nose. Shorbojoya laughed. 'Goodness me! Who's that there? I don't think I know him.' Opu blushed and swept the flower from his nose, 'Didi made me wear it,' he said.

He had no time to say any more for Durga burst out excitedly, 'Listen, Opu. It's a drum. Come on! They're going to have a monkey dance. Come quickly.'

They dashed outside, Durga in front, Opu close behind, and they ran along the path in front of the house; but it was not the monkey man, it was Chinibas the sweet-seller. He had his basket on his head and was doing a round of the village. He ran a small shop on the other side of the village, but he often went round from house to house hawking sweets, and sometimes paddy as well. He had not done very well in the past, never having enough capital to keep his business going for long. He had tried touring the markets with a basket on his head selling potatoes and beans, and betel; but that venture did not do well either. So he was forced to put a bag round his neck and go back to being a beggar as his ancestors had been. Then one day he suddenly reappeared selling rock-lime. People said he had had a go at selling everything except fish. The next day was the mid-summer festival known as Dasahara, and people would be wanting to buy sugared rice and sweets for it. That is why he was out. He usually went past Horihor's gate without stopping because he knew they never bought anything; but seeing Durga and Opu standing there he asked them if they wanted anything.

Opu looked at Durga, but she shook her head and said, 'No!'

Chinibas passed on at once to the next house, which was Bhubon Mukherji's, and set his basket down in the yard there. The children of the family let out a yell when they saw him and clustered round to see what he had brought. Bhubon

Mukherji was a rich man. He had five or six rice barns, and he owned more land and property than anybody in the district except Onnoda Ray.

His wife had been dead a long time, and it was his third brother's widow who was the mistress of the household. They called her Shejbou. She was over forty and was well-known in the neighbourhood for her shrewish temper. Seeing Chinibas in the yard she took a polished brass tray out with her and bought some sugared rice and several kinds of cream sweets for the festival; and as Bhubon Mukherji's children and her own son Shunil were standing there, she bought some for them too. Durga and Opu were in the yard when she came out—they had followed Chinibas in—but as soon as Shejbou saw them she gave her son a push saying, 'Run along indoors now and eat your sweets there. They are for the god's festival, you know; so mind you don't drop any of them from your mouth. They'll cause defilement if you do, and we shan't be able to make any offering to the god.' This she said to make sure that Durga and Opu did not get any of the sweets even by accident.

Chinibas put the basket on his head moved on to another house. Durga said to Opu, 'Come along; let's follow him to Tunu's.' But as they passed by her door Shejbou turned her head and said in a loud voice so that every word would be heard, 'Can't bear that sort of thing. Did you notice? What a greedy girl that Durga is! She's always hanging round other people's houses. You'd think from the way she behaves that she hadn't a home of her own. Why doesn't she buy her own sweets and eat them there? The brat of a girl's just like her mother.'

Opu was very upset, and when they got outside Durga tried to console him. 'Never mind,' she said, 'Chinibas hasn't got much any way. It'll be the Chariot festival soon, and

Daddy will be home by then. I'll get four pice from him when he comes, two for you and two for me; and then we shall be able to buy some sweets for ourselves.'

Opu thought for a while and then said, 'How many days are there left before the Chariot festival, Didi?'

TEN

It was several months later.

Shorbojoya had just come in with water she had drawn from the well at Bhubon Mukherji's house. Opu was just behind her, holding on to her sari and twisting it in his hand. She set down the water pot and said to him, 'Why have you taken to following me backwards and forwards like this? I've got to finish the housework and then I'm going to the tank for my bath; but I can't get on with anything if you hang on to me like this, can I?'

'The housework doesn't matter. You can do it this afternoon.' Then in the hope of wheedling her into forgetting about the work, he said plaintively, 'Do you think I never feel hungry? I haven't had anything to eat for four days, you know.'

'I know you haven't but what can I do about it? You go wandering about in the sun and get fever; and if I say anything to you, you don't take any notice. And Durga's just as bad. Anyway, I've got to get on now, I can't go for my bath until the housework's done; and I've no time to waste, so be off with you; and don't be such a naughty boy. I just cannot do everything you and your sister want. So run along now.'

Opu twisted her sari round in his hand and held it even more tightly than before. 'I'm not going to let go,' he said defiantly. 'You're always doing housework. It won't do any harm to let it be for one day, surely? Go for your bath now. If you don't I won't take any notice of whatever you say; and that'll stop you doing all this silly housework?'

Shorbojoya glared at him for a moment and then suddenly she saw the funny side of it and burst out laughing. 'Don't be such a naughty boy,' she said. 'I'll be finished in no time now. Just wait a minute or two longer, then I'll go to the tank and hurry back and cook some rice for you. What's the use of carrying on like this? Let go of my sari and tell me how much fried vegetable you can eat.'

About an hour later Opu sat down to eat so eagerly that if you had seen him you would have thought he was ravenous. He first picked up his glass and half-emptied it with a great gulp. Then he swallowed a mouthful or two of rice, moving the rest busily round his plate as though he were eating hard; then he finished the rest of the water and raised his hands to show he had had enough.

'You call that eating?' said his mother. 'All this time you've been clamouring for rice, and I've given you fried vegetables as well. And yet you've left them all. You've hardly eaten anything.'

Shorbojoya took a cup of milk, softened some rice in it, and began to feed him. 'Say "a-a-ah". I know you're not a lucky boy,' she said when she had got some of it into his mouth. 'I've no sweets to give you, just rice, a few grains of rice; I know that; but it worries me to see you like this. Day after day you sit down to your food and all you do is pull a face. You don't eat enough to keep body and soul together. You'll never grow into a man if you go on like this. But as far as I can see, you weren't born to grow into a man; you were only born to plague your mother. No, no! don't turn your face away like that. Open your mouth, my precious! Just this little bit and it's all gone. Oh!' she went on, 'this evening there's the Manasa party at Tunu's house. You didn't know that, did you? So eat up quickly, and we'll all ...'

Durga came into the room. She had just got back from one of her wanderings. Her feet were covered with dust, and a wisp of hair three or four inches long hung straight down over her eyes. She was always going off on her own, for she very seldom played in the village with children of her own age; but she knew what bush had ripe berries on it; and if there were green mangoes in anybody's garden, she knew that too, and what tree they were on; and where in the bamboo grove the jujube fruit was good to eat. Whenever she went along a path she was on the lookout, scanning both sides of the way at every step she took. For who knows? Perhaps she might come across some ripe fruit on a nightshade bush, and when she did she plucked it at once to make into egg-fruit for her toy house. Sometimes she squatted down in the path and picked up pieces of broken roof tiling. She weighed them in her hand first and then practised throwing them to see which ones would be accurate enough for Ganges and Jamuna; and when she had tried them out, she wrapped up the most promising pieces in the corner of her sari. She was always on the lookout for something to put in her doll's box or her toy house.

She came in and stood looking at her mother with a guilty look in her eyes.

Shorbojoya said, 'Oh, so you've come at last, have you? Come in then; your food's ready for you. Finish it off and let me get on; and then you can wander off to wherever you feel like wandering. It's the month of May now and everybody else's daughter—you can go and see for yourself—everybody else's daughter, I say, is making candles and getting ready for the festival. But not you! You go round the place like a vagabond, though you're old enough to be married now. What a girl you are! You went out as soon as it was light, and now it's past midday and you've only just come home. And look at the state of your hair. There's not a drop of oil on it, and it looks as if you didn't touch it with a comb either. Who would think you were a Brahmin's daughter? You look just like a girl from a low-caste house; and if you ever do get married that's the sort of family you'll marry into. What treasure is that you've got tied up in your sari? Take it out at once.'

Durga began to untie the corner of her sari, and as she fumbled nervously with the knot she tried to explain. 'Over there ... in front of the Rays' house ... on the kalkashunda tree'—she swallowed hard before she could go on—there are a lot of shop-ladies ...'

Unfortunately there are many people in this world who are so insensitive that they cannot understand a child's passion for shop-lady berries, as Durga called them. Shorbojoya was livid. 'You and your wretched shop-ladies!' she shouted. 'What is there ladylike wandering round all the hours of the day and night picking up I don't know what rubbish and tying it in your sari! You see if I don't drag your doll's box out of the house before the day is done and throw it in the pond in the bamboo grove! That'll make you ...'

But before Shorbojoya could finish there was an interruption. It was Shejbou, from Bhubon Mukherji's house. She marched right in through the front gate, and behind her came her daughter Tunu and her nephew Shotu, and there were four or five other children behind them. Shejbou did not say a word to anybody. She did not even look at anybody. She went straight across the yard and up into the porch. Then she turned to her nephew and said, 'Go and get that doll's box, and bring it out here so that I can see for myself.' Before anyone in the house could utter a syllable Tunu and Shotu had fetched Durga's doll's tin box out of the room and dumped it down in front of Shejbou. Tunu opened it and rummaged about inside, and presently she produced a string of beads.

'Here it is, Mummy! Look. This is my necklace. She came to play with us the other day and she stole it.'

Meanwhile, Shotu who went on digging about in a corner of the box had brought out several green mangoes. 'Look here Auntie! These are mangoes she's picked from our shonamukhi tree!'

The whole affair had happened so quickly, and what had been done had taken everyone in the house so much by surprise that until now none of them had said a word. At this point however Shorbojoya found her voice. 'What's all this about, Shejbou? What's happened?' And there was a look of bewilderment on her face as she came out from the kitchen to see for herself.

'Come over here and you'll be able to see what's happened. It's something that even you should be proud of. That daughter of yours came to play with the children the other day and she stole this necklace from Tunu's doll's box. The poor child was worried to death thinking she'd lost it until Shotu came and told her that he'd seen it in Durga's box. The impertinence of it! That daughter of yours is an absolute pest. She's a thief, an impudent thief! And look at these too. They're green mangoes from our garden. She couldn't even wait for them to fall. She had to steal them from the tree and then she hid them in her box.'

Durga was leaning against the wall, sweating. She was completely numbed by this double accusation. Shorbojoya turned to her and said, 'Did you take the necklace from their house?'

Before Durga could reply Shejbou exclaimed, 'What do you mean, "Did she take it?" Are you trying to make out that I'm telling a lie? And don't forget these mangoes either. You know what our shonamukhi mangoes look like, don't you? Or is that a lie too?'

Shorbojoya was so taken aback she could not find the words she wanted. 'No, Shejbou,' she said, 'that's not what I meant. I'm not suggesting that you're telling a lie at all. I'm only asking her.'

Shejbou waved her arms about and retorted hotly. 'You can ask her as much as you like, but I warn you that girl will come to no good. At her age she's taken to thieving. Goodness knows what she'll come to later on. But you'll find out. Come on, Shotu. Wrap those mangoes up. It's coming to something if we can't enjoy our own mangoes because this wretched creature steals them all. Tunu, have you got that necklace?'

Shorbojoya's patience was beginning to run out; and she was never one to back down in a quarrel. 'I don't know about the necklace.' She said, 'but those mangoes! You don't seem to have made up your mind whether she knocked them off the tree or only picked them up off the ground. In any case there's no name on them, is there? And children the whole world over collect mangoes. There's no crime in that.'

Shejbou was furious. 'What cheek you've got to talk to me

83

like that! You're just trying to argue yourself out of it. Of course there's no name on them. But what garden of yours did they come from? Tell me that. There was no name on the money you wheedled out of me over a year ago either. And what have you been saying about that? "I'll pay you this afternoon … I'll let you have it tomorrow … I'll bring it over at once!" I've had enough of all this, and it's got to stop. So pay up. I don't care where you get the money from, but get it.'

Shejbou stamped out through the gate with her regiment behind her. Outside on the path somebody asked her what the matter was, and she explained at the top of her voice to make sure that Shorbojoya heard what she said. 'The wretched girl from their house stole this bead necklace from Tunu's box and hid it in her own. And she took these mangoes too. Look at them. Our garden's next door to theirs, and they think they can take as many as they like. I only went to tell her about it, and she tried to talk me down. (Here she started mimicking Shorbojoya's voice.) She said "Children all over the world take mangoes. There's no crime in that. Besides you haven't your name on them, have you?" (Then she lowered her voice a little.) The truth is the mother's as big a thief as the daughter. The girl didn't learn all she knows without teaching. The whole family of them are thieves.'

Shorbojoya's eyes were full of tears, tears of humiliation and distress. That final insult had included her husband and that was more than she could bear. She swung round on Durga and grabbed hold of her by her long dry hair, and with hands that were still covered with dal and rice she began to thump and slap her, blow after blow. And she kept it up. 'You little fiend!' she screamed. 'You've brought a curse on all of us. Would to God you were dead! If you were I might be able to breathe again, and know some peace in my bones. Get out! Get out of the house! And stay out!'

Durga was terrified, and with the blows still falling on her she broke away and dashed out of the back door. Some strands of her torn dry hair remained behind in Shorbojoya's hand.

All this time Opu had been sitting over his food. He had watched and heard everything but he had not said a word. He did not know whether his sister had stolen the mangoes. He was quite sure that was not stealing. Last evening she had taken him with her to pick up some mangoes in Tunu's garden. A few had fallen from the shonamukhi tree, and she had picked them up. He knew all about that. Since then she had said to him a time or two, 'What do you think, Opu? Shall we pickle those mangoes?' But it so happened that their mother had always been in the house and they had not been able to do it. Now those very mangoes which she had so looked forward to eating had been taken from her in this way; and on top of that she had had such a terrible beating. He was furious with his mother for pulling her hair out. He loved Durga's hair. He could not say why, but he did, especially when it hung long and dry over her eyes or when the wind blew it straight up in the air; and as he thought of her hair he felt even fonder of her than before. It seemed to him that she had no one anywhere to care for her. Wherever she had come from she had come alone; and she had no companions here either. One thought only possessed his mind, how to drive away all her unhappiness and to make up to her for all the things she had to do without. He must do something to save her from all this suffering.

Nevertheless, Opu was afraid of his mother, so when he had finished his meal he sat down in his room and began to read; but his mind was not on his book, it was racing about outside. As evening drew on, he went to Tunu's house, to the Potlis' house, to Nera's house. He looked in at them all one by one, but his sister was nowhere there. Rajkrishna Palit's wife was coming back from the tank with water, so he asked her. 'Auntie, have you seen my Didi? She hasn't had a meal today. She hasn't eaten anything. Mummy gave her a terrible beating and she has run away somewhere. Have you seen her, Auntie?'

While he was walking along the path that ran by the house it occurred to him that she might be sitting in the bamboo grove, so he went there and searched for her. Then he went into the house again through the back door, but there was nobody in. His mother must have gone to the tank or somewhere. The evening shadows were creeping over the house. Near the front door there was a clump of bamboos, and on one of the dry swinging branches was perched a long-tailed yellow bird. He knew it well. Every day just before dark it came and settled down on that same bamboo branch. It did it every day, day after day. There were other birds about too, twittering in the jungle round the house. The place where Nilmoni Ray's derelict house stood was quite dark under the shade of the thick clustering trees. Opu stood in the yard and stared at the top of the banyan tree. It was still lit up, though faintly, with the last red glow of the sun. Something was swinging on the topmost branch. It might be a crane, or else a kite that had got caught there. The colours of the sky were deepening and darkness was near. Whichever way he looked he could see no one. There was not a soul in sight, only the gleam which was reflected from the dark green leaves of the kochu bush in Nilmoni Ray's compound. Panic came upon him. It was hours since she had gone, and she was not back yet. She had had nothing to eat. Where could she have gone to?

In Bhubon Mukherji's yard all the children of the household were playing hide-and-seek. Ranu saw him and rushed up to him. 'Look! Opu's come! He must be on our side. Come on, Opu.'

Opu shook off her hand. 'I don't want to play, Ranu. Have you seen Didi?'

'Durga? No, I haven't seen her. Isn't she under the bokul tree?'

He had not thought of the bokul tree. He knew that she did sit there at times. So he left the Mukherjis' house and went towards it. By now the night had come. The branches of the bokul grew close together and they spread out widely over a large area. The ground underneath was very dark. There was nobody there; but perhaps she might be standing on the other side of the tree, so he called, 'Didi, Didi! O Didi!' Only a few cranes in the dark tree flapped their wings. Opu was frightened as he looked up to see what it was. Not far from the bokul there was a date palm by the tank. The dates were half-ripe now, and he knew that Durga went there sometimes. But it was very dark, and there was a bamboo grove on either side of the tank, and Opu was afraid to go there and look. He moved nearer to the trunk of the bokul tree and called out nervously. An animal in the thickets was disturbed by the sound of his voice and rustled through the undergrowth as it ran towards the tank.

He turned to go home, but suddenly he stopped. There was a wild mangosteen tree in front of him. The path lay right under it, and he was alone and it was dark. He was terrified. Prickles of fear ran up and down his body. He did not know why he was afraid to walk under that tree. There was no reason, but because there was no reason he was all the more afraid. He had never been out so late before, though that thought did not occur to him at the time. Nevertheless, whether he thought of it or not, he would never have come this way alone if his mind had not been so preoccupied.

He stood looking at the dark tree for some time and then he turned away from it. There was another way home. It was a bit round about, past the Potlis' house, but it took him away from the unknown terrors that lurked beneath that tree. When he reached the Potlis' house, the grandmother of the family was out on the verandah with the children. They were sitting in the dark and she was telling them a story. Their mother was in the kitchen. Bidhu the fisherman's wife was standing near the vegetable rack trying to get payment for some fish.

Opu called out, 'I've been out looking for Didi, Granny. I went to look under the bokul tree ...'

'Durga? She's gone home. She went by some time ago. Hurry along. She must be there by now.'

He dashed off. As he ran, Raji, one of the Potli sisters, called after him. 'Come tomorrow morning, Opu. We've marked out a new court for Ganges and Jamuna. It's under the neem tree behind the husking shed. Tell Durga.'

As he approached the house he stopped dead in his tracks. Durga was running out of the door screaming at the top of her voice. Behind her came his mother. She had something in her hand and was beating her with it. Durga fled along the path that went under the mangosteen tree. His mother stood in the doorway and screeched after her as she ran. 'Go away, go away for ever; and never come back here again, curse you! You're the cause of all our troubles. I wish I could have you taken to the chatim tree.'

The chatim tree stood in the village cremation grounds. Opu knew that and his body froze in horror. He went stiff and heavy like a stone. Shorbojoya took down the lamp that was in the porch and went inside. Opu tiptoed in after her, hoping she would not see him, but she did. 'It's very late,' she scolded. 'Where have you been to? You know you've had fever and that you're not eating properly yet!'

Many questions were milling round in Opu's mind. Why had Didi been beaten again. Where had she been all this time?

Had she had anything to eat at midday? Had she stolen anything else? But he was too frightened to ask. He did everything his mother told him to, automatically like a clock-work doll, and then he went to his room. Still trembling he turned up the lamp and took down his bundle of books to read. He had only got as far as the *Third Reader*, but his library contained two very heavy tomes in English, a list of doctor's medicines, a long poem by Dashu Ray—its pages were badly torn—and an old almanac, which was at least fifty years old. These he had collected by asking various people for them, and though he could not read them not a day passed without his taking them down and looking at them at least once.

For a while he sat staring at the wall lost in thought. Then he turned the lamp up a little further and began to finger the pages of his poetry book absentmindedly. While he was doing it his mother came into the room with a glass of milk in her hand. 'Come on, drink this up,' she said. Opu took the glass without a word and began to sip at it. On any other day it would not have been so easy to get him to drink milk. Nevertheless when he had had a few sips he took the glass away from his mouth and put it down.

'What's this?' Shorbojoya said. 'You must drink all of it. If you can't drink a few mouthfuls of milk like this how do you expect to get well and strong again?'

Opu made no protest. He raised the glass to his mouth again, but Shorbojoya noticed that though it was touching his lips he was not drinking. Both hand and glass were trembling. He held the glass there some time, and then abruptly he put it down and turning towards his mother burst into tears. Shorbojoya was surprised. 'What's the matter?' she said. 'What have you done? Have you bitten your tongue?' Opu forgot his fears and said sobbing, 'It's Didi! I'm sad for Didi.'

Shorbojoya remained silent for a little while; she moved close up to him and put her arm round him. 'Don't cry like that,' she said gently. 'Don't cry. She's probably sitting in the Potlis' house, or at Nera's. She's not likely to have gone far on a dark night like this. But she's a very naughty girl, you know. She went out this morning, and she hasn't been back the whole day. She didn't come in for her meal. She was sitting in the Palits' garden at the other end of the village, and she ate some green mangoes and some wild plums. But don't be so upset. I'll send for her at once. You'll make yourself ill again, you silly boy!'

She wiped his tears away with her sari, and took up the glass and tried to get him to finish the rest of the milk. 'Open your mouth, darling! Your father'll go and fetch her as soon as he comes in. You are a silly boy! I don't know why I should have such a silly boy. One more sip now. Yes, that's it!'

It was late that same night. Opu and Durga were sleeping in a bed in the north room of the house. There was an empty place in the bed by Opu's side. It was his mother's. She had not yet finished her work in the kitchen. His father was back; he had had his meal and was sitting in the next room smoking. Horihor had returned earlier in the evening, and when he heard what had happened he went out into the village to look for Durga.

Durga did not say a word to anybody when she came in. She had her meal in silence and went to bed. Opu put out his hand to touch her. 'Didi,' he asked, 'what did Mummy beat you with this evening?' She did not reply. So he spoke to her again. 'Are you cross with me, Didi? I haven't done anything.'

'Oh, haven't you? Then how did Shotu find out that the bead necklace was in my box?'

This accusation made Opu sit straight up on the bed. 'No, honestly, Didi, I didn't show it to him. I promise you I didn't

90

even know it was there. Shotu was here yesterday afternoon. We were playing with that big red marble of his. It was then that he opened your box and began to look for something. I told him not to touch it, or you'd be angry with me. That's when he must have seen it.'

The he began to stroke her with his hand. 'Does it hurt a lot, Didi? Where did she hit you?'

'She hit me behind the ear and made it bleed. It's still throbbing. Here it is! You can feel it. Yes, that's the place!'

'Here? Yes, now I can feel it. You've got a cut there. Shall I get some oil from the lamp and put on it?'

'No, it doesn't matter. I'll tell you what. Tomorrow afternoon we'll go to the Palits' garden. The berries there are ever so ripe. They're as big as big. But don't tell anybody. We'll go when nobody's looking just you and me. I pulled one or two of them off today. They're sweet like sugar.'

ELEVEN

❦

It was another day, and this is what happened.

Opu's father had told him to write out the alphabet seven times on some palm leaves and as soon as he had finished he went wandering round the house looking for his sister and wondering what they were going to do; but Durga was not in. She had slipped out and had her bath early in the morning to get away from her mother, and then went to say her prayers under the papaya tree in the inner yard. It was the festival of the Holy Pond, when sisters pray for their brothers. There was a small square pit in the yard. Some days before she had planted pulse and peas in it, and already the shoots were showing in the damp soil. She had also set some banana suckers outside the pit, and when Opu found her she was tracing pictures round them; lotuses, birds, bundles of rice, and the rising sun.

'Wait a minute,' she said to him. 'Just let me finish my prayers and then we'll go somewhere.'

'Where, Didi?'

'Never you mind. I'll take you very soon now, and then you'll know.'

So saying she went on with her prayers. First she went through a number of ritual acts which were prescribed for this festival; then, drawing a deep breath, she began to intone:

'Oh, holy pond; oh, holy flower!
I worship you neath the noon-day sky.
A maiden's purity is my dower;
My brother lives and blest am I.'

Opu stood not far away listening. The words sounded odd to him and he gave a little laugh of surprise. Durga stopped at once and smiled, but she was clearly embarrassed.

'What did you laugh like that for ? Go away. You've no business to be here. Go away.'

Opu laughed again and went away, but he mimicked her as he went—'My brother lives and blest am I ... blest am I ...' He thought it was very funny.

'You think you're being clever, don't you? Just wait till I tell Mummy. You won't find it so funny then. You wait.'

Nevertheless she went on with what she had to do, and when it was over she called out to him. 'Come on. The water fruit's out near the Moat Lake. Bhonda's mother told me. Let's go and get some.'

At the extreme northern end of the village there was a path which ran through some very old mango and jackfruit orchards. There were bamboos too, and the undergrowth was very dense. If you went along that path, far from the houses, to where the jungle ended, you would come to a tank near the open field. In the old days a family named Mojumdar used to live there, and they had dug a moat round their house. Most of the moat was filled in now, but in one place there was a hole which was full of water all the year round. That was what they called the Moat Lake. Of the Mojumdars' house, however, no trace remained.

When the children got to the lake they saw a lot of water fruit, but none of it was down near the water; it was mostly very high up.

Durga said, 'Opu, we shall need a pole to get the fruit with. Go and see if you can find a piece of bamboo.' While she was waiting for him she pulled some ripe berries off a bush by the water's edge and began to eat them. Opu saw her from where he was among the bamboos and called out at once, 'Don't eat those berries, Didi. Leave them alone. They're not good to eat. They are sheora berries, and only fit for birds to eat.'

Durga squeezed the seed out of a ripe berry and said, 'Who says they're not good to eat. I've eaten lots of them. Come and see for yourself. They're as sweet as sugar.'

Opu had collected a number of bamboo canes by this time, but he put them down and went to where his sister was standing. 'Don't they say you go mad if you eat them, Didi? Just one then, to see how they taste.' He put one into his mouth but the moment he got his teeth into it he wrinkled up his face. 'It's bit... bitter, isn't it, Didi?'

'What did you expect? Of course it's a bit bitter, but it's very sweet too, don't you think?' And she stuffed some more ripe berries into her mouth and ate them with obvious relish.

They had never in their short lives had nice things to eat. They were young and their palates were untrained, that is why they were eager to sample everything they could, particularly things that tasted sweet. They had never been able to afford to satisfy their craving for delicacies with cream and sugared curds. They were the children of a poor home, and like poor children everywhere they were driven to find their sweets on the jungle bushes; yet coarse and astringent though these simple fruits might be in a world which lives on luscious food, the kindly goddesses of the forest had contrived to fill them with a honeyed nectar all their own.

Durga went down a little into the water. 'There's a lot of water fruit here, Opu,' she shouted. 'You stand there and I'll get some.' She went in a little further and tore several plants up by the stems and threw them on the bank. 'Catch, Opu.'

'The water fruit's right out over the water, Didi. How are you going to get at it?'

The water fruit was indeed far out over the water. Durga did her best to reach it with a bamboo cane, but with no success. 'The bank's very steep here,' she said. 'I shall slip down into deep water if I go further out. What can I do to reach it? Oh, yes, I know, you can help. Hold on to the end of my sari and I may be able to reach them with the pole.'

Inside the jungle a yellow bird was sitting on a twig in a moynakanta tree. It was singing very sweetly and making the leaves dance. Opu was fascinated. 'What bird is that, Didi?'

'Don't worry about birds! Hold on to my sari for all your worth or I shall slip in. Hold on tight now.'

Step by step Durga went down into the water, stretching out with the cane as far as it would go. Her clothes were wet through but still she could not reach. She went a little bit further and tried again, this time holding the cane with the tips of her fingers. Opu stood behind her pulling as hard as he could, but suddenly he realized that he was not strong enough to hold her and burst out laughing. He laughed so much that he let go and Durga began to slide in, but she managed to save herself in time. Then she laughed too. 'What a wash-out you are!' she exclaimed. 'You're utterly useless!

95

But come on, let's have another go. Hold on again.' With
an enormous effort she succeeded in hooking a cluster of fruit
and pulling it near. She examined it eagerly to see how much
fruit there was on it, but in a minute or so she flung it on
the bank. 'They're quite raw. They haven't got any milk in
them yet. Let's try once more. Hold on now.' Opu held on
again, but he could not counter his sister's pull as she leaned
forward, and little by little he found himself slipping into
the water. His clothes began to get wet, so he gave up and
stood there shaking with laughter. Durga laughed too. 'Silly!'
she said; and for some time the lonely bamboo grove by the
side of the pond echoed with the happy laughter of brother
and sister.

'If only you had a little strength in your body!' Durga said
with a laugh, 'but you haven't. You're no stronger than a dry
stick.' Thereupon she went down into the water to have
another try, but Opu who was still standing on the bank
suddenly screamed out and pointed with his finger in the
direction of a bush nearby, 'Look Didi! What's that there?'
And he rushed to the place and started to dig something out
of the ground. Durga climbed out of the water, but before
she got to him he had unearthed something and was rubbing
it clean on his clothes. He was very excited. 'Look at this,
Didi!' he said and held it out for her to see. 'See how it shines.
What is it?'

Durga took it in her hand. It was roundish, had sharply
cut facets, and it sparkled. She turned it this way and that
and examined it intently for a while, when an idea suddenly
flashed into her mind and her face shone bright through the
dry hair that flopped over it. She looked round nervously to
see if anybody was watching, and then she whispered, 'Opu,
I think it's a diamond. Sh! Don't shout.' And once more she
looked around nervously. Opu did not say a word. He just

stood and stared at her. He knew what the word meant though. His mother, and his sister too, had told him lots of fairy stories about princes and princesses, and they were always dressed in diamonds and pearls. He had however a somewhat wrong notion of what a diamond looked like. He thought it was yellowish, somewhat like fishes' roes, but hard not soft.

Shorbojoya was not in the house, but when she got back from the village she saw the two of them standing near the door. Durga crept up to her, 'Mummy,' she whispered, 'we've found something. We were near the Moat Lake picking water fruit and it was buried in the jungle.'

Opu said, 'I saw it first, Mummy, and told Didi about it.'

Durga untied the knot in her sari and put the stone in her mother's hand. 'Look at it, Mummy. What is it?' Shorbojoya turned it this way and that, and Durga whispered to her, 'It's a real diamond, Mummy, isn't it?'

Shorbojoya knew no more about diamonds than that they did, so she said dubiously, 'What makes you think it's a diamond?'

'The Mojumdars were rich people, weren't they, Mummy? And people used to pick up gold coins in the jungle near their house. Auntie used to tell me about them. We found this buried in the jungle close to the lake. The sun was shining on it and it sparkled. It must be a real diamond, Mummy!'

Shorbojoya said, 'Wait till your father comes home and we'll show it to him.'

It was a very excited and happy Durga that went out into the yard, and she said to Opu, 'If it's a real diamond, Opu, we shall be rich. You wait and see.'

Opu did not know what she meant by rich, but he laughed all the same, a wild excited laugh.

When the children left her, Shorbojoya took the thing out and had another look at it. It was roundish and had bevelled edges. One face was pointed like the stone on the top of her vermilion powder box. It really did sparkle. She thought she could see all kinds of colours in it, so it certainly was not glass, at least she did not remember ever having seen glass like that. A wave of excitement thrilled through her, and deep within her a hope, an impossible hope, came to life, brushing all her doubts and hesitations away into the back of her mind. 'If it really is a diamond ...'

To her diamonds belonged only to fairyland. They hardly ever came into real life. They were like a touch-stone or the fabulous jewel in a serpent's head. The wealth of the whole world could be exchanged for one little diamond.

A little later Horihor came in carrying his bundle in his hand. 'Come here,' she said. 'Look at this. What is it?'

Horihor took it in his hand. 'Where did you get it?'

'Durga went to pick some water fruit at the Moat Lake. She dug it out of ground there. What is it?'

Horihor turned it round a time or two and then said, 'It's a piece of glass, or maybe a stone. It's so small I can't be sure.'

A thin ray of hope shone in Shorbojoya's mind. If it were glass, she asked herself, wouldn't her husband be able to recognize it? So she whispered to him nervously, hoping that he would not contradict her, yet fearful that he might. 'Could it be a diamond? Durga says that lots of people have picked up all sorts of things in the moat near the Mojumdars' house. It might be a diamond, mightn't it?'

'Yes, it might be; but if diamonds could be picked up by the roadside, there'd be no need for anybody to worry about anything. What a woman you are!' He was convinced at first that it was only glass, but as he reflected further a doubt assailed him. 'It's just possible. Who can be sure? The Mojumdars were rich. Is it entirely impossible that a stone from one of their many ornaments may by some chance have got buried in the ground? They say that an unlucky man is one who does not recognize hidden treasure even when he has it in his hand. Is this going to turn out to be another poor Brahmin story?' Then he said aloud, 'All right, and I'll go and show it to the Gangulis.'

Shorbojoya prayed to herself as she went on with the cooking, saying again and again, 'Please God! Lots of other people pick up things. And times are so hard for us. Have mercy on the children. Please God!' And her heart beat more quickly as she prayed.

Durga came in and asked excitedly, 'Has Daddy come home yet?'

Horihor entered at that very moment. 'It's just as I thought,' he said. 'It isn't anything. Shottobabu, the Gangulis' son-in-law, is back from Calcutta. He had a look at it. He says it's a kind of crystal glass, the sort they use in chandeliers. If you could pick up diamonds and such things by the roadside.... What a woman you are for wild ideas!'

TWELVE

◦⟨◉⟩◦

It was almost noon on a day in the hot month of May. Shorbojoya was grinding spices which she took, as and when she needed them, out of a flower basket—it was a long time since it had been used to hold flowers—placed within easy reach of her right hand. She turned to get some more spices.

'Oh, you're at it again, are you?' she said. 'Where have you run off to with that bundle of fennel and pepper? What a tease you are, Opu! I can't get on with my cooking; and in a few minutes you'll be saying you're hungry.'

There was no sign of Opu.

'Please bring them back, darling,' she pleaded. 'Why must you be such a nuisance? Can't you see it's getting late?'

Opu peeped round the kitchen door, his bright little face wreathed with the naughtiest of smiles, but the moment his

100

mother caught sight of him he disappeared behind the door again like a snail into its shell.

Shorbojoya said, 'What naughtiness is this? Why must you tease me in the middle of the day when I'm busy. Come and give them to me.'

Opu peeped round the door again a second time. He was still smiling.

'I can see you. There's no need to hide any more. Give them to me.'

Shorbojoya knew her son well. She could see him as he was when he was eighteen months old. He was even fairer to look at then than he was now. She recalled how she used to darken his eyes with kohl and put a spot of it in the middle of his forehead. She could see the woollen cap she used to put on his head. It was only a cheap cap, but it was blue and had buttons on it. And in the evening she took him in her arms and went out onto the verandah where she droned a song to put him to sleep.

'Sing, little birdie, on your tree top;
Swing your long tail and my little one rock.'

His cheeks were round and podgy, and he lay staring up into her face. All at once as some whim took him, he chuckled with joy and showed all his toothless gums. Then he gripped his mother with his absurdly tiny feet—they had anklets on at the time—and hid his face behind her back. She smiled and said, 'Goodness me! Where's baby got to? I can't see him anywhere.' When she turned to look behind her, he brought his smiling face round to the front of her and chuckling with glee tried to hide himself against her shoulder. The more she said, 'Where's baby got to? Where can he be?' the longer the little game went on. Shorbojoya twisted her neck this way and that until it ached, but the game still went on. He was

new, and the world was new; and he had just come into it.
And now that he had got a grain of pleasure from the world's
endless store, his childish mind never cloyed of savouring the
joy of it, over and over again, like a glutton. What mother
could possibly bring herself to stop him? For a long time he
kept it up until his tiny body ran out of energy, and then
suddenly he yawned and forgot to do it any more. When she
saw him yawn, Shorbojoya snapped her fingers, as mothers
often do, and prayed to Shashthi, the goddess of children,
to watch over him now that his play was done and sleep had
come. Her eyes were warm with love as she looked down
into his baby face, its kohl mark still there. 'What games you
play, my darling!' she said; 'and Shashthi's pet is only eighteen
months old.' And she smothered his glowing cheeks with a
flurry of kisses; but his eyes were heavy with sleep and he
received this demonstration of her affection with complete
indifference. Very tenderly she put his head on her shoulder
and murmured, 'Bless you, darling! It's only just dark and
you're fast asleep. I was going to give you some milk when
it got dark and then put you to sleep, but you were too quick
for me.'

Shorbojoya knew full well that though he was now eight
years old he was just as fond of playing hide-and-seek with
her as he had been as a baby. He would hide in places that
would not have deceived even a blind man, yet she had to
pretend not to know where he was. What she usually did was
to sit down somewhere, look this way and that and then say,
'I wonder where on earth he's got to. I can't see him anywhere.'
Opu was quite sure that she did not know where he was; and
that is what made it such fun. But today she was busy and
she knew that if she let him think she was going to play with
him, the game could go on all day. So she spoke severely, 'If
you go on like this, Opu, I shall never get the cooking done.

102

You may think it fun now, but it won't be so funny when you want your dinner and find it's not ready for you.'

Opu came out from his hiding place with a laugh and dumped the bundle of spices down in front of her. 'Go and play outside for a while,' she said. 'Go and see where Didi is. Call out to her from the mangosteen tree. Today's her special festival day and she's probably having her bath. I scarcely ever see the wretched girl nowadays. Run along now, darling!'

Opu might be a darling but he made no attempt to behave like one. He took no notice at all of what his mother told him. He went behind her and began to play with something there, and as he played he hummed a tune. She was too busy grinding the spices to pay much attention but when she did look round she saw him crouching on the floor on his hands and knees. He was covered with a piece of sacking she usually kept on the rafters. 'That's very naughty of you, darling! That sacking must have the dust of ages in it. Throw it away. There may be spiders in it, or even a snake. Goodness knows how long it's been up there!'

The humming went on, but in a slightly lower key.

'I do wish you would do what I tell you, my pet! Do throw it away, please. You know I can't touch it. My hands are covered with paste. Do stop being so naughty.'

The sack-covered figure crawled slowly towards her. 'Careful now!' she called out to him. 'You might touch me, and you mustn't do that. You know you shouldn't touch me while I've still got food on my hands. Stop it! Can't you see how frightened I am! I'm frightened to death.'

Opu chuckled and threw off the sack. Then he came and stood by her side. His hair, face, eyebrows and ears were all thick with dust; but he pulled a face when he felt some of it gritting between his teeth.

'What on earth am I to do with you, silly boy? You look like a ghost with all that dust over you. And it's dust from that awful old sack too! You're quite mad!' As she looked at the silly child standing there white with dust, Shorbojoya's heart filled with tenderness, even though it was difficult for her to do anything for him. She had already had her bath and if she touched him now she would have to go and have another. Fortunately however, all he had on was an unwashed towel round his middle, so she said, 'Take that towel off and wipe the dust off your body with it. What a child you are!'

She had to leave him then to see to something in the kitchen. When that was done she went out to draw some water, and as she was going she spotted Durga coming in through the gate. Her face was sunburnt, her hair tangled and untidy, and her feet were thick with dust; but in spite of the dust she had painted the edges of her feet red with alta dye. Durga swallowed hard as she came face to face with her mother, and then she showed her some mangoes which she had tied up in her sari. 'I went to Raji's house to get some grain seeds for my Holy Pond day,' she explained. 'They had picked some mangoes from one of their trees and were sharing them out. Raji's aunt gave me some.' 'Yes,' replied Shorbojoya, 'but look at the condition you're in. Your skin's dry and you're covered with dust. And as for your hair, it makes me sick to look at it. Holy Pond indeed! I suppose you didn't sleep a wink last night thinking of your Holy Pond and what you were going to do to celebrate it.' Then she caught sight of Durga's feet. 'You've got alta on your feet. You've been at my basket again, have you?'

Durga rubbed her face with her sari and brushed back her untidy hair, 'No, I didn't get the alta from your basket. The other day I asked Daddy to get me a pice worth from the market, and I saved up two leaves of it in my doll's box.'

104

At that moment Horihor came out on to the kitchen verandah. He had his hukkah in his hand and wanted a burning ember from the fire to get it going with. Shorbojoya turned on him angrily. 'You seem to think that you can come here for wood to light your pipe with any hour of the day or night. Where am I to get it from? It would be all right if you'd get me some decent wood for my fire, but these bamboo chips! They burn out in no time. They certainly don't last long enough for me to supply you with a light for your pipe whenever you happen to want one.' Nevertheless peeved as she was she put a few glowing embers in a broken brass ladle she used to poke the fire with and thrust it at him. In a little while she calmed down and asked him how things were going. 'All right up to a point,' he said. 'The whole household wants me to act as their family priest. But there's been a bit of a hitch. There's some dispute about the income from Mohesh Bisvas's father-in-law's house. Bisvas has gone there himself to see about it. After all he's the sole owner. That means that the initiation ceremony has had to be put off till later; and the period from the beginning of June is inauspicious. So you see there's some difficulty about it.'

'But they said they wanted you to settle down there and promised you a place to live in. What's happened about that?'

'That's where it's difficult. If the initiation ceremony is put off, I can't very well raise the other matter, can I?'

Shorbojoya had been very hopeful, so what her husband told her now came as a great disappointment to her. 'In that case why don't you look somewhere else. There's certainly nothing doing here. You know what they say about a priest not being respected in his own village. Moreover look how we have to live here. It's the season for mangoes and jackfruit, but we haven't a single mango or jackfruit tree of our own. Durga came back today with two miserable half-rotten

mangoes that somebody had given her. And yet'—here she
pointed with her chin in the direction of the Mukherjis' house
next door—'they carry basket loads of mangoes past our gate
everyday, and the poor children have to stand and watch. It's
not easy for them.'

At the mention of the fruit orchard Horihor exploded.
'That man. He's a swindler. The ground rent for that orchard
used to be twenty-five rupees a year at least, but he's written it
down as five rupees. I've got a son and daughter, and that I need
the income from the orchard for their education, and that is all
the income I have. "Moreover," I told him, "the land belongs
to my family; it's all we have, and God has been kind to you.
You have two other orchards, large ones, with mangoes, plums,
coconuts and betel; in fact everything you need. Can't you
possibly see your way to letting me have this orchard?" And do
you know what he said? He said that my cousin, Nilmoni,
while he was alive, borrowed three hundred rupees from him,
and didn't pay him back, so he's taking the rent for the orchard
as interest. Did you ever hear anything like it? To suggest that
Nilmoni was hard up and went with his hand out like a beggar
to borrow three hundred rupees from the Mukherjis! No, my
cousin's wife is a simple soul, and he's talked her into believing
what he said. That's what must have happened.'

'Simple soul indeed!' retorted Shorbojoya. 'I'm pretty
sure that what she told him was that she couldn't get on with
you, and that if you got hold of the orchard she wouldn't
get anything out of it, but that you would keep it all, fruit
as well; and that it would therefore be better for her to come
to some agreement even at a lower rent to make sure that
she got something out of it.'

'Do you mean to say that she thought I wouldn't have
paid her the rent? And that she let him cajole her into
mortgaging the property to him without saying a word to me?'

That afternoon a violent summer storm blew up and it became quite dark. There had been clouds about for some time, yet when the storm came it came very suddenly. The bamboos that grew just the other side of their wall were blown down and carried away by the great gust of wind, and left the house looking quite naked. The gale swirled round the yard, filling it with dust, bamboo leaves, jackfruit leaves and straw. Durga ran out of the house to pick up some mango windfalls, and Opu dashed after her. As they ran Durga said to him, 'Quick, quick! You go and stand under the shindurkoto tree, and I'll go to the shonamukhi. But hurry!' There was dust everywhere. The branches of the big trees writhed in the storm which stripped them of their leaves, and the trees themselves creaked and groaned as the wind battered against them. Dry branches crashed down in the orchard, their points up, soared spiralling into the sky. White feathery flowers from the kukshima trees circled in the face of the storm like cotton, this way and that, endlessly. And the noise was deafening.

Meanwhile Opu under his tree was shouting wildly, jumping up and down and dashing here, there and everywhere. 'Look, Didi, one's fallen here. And oh! There goes another one.' But he did much more shouting than collecting. And the roar of the storm got louder and louder. The noise of it made it impossible to hear a mango fall or when they did hear one fall to tell where it had fallen. Durga by this time had got eight or nine, but Opu for all his rushing about had managed to find only two. These he showed to his sister with great glee. 'Look, Didi, what a big one I've got! And there's another one.'

While they were at work they heard the shouts of the Mukherji children who were also coming out to pick up the fallen mangoes. Shotu yelled to the others, 'Look, Durga and

Opu are picking up our mangoes,' and they arrived in a body under the shonamukhi tree. Shotu said, 'What are you doing picking up mangoes in our orchard? Didn't Mummy tell you you weren't to come here any more? Let me see how many you've got?' When he had seen he turned to the others and said, 'Tunu, can you see how many shonamukhis she's got? Go away, Durga, get out of our orchard. If you don't I shall go and tell Mummy.' Ranu said, 'What do you want to send them away for, Shotu? Let them be; there are plenty of mangoes for all of us.' 'Why should they pick our mangoes?' Shotu replied. 'If she stays she'll get them all. Besides she's no right to be here at all. Go away, Durga! I won't let you stay under our tree.'

At any other time Durga would have not accepted defeat so easily, but it was only the other day that they had complained about her to her mother and her mother had beaten her; so she was afraid to quarrel again. This was why she gave in at once. She said to Opu a little sadly, 'Come on, Opu; let's go.' Then suddenly feigning excitement she said to him, 'They won't let us stay here, but it doesn't matter. We can go to that other place. Do you remember? The mangoes there are much bigger than here; and we can have such fun gathering them. Come on.' She seemed to be all eagerness as she took Opu by the hand and led him through the hole in the hedge. The look she had on her face seemed to convey that they had been wasting their time there and that it was really a blessing in disguise that they were having to go somewhere else. After they had gone, Ranu said to Shotu, 'Why did you drive them away? It was most unkind of you.' The look of disappointment on Durga's face had hurt her.

Opu did not understand what all the unpleasantness was about, so when the two of them got to the path on the other side of the hedge he said to Durga, 'Where's that place with the big mangoes, Didi? Is it under Putu's tree?' Durga did not know either, but she thought for a minute and then said, 'Come on, we'll go to the orchard near the Moat Lake. There are a lot of big trees there.' It was nearly fifteen minutes walk to the Moat Lake, and to get there they had to go along a narrow path through almost continuous jungle. It is true that there were many mango and jackfruit trees there, but they were very old, and underneath them was an almost impenetrable wall of thorn bushes and other undergrowth. Scarcely anybody ever went there to look for mangoes because it was such a lonely and remote place. Old creepers as thick as ropes hung from tree to tree, and it was far from easy to ferret out the mangoes that had fallen into that tangle of undergrowth beneath the giant old fruit trees. To make things more difficult they could not see very well, what with the thick black storm clouds overhead and the dark shadows where the trees sagged down over the bushes below. Nevertheless Durga would not give up and in the end she managed to find eight or nine mangoes.

Suddenly Durga shouted out, 'Oh, Opu! It's going to rain.'

With the rain the force of the wind abated a little, and soon they got the smell that comes when rain falls on parched earth. Before long heavy drops were splashing down on the leaves of the trees.

'Let's stand under this tree. The rain won't get through here.'

The words were hardly out of her mouth when the rain was coming down in a solid stream. It looked just like a thick curtain of smoke round them. The drops were so heavy that they snapped leaves off the trees, and everywhere there was the fresh wet smell of the earth. The storm had slackened a little when the rain first started but soon it became as violent as ever. It is true that it did not fall heavily through the tree where the children were standing but the east wind drove the spray of it in under the branches and they were soon soaked through. They were a long way from home, and Opu was frightened. 'Oh, Didi,' he whimpered. 'The rain's very hard.'

'Stand close to me,' she said, and she drew him right up to her and wrapped the end of her sari round him. 'I wonder how much longer it will last. It can't go on much longer. Besides it's good to have the rain, isn't it? What about going back to the shonamukhi tree as soon as it's over?'

Then to keep their courage up the two of them began to sing at the top of their voices.

'Rain, rain go away from me,
There's a koromcha fruit on our lemon tree;
And—'

Flash! The wide curtain of darkness which covered the forest was split from end to end, and in that moment it was bright everywhere. They could even see the bunches of berries which were swinging on the branches at the top of the tree in front of them. Opu clung to his sister in terror and whimpered again. 'Oh, Didi!'

'Don't be frightened. Say a prayer and sing.

Rain, rain, go away from me,
There's a koromcha fruit on our lemon tree.'

But still the rain drove in on them. Their clothes and hair were soaked and dripping. Then boo-oo-m-m! A deep low roar as if someone were dragging a huge metal roller backwards and forwards over the iron floor of the sky. Opu's voice was very frightened. 'There it is again, Didi!'

'There's nothing to be afraid of. Stand a little closer to me. The water's pouring down from your hair.'

All they could hear was the lashing torrent of rain on leaves, the hiss and moan of the gusts of the gale, and the booming cannonade in the clouds. Once or twice Durga wondered whether the whole forest would be uprooted by the wind and come down on top of them with a rending crash.

'Didi, supposing it doesn't stop!'

A long flickering tongue of fire rent through the sky's dark mantle from one end to the other, and was gone in an instant; and they could hear the harsh mocking laugh of the demon of the storm. Cra-a-ck! The lightning came again, and the eyes of the two helpless children were blinded by a stabbing blue flame which tore aside the smoke screen of the rain which hid the forest, and they stood there trapped in the terrifying pandemonium of Nature gone mad.

Opu was too panic-stricken to look, and Durga's throat was dry. She peered round to see if it was a thunderbolt that had fallen, and once again she glimpsed the berries swinging at the top of the tree; and they heard that iron roller being dragged across the floor of the sky. Opu's teeth chattered with terror. Durga pressed him closer to her, and not knowing what else to do to console him, she repeated their song.

'Rain, rain, go away from me,
There's koromcha fruit on our lemon tree.'

Three times she sang it, but her voice trembled as she sang.

Night was not a long way off. The cyclone had ended a little while before. Shorbojoya was standing at the outer gate. Rajkrishna Palit's daughter, Ashalota, was splashing through the pools that had formed on the path which led down to the tank. Shorbojoya called out to her. 'Have you seen Durga and Opu anywhere, my dear?'

'No, Auntie; I haven't. Where did they go to?' Then she smiled, 'This rain will bring the frogs out, won't it, Auntie?'

'The two of them went out before the rain started. They

111

said they were going to collect mangoes; but they haven't come back yet. The storm's been over for some time now, and it's getting dark. I don't know where they could have got to, and I'm worried.'

Shorbojoya was indeed very worried, but there did not seem to be anything that she could do, so she started to go back into the house. As she did so she heard the back door open. It was Durga with Opu behind her. They were soaked from head to foot. Durga had a ripe coconut in her hand and Opu was dragging a coconut branch after him. Shorbojoya ran to meet them. 'Goodness me!' she said. 'What will happen next? You must be wet through to the marrow. Where were you when it rained?' She felt Opu's head with her hand and said, 'You're dripping. You look just like a drowned rat.' Then her face lit up. 'Where did you get that coconut, Durga?'

'Sh,' the two of them whispered together. 'Speak quietly, Mummy. Shejbou's out in the garden. Look, you can see her from here. You know that coconut tree up against the fence? Well, it was lying at the foot of that. But just as we were getting away Shejbou came out. She must have seen Opu and I think she saw me too.' She paused for a moment to control her excitement. 'It was just at the foot of the tree. I hadn't noticed it before. I had gone there to see if there were any mangoes under the shonamukhi tree. There was a branch lying there too, so I told Opu to bring it for you. I knew you wanted a broom.' Her face glowed with pleasure. 'It's a lovely big coconut, isn't it, Mummy?'

Opu was as delighted as she was. He waved his hands about and beamed all over his face. 'I did it too, Mummy, I rushed off with the branch as soon as ...'

'Yes, it's a fine big coconut, but it isn't quite ready yet. Put it under the eaves. I'll wash it and take it inside later on.'

'No Mummy!' pleaded Opu. 'You're always saying we

112

have no coconuts. Now we have got one, and you must make us some sweets. I won't let you get out of it this time. I just won't.'

The rain had made the children's faces as lovely as jasmine flowers after a shower, but their lips were blue with cold and their wet hair was plastered down over their ears.

'Come here, both of you,' said Shorbojoya, 'and let me take your clothes off. And then you're to go out on to the verandah and wash your feet.'

Shortly afterwards Shorbojoya went across the Mukherjis' compound to draw water from the well there. When she had got as far as the back door she heard Shejbou shouting inside the house. She was making enough noise to raise the roof. 'It cost us a small fortune to get that orchard. We didn't get it for nothing; and yet there isn't a single tree in it we can call our own. Why, I can't even walk through it into the house without falling over those poverty-stricken wretches. And as for that dreadful daughter of theirs, she hangs about the orchard all day and night. She'd steal anything, even a wisp of straw. But it's her mother that puts her up to it. That hag of a woman is as big a thief as the daughter. What do you think they did today? The rain had just stopped and I went out into the orchard to have a look round, and there, under my very nose, they grabbed a large coconut, a very large one, and dashed off with it. I pray to God to punish them for the way they're persecuting us. May He damn them for ever. And this is the curse I put on them now in the quiet of the evening when God hears our prayers: "May they never eat that coconut, or if they do may they die and be burned to ashes!"'

Shorbojoya stood still outside the back door. She was petrified. She thought of those two sweet rain-washed faces and of this dreadful curse that had been put on them. 'What a terrible woman she is! Her tongue is more poisonous than

113

a serpent's fang. What can I do about it? I must do something.'
The mere thought of that potent curse sent a shudder through
her body, and all the strength seemed to drain out of her.
She did not go into the Mukherjis' house; she could not. The
evening was still after the rain, and in the thickets nearby and
under the bamboos the fireflies were glowing; but still she
could not move. It was fear that ultimately gave strength to
her limbs; and she picked up her small bucket, put the water
jar on her hip and turned back home. And as she walked she
tried to think it out. 'Supposing we return the coconut ...
surely the curse will not work then? How can it? If a thing
is given back to its owner, it can't possibly ...'

The moment she set foot in the house she said to Durga,
'Go to Shotu's house and give them that coconut back.'

Durga and Opu stared at their mother speechless; and
then Durga said, 'Now?'

'Yes, go at once. Their backdoor's open. Hurry. Tell them
you picked it up and are returning it.'

'May Opu go with me, Mummy? It's dark. Come on,
Opu.'

When they had gone Shorbojoya lit a lamp near the holy
basil, folded the end of her sari round her neck and bowed
in prayer. 'O Lord, thou knowest that they meant no harm
when they took the coconut. Don't let this curse fall on them.
Let them live, O Lord, I implore thee. Be merciful to them.
Look kindly upon them, I beseech thee, good Lord!'

THIRTEEN

The village schoolmaster Proshonno ran a grocery shop as well as a school. The two were in adjoining rooms and there was no partition. The classroom had none of the usual appurtenances except a cane; but the faith of the parents in the efficacy of the cane was no less than that of the schoolmaster: in fact they gave him authority to use it as much as he liked subject only to the trifling reservation that the boys did not become lame or lose an eye in the process. Proshonno's ability with the cane more than made up for his ignorance of educational methods and the absence of proper equipment. He used it with such careless abandon that it is a wonder that the students escaped with their lives, let alone being lamed or blinded.

Very early one morning at the beginning of January Opu

was lying in bed waiting for the sun to rise. It was cold and he was wrapped up in a quilt. His mother came in and called him.

'Opu, get up quickly. You're going to school today. Your father's going to take you there. Isn't that nice? You'll have lots of books and a slate. So get up and go and wash your face.'

At the mention of the word school Opu opened a pair of very sleepy eyes and looked at his mother with utter incredulity. He had an idea that only naughty boys were ever sent to school, boys who disobeyed their mothers and fought with their brothers and sisters. He had never done those things, so why should he go to school?

After a while Shoibojoya came in and called him again.

'Get up, Opu. Go and wash your face. I'm just wrapping up some crispy baked rice for you. You can eat it while you're in school. So do get up, darling.'

In reply Opu grunted and put out the tip of his tongue to let her know that he did not believe a word she said and was not going to do as she said anyway. Then he closed his eyes again and there was an odd expression on his face; but he made no move towards getting up. In the end his father came in. That took the matter out of Opu's hands. He had to go to school. He was sure it was his mother's doing and he was very cross with her, so when she gave him the food she had wrapped up for him, he said with a sob, 'You watch! I shall never come home again.'

'Good gracious me! You won't come home again? Why, you silly boy! You mustn't talk like that.' And she put her hand under his chin and kissed him. 'You'll be able to learn lots of things. So you must work hard, and then when you grow up you'll get a good job and earn a lot of money. I'm quite sure of that.' Then turning to her husband, she said, 'Tell the schoolmaster not to be too hard on him.'

When they got to the school his father said to him, 'I'll come for you when school's over, Opu. So work hard and listen to your teacher; and don't be naughty.'

Horihor turned and went back. Opu followed him with his eyes until gradually he passed out of sight round a bend in the road. He was alone, alone on an endless sea! For a long time he sat looking down. Then timidly he raised his eyes and saw the schoolmaster weighing out some salt for a customer. There were some big boys seated near Opu. They were sitting on grass mats reciting something. Their voices were harsh and strident, and as they recited they swung their bodies backwards and forwards in a way that frightened him. There was only one other boy as small as he was, and he was sitting by himself leaning against a pillar and chewing one of the palm leaves he had brought to write on. There was another big boy in the class. He had a mole on his cheek. He was staring hard at something under the bench in the shop. Just in front of Opu there were two other boys. They were playing house on a slate. One of them whispered, 'This is my cross.' The other said, 'This is my circle.' And as they went on with the game the house grew larger. The teacher was busy with his customers and from time to time the two boys cast glances in his direction out of the corner of their eyes. Opu began writing letters in a large hand on his slate. Some time later, he had lost count of time by then, he was startled to hear the teacher call out, 'Phoni, what's that you're drawing on your slate?'

Immediately the two boys who were sitting in front of Opu covered their slate, but it was hard to conceal anything from the teacher's eagle eye.

'Shotish, bring Phoni's slate to me.' The words were scarcely out of his mouth when the boy with the big mole swooped down on them like a hawk. He seized the slate and bore it off to the bench in the shop.

117

'Oho! This is what you're up to, is it? Shotish, take hold of them by their ears and bring them up to me.'

The way the big boy swooped down on their slate and the way the two were being dragged step by step up to the teacher and the look of dismay on their faces suddenly struck Opu as funny, and he began to giggle. For a moment he succeeded in checking the giggle, but then it began again.

'Who's that laughing? What are you laughing at, boy? Do you think this is a playhouse? A playhouse, boy? Is that what you think it is?'

Opu did not know what a playhouse was, but his face went white with fear.

'Shotish, bring me a brick. There are some under the tamarind tree. Make sure it's a big one, and I'll make him hold it over his head.'

Opu was terrified, and his throat went dry; but when the brick was brought he realized that it was not for him but for the other two. Either because he was so young or because he was a new boy the teacher had decided to let him off this time.

The afternoon session of the school was attended by some eight or ten students, both boys and girls. Except for Opu, they had all brought mats to sit on. Opu had no mat but his mother had given him an old threadbare rug. The classroom was open on all sides. There were no walls, neither was there a fence outside to limit the view. Inside were the students sitting in rows; outside was the jungle. Behind the house to the west lay the orchard which the schoolmaster had inherited from his ancestors. The afternoon sun was bright and warm. It shone into the room through the orchard trees, pomelo, mangosteen, guava and mango, lighting up the bamboo pillars which supported the roof. There was no other house in sight, nothing but just jungle and the orchard, and the narrow path which led to the school.

The pupils were memorizing their lessons by reading them aloud. Their voices were pitched in different keys and as they chanted they swung their bodies backwards and forwards to aid the process. Now and then the schoolmaster's voice rose above the din.

'Eh, Kebola! What are you looking at somebody else's slate for? I'll twist your ears for you if you do it again ... Nutu, how many more times are you going to go out to wet your duster? If I catch you going out again ...'

The schoolmaster usually sat on a palm-leaf mat leaning back against one of the pillars, and the pillar he leant against was dark with the oil the he put on his hair. In the late afternoon Dinu Palit and Raju Ray often used to walk over from the village to talk to him. Opu found these conversations much more interesting than his lesson. Raju Ray said that when he was a young man he heard an adage which said that the goddess of wealth lived in business houses, and he described how relying on that adage he had opened a tobacco shop in the market at Asharhu. Opu listened spellbound. Raju told them how he opened the matting door of his little shop and sat inside slicing up the tobacco with a knife; how at night he went down to the river and then cooked and ate fish soup from a small bowl; and how sometimes he used to light an earthenware lamp and sit reading the Mahabharat or his father's copy of Dashu Ray's ballad. At night during the monsoon it was very dark outside with the rain pouring down. There was no one about and the frogs croaked in the pond behind his house. How beautiful it was! Opu told himself that he would open a tobacco shop when he grew up.

Sometimes Rajkrishna Shanyal, who lived at the far end of the village, used to come over; and when he did the story-telling had a much more moving and imaginative quality. Whatever the story was about, indeed however commonplace

119

it was, he had the extraordinary ability to tell it in a way that made it come alive. Shanyal had a passion for travelling. Sometimes it was to Dwarka, sometimes to the Savitri hills, sometimes to Chandranath; but he did not like travelling alone. He always took his wife and family with him. He stayed away until he had spent all his money, and then he came home again. On the other hand he was a great home-lover, or at least people thought he was. One thing above all that he seemed to find enjoyment in was to sit at ease in his room smoking a flat-bottomed hukkah. But whether he was truly a home-lover or not, there were not many people in these days, even in an old-fashioned village, who were content to spend so much time at home as he was. Then suddenly one day it was noticed that the door was locked on the outside and there was no sign of life in the compound. Shanyal had once more taken his family and gone off to the Vindhya hills or Chandranath. For a long time they would not be seen, and then one day about noon the neighbours would hear a creaking sound and looked out with surprise to see two loaded bullock carts. Shanyal had brought his family home from their travels; and soon he was calling for people to help him cut back the knee-high jungle of weeds and creepers that had grown up in the yard during his absence, so that he could get into the house.

He used to come striding down to the school with a thick stick in his hand. 'Here we are, Proshonno! How are you?' he would say. 'You've been spreading that excellent web of yours, I see. How many flies have you caught this time?'

Opu was doing his multiplication tables and his face lit up with pleasure. He edged forward eagerly as near as he could to where Shanyal was seated on a palm-leaf mat. He bundled up his slate and books and put them to one side as if school was over. There would be no more class that day.

120

His eyes were wide-open and longing, and he swallowed every word that was said as greedily as a starving beggar.

'On the road to the indigo factory, you know where it is, there is a place they call Naltakuri's Jol. Out beyond there—this happened a long time ago—a villager named Chondor Hajra—his brother was Moti Hajra—had gone to cut trees in the jungle. It was during the monsoon and the rain had caused a number of earth-slides. All at once his eyes fell on a certain patch of mud and he saw something in it that looked like the brim of a brass jar. That's what it was, so he dug it up and when he got it home he found it was full of old coins. That's why Chondor Hajra was able to live for so long like a lord.' Shanyal had seen all this with his own eyes.

Some of the stories were about his railway journeys. He told them where the Savitri hills were. His wife apparently had had considerable difficulty in climbing them, and he himself had once had a scuffle with the temple attendants at Nabhigaya while he was making an offering at the shrine. In one place they had had some wonderful sweets to eat. Shanyal named them. It sounded like 'pyanra', and it made Opu laugh; but he made a point of remembering it. When he grew up he would get some 'pyanras' to eat.

Another day Shanyal was telling a story about a certain place—he had forgotten its name—but a large number of people lived there in times gone by. It was about nightfall and he and his party were going through a forest of tamarind trees. The thing they were going to see was called 'Chika mosque'; he repeated the name several times. Opu was not clear at first what the thing was, but as the story developed he realized that it was an old ruined house. It was almost dark by then, and as they were entering a swarm of small bats swished past them. Opu could picture it all: darkness everywhere—a tamarind jungle—not a soul about—an old broken door—a swarm of bats swishing past them as they went in—and inside it was as dark as the inner room on the west side of Ranu's house.

In one place Shanyal had met a fakir who lived under a banyan tree. He was highly delighted if anyone gave him a pipe of opium to smoke, and in return he would ask them what kind of fruit they liked best. When they mentioned the name of the fruit he would say, 'If you will go to that tree over there you will find one.' When they got there they would see, say, a mango tree, but if they had mentioned pomegranates there would be pomegranates on it; or it might be a guava tree and if they had said bananas they would find a bunch of bananas hanging from it.

Raju Ray said, 'That must have been some sort of magic. Once an uncle of mine ...'

Dinu Palit interrupted him. 'Now if you're going to talk about magic, let me tell you a story. It's not a made-up story. It actually happened; I was there myself. Have any of you seen Budho, the old cart-driver at Beledanga? Raju may not have seen him, but you, Rajkrishna, must have seen him often. He used to go about in wooden mules which he tied to his feet with string. He was an old man then but he went regularly to Nite the blacksmith's shop to sharpen his ploughshare. He was a hundred when he died and that's over twenty-five years ago now. His hands and wrists were so strong that even though we were young men we could not match his grip. Once a long time ago, I was not more than nineteen or twenty at the time, we were returning from Chakda by cart after bathing in the Ganges. It was Budho's cart and the party consisted of my aunt, Ram, Ononto Mukherji's nephew, and myself. Ram has left this village now and is living at Khulna. We were in the open country near

Kanashona and the sun had almost set. Rajkrishna, you must know well how frightening it was all round there. For one thing it was a lonely road, and for another we had a woman with us and quite a lot of money too. We were very anxious. There's a new village there now, but there was no village then; and you can guess what happened. Four men, black and as strong as bulls, came charging down on us, two from one side and two from the other; and they seized hold of the bamboo pole at the back of the cart. We were too terrified to utter a sound, but somehow we managed to remain sitting in the cart. And all the time they were there, still holding on to the pole, and coming along with us. Budho the cartman kept glancing at them. I saw him doing that but he signalled to us not to make a sound, and indicated that everything was all right. Slowly Nawabganj bazar came into sight, and then the village police station, and the cart went steadily on. At this stage the men began to shout to Budho, "Master, forgive us. We didn't know. Let us go." Budho replied, "Why should I do that, you scoundrels? I'm going to take you to the police station and have you locked up." They went on pleading with him and in the end he yielded. "All right," he said, "I'll let you go this time; but you must promise never to do it again". At that moment they were set free. They bent down to take the dust from Budho's feet and made off as fast as they could. And all this I saw with my own yes. What it was I don't know, but Budho must have had some magical power, because once the men had laid hands on the pole they were caught. They could not let go and had to go along with the cart. It looked for all the world as though they were nailed to it. So you see, when it comes to talking about magic ...'

The stories went on for a long time and it was now late. The afternoon sun was low in the sky but its red rays still shone through the trees that surrounded the school house.

Tailor-birds with their heads thrown back sat swinging on the creepers that hung down from the jackfruit and jagadumar trees; and inside the air was heavy with many scents, the unmistakeable smells of the rush mats and the old tattered books and the earth of the floor, the pungent aroma of the tobacco that had been sliced with the large knife, all mingling with the odours which the wind brought in from the trees and bushes outside.

On the dusty path which led to the village there was yet another picture: a little boy who seemed to be walking on air was going home from school a few paces behind his sister, a bundle of books held tightly under his arm. His clothes were old and patched, and had been much washed with fuller's earth. The hair on his little head, which his mother had combed so lovingly, was as soft as silk, gleaming and so gentle to the touch; and in his big beautiful eyes there glowed the light of speechless wonder, as if they had just opened and looked for the first time on some other world, where everything was strange and new. All he knew was a little plot of land with trees all round it, where every day his mother fed him with her own hands and his sister helped him to dress; but outside this tiny circle was the ocean of the unknown, endless and unfathomable, where there was no base the feet of a child could stand on.

Beyond the orchard outside their house was a bamboo grove, and a narrow path ran through it. But where did that path go to? If you went along it and kept straight on, you would come to the unknown land of hidden treasure by the banks of the Shankhari pond. Big trees grew there, and under them the monsoon rain had washed away the earth, exposing the brims of jars which were full of old gold coins; but nobody knew they were there because they were hidden from the eye by the darkness of the jungle thickets and the shining green overgrowth of kochu and ol and jasmine creepers.

One day something happened at school that was an altogether new experience in Opu's life. It was afternoon but no one had come to visit the schoolmaster and consequently there could be no conversation. So they had class instead. Opu was reading his primer when the teacher called out, 'Take up your slates and write a dictation.'

Proshonno spoke without reference to a book, but Opu knew that the words were not his own; he was reciting something from memory just as Opu himself could recite lines from Dashu Ray's ballad. As he listened Opu realized that he had never heard so many beautiful words so beautifully strung together. He did not understand everything in the passage: there were too many long words he did not know; but the lilt of its rhythm and the music of its weighted syllables fell on the ears of the untutored child with the fresh charm of beauty newly discovered; and because he did not understand it all, it created for him a picture only partly discerned through a curtain of mist.

Deep in the heart of Janasthan the lordly mount Prasravan stands. Its godlike summit wears as a crown the rich blue radiance of the empyrean; its massive shoulders are mantled o'er with ever-moving clouds which ceaseless gales urge down the paths of the air; while unlifted along its flanks, cool, fragrant, beautiful, soar the monarchs of the forest, tall and thickly clustering; and at its feet clear, crystalline, the waters of the broad Godavari flow.

Opu could not say why, but deep within himself he knew that the path he was looking down now was the same path that he had seen running through the open country and disappearing into the distance two years before, on the day of the Sarasvati festival, when he had gone with his father to see the blue-throated jay near the indigo factory. On either side of the path were many birds, bushes he had never seen before. He had spent a long time that day staring along it, but though he asked himself often where it went to, the question remained unanswered. His father had told him that it was the Shonadanga road, and went by way of Madhobpur and Dasghara down to the ferry crossing at Dholchite. But that could not be right. He knew it was not just an ordinary road to the ferry at Dholchite: it went much further than that; it went all the way to the land of the Ramayan and Mahabharat, that land of faraway which came to his mind whenever he looked at the branches at the top of the banyan tree.

The dictation threw more light on the path he had seen two years before. Somewhere far down it was the mountain Prasravan, deep in the heart of Janasthan. The fragrant odours of trees and bushes, the shimmering light of evening when the mystery of dark began to descend, were all part of his dreamland as a whole. How far off was the lofty summit of Mount Prasravan, whose still, blue loveliness lies ever veiled by the mantle of clouds that the wind blows down the path of the sky?

When he was grown up he would go and see it.

But that mountain side thick with undergrowth, the Godavari with its many sandbanks, that dark abode of man, that mysterious rocky peak wrapped round with a garland of blue clouds, are not to be found in any country described in Valmiki's Ramayan. Valmiki did not create them; nor did the poet Bhavabhuti. They came to life at eventide in the enchanted mind of a little-schooled village boy when a bird from the past was calling. They were all so real; he knew them all so well. Mount Prasravan may not be marked in any of the atlases of this world; but a Mount Prasravan from a world of fancy, its blue peaks hidden behind a curtain of ever-moving clouds, appeared in a dream to a child who knew no geography, and took up its abode in his mind, there to remain for ever.

FOURTEEN

❦

Durga was out looking for her brother. She had been to all the usual places nearby, but he was not to be found anywhere. Eventually she came to Onnoda Ray's house and it occurred to her that here was an opportunity to kill two birds with one stone, to go and see if Opu was there and perhaps at the same time have a talk with Onnoda Ray's daughter-in-law, her auntie or boudi as she called her. Before she got inside however, she heard somebody crying, and somebody else shouting; so she did not go in but stood where she was, outside the door. Onnoda Ray's widowed sister Shokhithakrun, was standing at the end of the verandah screaming loudly enough to bring the house down.

'She doesn't seem to have the slightest idea what fear is, I've come across some pig-headed women in my life, but I've never met one like her, never! I've done all I can, but it's no good. I've told her that her husband has a fiendish temper and that when he's in a rage he's quite capable of breaking every bone in her body. I've pleaded with her time and time again to remember what he's like and be careful. She knows as well as I do that for the last three days he's been telling her, not once but many times, to put the paddy out to dry in the sun; but she takes no notice. She doesn't seem to listen to what anybody says. The wife of the family is supposed to look after the rice and do the housework, everybody knows that; but all she does is to sit out in the sun doing herself up like a bride in a picture.' Here she broke off and did a mime to make quite sure that everybody knew what she meant by a bride in a picture. 'I tell you I've never seen a woman like her anywhere; I've never heard of one either.'

The daughter-in-law was inside the house. It was she who was crying, and when she spoke her voice was creaky and nasal. 'You say I'm like a bride in a picture. I spent the whole of yesterday afternoon frying daal, twenty pounds of it. I started immediately after the midday meal and I was still sitting over the fire when the five o'clock train went past. Don't you call that work? Two whole baskets of daal to grind and fry, and I didn't get done till dark. I was tired in every limb. My whole body ached, and last night I had fever. But do you think anybody took any notice of that? And what is more, this morning he beat me for nothing at all. He seems to think I spend all my time sitting about.'

Onnoda Ray's son, Gokul, came into the yard just in time to catch the last few words. He had a newly cut bamboo in one hand, the leaves were still on it, and in the other he carried the kitchen chopper. 'So that's it, is it?' he yelled. 'You haven't had enough yet, getting me worked up into a temper at this hour of the morning. I've been at you for three days now to put the paddy out in the sun, until I'm completely worn out. And now the clouds are coming up. What do you think is going to happen if the paddy starts to sprout? Do you think your precious father or somebody'll come and stop it. If it does sprout what are we going to live on for the rest of the year?'

His wife stopped crying instantly and screamed back in a rage, 'Don't you dare insult my father! What's he done to you that you're always abusing him?'

Gokul barely waited till the words were out of her mouth. He dropped the bamboo and leapt up the steps into the house with the chopper still in his hand. 'Now you're going to get it! It's either you or me this time. If I don't put an end to this hankering for your father's house once and for all, I'll ...'

One of the farm hands in the yard, fearing that murder would be done, shouted out, 'What are you doing, sir? What are you doing? Stop, stop!' He sprang up the steps. Durga rushed in too. Shokhithakrun hid herself in the built-up part of the verandah. Everybody was yelling and screaming. Gokul's wife jumped to one side as her husband charged in to attack her. She raised her hands over her head to ward off the blow and stood cowering against the wall. She was terrified. But the farm hand snatched the chopper out of Gokul's hands and began to drag him out of the room. 'What are you doing, sir? Stop it! Calm down now, and come out into the yard.'

Gokul was a fully grown man. He must have been at least thirty-five or thirty-six years old, but physically he was not very strong. He had had malaria too often for that. He realized that if he tried to wrench himself free from the hands of the burly labourer everybody would see what a weakling he was. So he let himself be taken outside, but he did not stop talking, even though what he said was barely articulate. 'Look at her—look at her—a basket of paddy—seed paddy—

129

if it gets wet how shall we plant it? I've been telling her for three days—and all I get is a cheeky answer—didn't you hear? And as for your butting in …!'

Durga heaved a sigh of relief; but as the moment did not seem propitious for a chat with her auntie she slipped away without saying anything to anybody.

Under the rose-apple tree near Panchu Banerji's house a man was repairing kitchen pans and utensils. People from the houses close by had brought him a lot of work to do and the charcoal in his fire glowed red. He was a dwarfish little fellow and very thin, hardly more than skin and bone. It was difficult to tell how old he was. He might have been thirty but on the other hand he could easily have been fifty. There was no doubt however what sect he belonged to, for he wore a three-strand garland of basil plaited round his neck, as many Vaisnavas do. He had the scar of an old knife wound on his right cheek, and the veins in his wrist stood out like ropes. His only garment was a dirty loin cloth. The children from the nearby houses had gathered round to watch him work, and Durga joined them.

He noticed her and asked, 'What is it, my dear?'

'Nothing. I was only looking.'

When Durga got home she went straight in to her mother, 'Mummy,' she said, 'I can't tell you what a terrible beating Uncle Gokul gave Auntie today.' And she told her mother all about it.

Shorbojoya said, 'He's an absolute brute. To think of such a nice girl marrying into a family like that and especially to a man like him! Her life's just one beating after another.'

'She's very fond of me, Mummy. Whenever there's something nice in the house she always keeps a bit for me. I feel so sad when I see her cry. And instead of being kind to her Shokhithakrun scolds her too.'

Children Make Their Own Toys

The next three or four days Durga went to see how the work was getting on under the rose-apple tree. The metal-smith asked her all sorts of questions: 'Where do you live?' and, 'What's your father's name?', etc. Then he said, 'Haven't you got any things at your home that need mending, my dear? If you have why don't you bring them here?' Durga spoke to her mother about it when she got home. 'Don't you want our broken pans repaired, Mummy? Such a nice man's come. He's working under the rose-apple tree on the other side of the village. He says his name is Pitom. I imagine he's a Kansari by caste. When he blows up his fire with the bellows he sits straight up and says, "Hail Radha! Radha Govinda!"

'Crowds of people went there to watch him from quite early in the morning; and when there were any gentlemen about he used to take a bit of burning charcoal from the fire with his tongs and get their pipes going for them. He made quite a ceremony of it, for when he handed them back their pipes he tilted his head to one side and said "Nothing could give me greater pleasure. May you enjoy your smoke, respected sir? May the holy Radha bless you!" ... Once somebody started talking about coconuts. "Coconuts!" he said. "Please don't talk to me about coconuts, sir. I put down a few young plants last summer, six or so in a sixth of an acre of land. And then we had a plague of frogs. They ate them all up, roots and all. That cost me quite a lot of money."

'Mr Mukherji goes there every day, and very early too, hoping presumably that if he talked to the man nicely he would get his brass jar repaired for nothing. He was sitting there smoking when they started to talk about coconuts, so he joined in. "That was most unfortunate, wasn't it? I thought of planting twenty or so this year, but I couldn't. I had a go of malaria. What's the malaria like in your part of the world,

131

Mr Metal-Smith?" (He called him Mr Metal-Smith all morning.)

' "Full of it. Absolutely full of it, sir! Please don't talk to me about malaria. I've had it so badly that it's burnt right into my bones. But here's your jar, sir. It's ready now. That'll be six pice, please."

'Mr Mukherji took the jar from him and stood up. "Oh, is that so? I didn't think you would want to be paid for a little job like this, especially as it's for a Brahmin, and at this season of the year too. Surely you can't expect ..."

'Pitom quickly took the jar back, though he smiled very politely as he did so. "Oh, no, sir!" he said. "You must forgive me, but I can't repair things for nothing. Besides, this is my first job of the day, and it would be unlucky for me not to be paid for that. You do understand, don't you, respected sir? So please leave the jar here and you can send someone with your esteemed money when you get home."'

Shorbojoya said, after she had heard Durga's story, 'I wonder now. I believe that sometimes they'll let you have new pans in exchange for old ones. I wonder if he will. Go and ask him.'

Pitom agreed at once. Durga made several trips and brought quite a little pile of pans, jars and pitchers which she set down beside him. She spent the rest of that day under the tree watching him blow up his fire and get his solder hot. Pitom promised to make her a brass ring and said that he would repair their things for nothing. 'What a nice man he is!' Shorbojoya said when she was told. 'Next Wednesday is Opu's birthday. Ask him to come to the house, and I'll give him a good meal of daal and rice for all his trouble.'

So next Wednesday Durga went back to the rose-apple tree, but the man was not there. She asked the people who lived nearby and they told her that he had closed down his forge some time the previous night and gone away. All that remained to show that he had been there was a heap of charcoal ash and a hole in the ground where his furnace had been. Durga searched all around, and asked everybody she met, but nobody knew where he had gone to. Her face went white with fear. How would she tell her mother, and what would she say? He had got away with half the family utensils. Then she remembered that he had told her that he ran a forge in the market at Jhikarhati. He said he had sent word there to his brother and that his brother would come in a day or two with some new utensils which he would change for their old ones. But where was he? And where was his brother? She asked everybody. But nobody knew. And to make matters worse it was only their things that had gone. Other people had been more cautious and they had not lost a single vessel.

Durga spent the whole day there, but in the evening her eyes streaming with tears, she went and told her mother what had happened. Horihor was out of the district, so there was nobody to organize a search to try and find the man. Shorbojoya was flabbergasted. 'I've never heard anything like it,' she said. 'Go and tell your old Uncle Ray, and see what he says.' When Horihor got home he had a search made in the market at Jhikarhati, but no one of the name of Pitom had a forge there, neither was there any one who answered to his description.

Several months went by. It was now August.

Opu was just about to go out for the afternoon when his mother called to him from inside the house. 'Where are you off to, Opu? Don't go just now. I'm preparing some rice and gram for you. They'll be ready in a minute.'

Opu pretended not to hear. He knew that his mother was making the rice and gram as a special treat because he was fond of them; but what was he to do? There was a marvellous going on at Nilu's place, and he could not possibly miss that, but before he got out of sight his mother called him again. 'I can see you going off, Opu. Please don't go yet. Don't be a naughty boy. Have your food while it's hot. I hurried back from my bath as fast as I could so that I could get it ready for you. Opu-u-u!'

But he was already out of the yard, and he did not stop running until he reached Nilu's house. There were a number of children about but the game was over when Opu got there. 'Come on, Opu,' Nilu said to him, 'what about going to the south field? I've seen a nest there with some young birds in it.' Opu was most enthusiastic and the two of them set off at once. They went across the rice fields and over the long metalled road to Nawabganj which ran east-west right through the middle of the open country. They must have had to walk more than a mile. Opu had never been so far from home before. He felt that Nilu was taking him a long way, far beyond the boundaries of the world he knew; so in a little while he said, 'Let's go home, Nilu. Mummy will be cross with me. It'll be dark soon, and I'm too frightened to go past the mangosteen tree by myself. Take me back home.'

So they started back, but Nilu missed the way. They wandered about for a long time until eventually they came upon a path which skirted somebody's large mango orchard. It was beginning to get dark by now, and there were some heavy clouds in the sky too, when Nilu stopped suddenly and nudged Opu with his elbow. He was looking straight ahead. 'Oh, Opu!' he said; and there was fear in his voice.

Opu did not know why his friend was frightened so he asked him, 'What is it, Nilu?' Then he looked ahead himself and saw that the path they were following came to an end in somebody's compound. There was a thatched cottage in the yard, and an English plum tree; but before Opu could question him further, Nilu spoke again, his voice trembling with fear, 'It's the house of Aturi the witch!'

Opu went pale. 'Aturi the witch!' And they had come there just as it was getting dark. Everybody knew the story of the fisherman's son. He went to steal some of her English plums and she caught him. She sucked the spirit out of his body, wrapped it up in leaves, and threw it into the water; and the fish ate it. That put an end to his fondness for plums for ever. Everybody knew also that if she wanted to she could suck a little boy's blood by just looking at him, and then she would let him go. He would not realize at the time that his blood had been sucked, but when he got home and had his dinner and went to bed he would not be able to get up again. How often on a cold night had he sat with his quilt wrapped round and listened to his sister telling him stories about Aturi the witch! 'Don't tell me stories like that at night, Didi,' he would say. 'They make me frightened. Tell me the story of the princess who was as pink as a kunch seed.'

He could not see very well; he seemed to have a film over his eyes; but he peered through it as hard as he could to see if there was anybody in the house or not, and as he looked his body turned cold, like a lump of ice. There was somebody standing near the gate in the bamboo fence—it must be Aturi the witch herself—it could not be any one else; and she was looking straight at them, no, it was at him. When he saw her, the one woman in the world he was most frightened of, Opu felt himself rooted to the ground. He could not move a step, either forward or backward.

The old woman screwed up her eyes. Her sunken cheeks were quivering. She thrust her face forward to see them better, and then she began to move towards them, one step at a time. Opu knew he was caught. Escape was impossible. She was angry, and for some reason or other it was with him. Any minute now she would suck the spirit out of him and wrap it up in leaves. In a flash he saw why this disaster had befallen him. He had been unkind to his mother and refused to eat his food. She had called him not once but several times, and he had taken no notice. She had asked him not to go out and he had gone; and this was to be his punishment. He looked about him helplessly. 'I don't know anything about it. Oh, Auntie! I'll never come here again. Let me go, please, Auntie!'

Nilu was frightened too. He was on the verge of tears; but Opu was dry-eyed. He was too terrified to cry.

'Why are you afraid of me, my dears?' said the old woman. 'There's nothing to be frightened of.' Then she laughed and tried to make a joke of it. 'Did you think I was going to run off with you? Come into my house and I'll give you some dried mango to eat.'

Dried mango! The old witch is pretending and trying to get us inside her house. Blood-sucking witches always try tricks like that. At any rate they did in the stories his mother told him. But what could he do now? There was no hope of getting away.

The old woman came a little nearer, talking as she came. 'There's nothing to be afraid of, little one. I shan't tell anybody. Don't be frightened!'

This is the end, he told himself. It will not be long now before I am punished for not listening to Mummy. Any minute now she will suck the spirit out of me and wrap it up in leaves. He was terrified. Every moment he expected her to stop smiling and burst into a fiendish cackle. It was like the story of the princess and the witch. He had been told that baby deer cannot move their eyes when a python looks at them. He was just like that. He could not turn his eyes away from the bewitching stare of the old woman. His throat was dry, and he was frantic with fear. 'Oh, Auntie! Mummy will cry for me. Don't do anything to me today. I didn't come to steal your plums. Mummy will cry!'

He was blue with fright. His home, his own room, the trees and even Nilu faded into a mist. There was nobody with him, only the old witch and the cruel look in her eyes. Far away, somewhere a long way off, he thought he heard his mother calling him to eat his baked rice; and then, suddenly with a courage born of sheer panic, the sort of desperate courage that comes to a man about to die, he screamed in wordless terror and dashed blindly away. He did not know where he was going. He crashed through undergrowth and tangled bushes, anywhere his eyes could see a way; and Nilu ran after him.

The old woman was puzzled. She could not make out why they were afraid. 'I wasn't going to hurt them or run away with them. Poor dears! Why do they get so frightened of me when it's dark? I wonder whose child he is.'

It was quite dark when Opu got home. Shorbojoya was getting ready to make some date cakes, and Durga was sitting by her side squeezing the juice out of the fruit. 'Where have you been to?' Shorbojoya said when she saw him. 'You went off this afternoon without anything to eat. Do you never feel hungry or thirsty?' Opu was bursting to tell her what had happened but he wanted to say it all at once, and the words got in one another's way; so that in the end he did not tell her anything. When he did manage to speak all he could say was, 'Can I change my clothes, Mummy? I've had these on all day.'

Later on when he got back into the room he noticed with hurt surprise that his mother was in no hurry to give him any baked rice. She was testing the date syrup to see whether it was thick or thin, and she seemed to have eyes for nothing else. When she had finished she said to Durga, 'Let's try frying one or two. You'll find some rice flour under the big bed. Go and get some of it.' At this point she looked up and saw Opu standing there. 'Wait a minute,' she said. 'You can have some as soon as they're done.'

Opu said, 'What about the baked rice, Mummy. Can't I have some of that?'

'Oh, that? It was ready for you this morning, and you didn't eat it, did you? I called you often enough, but you went out. There isn't any left now. It got cold, so Durga finished it off. But the cakes will be ready in a minute now, and I'll give you some of that.'

His mother was not behaving at all as Opu had anticipated she would. He had been building up an imaginary welcome for himself ever since he got away from the witch. He had been talking about it to himself all the way home. 'My Mummy loves me,' he kept telling himself. 'She'll have been worrying about me ever since I went out this afternoon. She must have been very upset, saying to herself time and time again, 'Why hasn't my darling Opu come back? I came back from my bath as quickly as I could to cook some rice for him; and he went off without eating any of it, the poor child!' Yes, he had told himself, she must have been in great distress, and probably had not slept for worrying about him. But now the home-coming he had planned for himself collapsed like a house of cards. His mother had not been worrying at all. She had given all that lovely rice to Durga. He was the one who had been worrying, and all for nothing too.

Durga said, 'Hurry up, Mummy. Put them on to fry at once. It's getting very cloudy, and if it rains as it did the other day you won't be able to do any frying. It'll be too wet.'

Even as she spoke it got darker. Clouds spread rapidly across the sky, and their thickening shadows lay black over the bamboo grove. Mass upon mass piled up in the sky and it suddenly became very dark; but still it did not rain. At times such as these, a feeling of joy would spring up in Durga's mind, mixed with curiosity. She wondered how hard it was going to rain, and whether it would be heavy enough to wash the earth away. Yet day after day it rained and the earth was never washed away; but the wondering uncertainty still remained, because she could never be sure. She was aware of a strange sense of excited elation; and she went out on to the verandah and peered at the cloud-darkened sky from under the eaves.

By now Shorbojoya had got a few cakes fried and she said to Durga, 'Put them in this bowl and give them to Opu. He must be hungry. He's had nothing to eat since this afternoon.' This was the last straw. All this time Opu had somehow or other managed to keep control of himself, but the casual kindness in his mother's voice was too much for him. The dam which had held his temper in check so far suddenly gave way, and he flung the bowl with the cakes in it out into the yard. 'I won't eat any of your cakes. I won't—ever—so there!'

His sudden tantrum took Shorbojoya by surprise. She could not make out what had come over him. They were a poor family, but none of the others really knew how difficult it was for her to get enough for them to eat; and now twice in one day the wretched boy had ruined food which she had been to such pains to get ready for him. She was angry as well as distressed.

'What's the matter with you today?' she said as she stared at him. 'It looks as though you're fated to eat only the ashes from the fire. There's nothing else left for you now, so I hope they're hot.'

Now it was Opu's turn. He had never thought to hear his mother use words like this to him. What he really expected was that she would pet him and try to coax him to have his

food. She had always done so before. How could she be so
cruel this evening! He sprang to his feet and began to speak.
'Right! I know I didn't eat my baked rice. I suppose that's
what you're talking about. But do you think I wasn't sorry
about it? I've been worrying about it ever since. I don't
suppose that ever occurred to you, did it? I'll never set foot
in this house again. You say I shall have to eat ashes. Why
should I? Just so that Didi can have all the nice things? I won't
come home again, I tell you. I won't—ever—'

He was beside himself with rage. He jumped down from
the verandah and dashed away across the yard with the same
desperation as he felt when he broke loose from Aturi the
witch earlier in the evening; and he ran off, regardless of the
dark or of thorn bushes or mango trees or whatever obstacles
there might be in his path.

Durga was doubled up with laughter. It all struck her as
being too funny for words, the angry look in Opu's eyes, his
trembling lips and the way he spoke. 'That Opu!' she said,
'he's quite mad, Mummy. What was it he said?'—and she
tried to mimic him—' "I know I didn't eat my baked rice" '—
She could hardly talk for laughing. ' "But do you think I
wasn't sorry about it?" He's completely off his head—Opu,
listen to me. Opu—u—u—'

Opu's flight had taken him down the path that ran along
the other side of the fence towards the bamboo grove. The
sky was still black with clouds, and because of that and
because the trees grew so close together and there was so
much undergrowth, it was pitch dark under the bamboos.
Ordinarily he would never have dreamed of coming to such
a place on his own at this hour; but on this occasion he was
so worked up that he was quite oblivious both of the dark
and of the loneliness of the place. He did not even hear the
loud cracks that the bamboos made, and he never gave a

thought to the ghost that always lives in mango trees. 'No,' he said to himself, 'I'll never go back home again, never as long as I live.'

When the first spasm of his rage had spent itself however, he began to feel less sure of himself. Just in front of him was the old mango tree where the ghost lived, and he looked at it a little nervously. 'I don't care,' he told himself, 'even if a ghost does come and take me to the top of the tree. It'll serve her right, she'll come to look for me and she'll cry herself to death. And she'll remember what she said to me, "I told him he would have to eat ashes for his supper. That's what made the little darling so angry; and that's why he went out into the dark on a stormy night like this and hasn't come home again."' He told himself how upset his mother would be if a ghost came and killed him; and for a time the thought of her distress buoyed him up with a sort of vindictive pleasure. But the sensation did not last long, and he crept slowly back towards the house and stood on the path near the wall. He was thoroughly frightened by now. He heard a muffled noise in the bamboo clump just in front of him, and there was panic in his eyes as he looked to see what it was. His mother and Durga were calling out to him near Ranu's house. He could hear their voices. But there was that noise in the bamboos again. He was caught in a cleft stick. He had left the house in a fit of temper and he could not possibly go back now unless they coaxed him to go. After all there was such a thing as self-respect. At that moment he thought he saw Durga coming out of the back door at Ranu's house, so he ran off and stood behind the gate near the corner of the wall. Durga was walking in that direction when suddenly she caught sight of him. She called out at once. 'Here he is, Mummy! Look; he's standing near the wall.' She dashed up to him and seized him by the hand, though there was no need to dash. 'You naughty boy!' she said. 'What are you standing there for? Why didn't you call out? Mummy and I have been looking all over the place for you. And here you are.'

Then the two of them took him by the hand and led him back into the house.

FIFTEEN

It was time for Horihor to visit one of his clients but on this
occasion he decided to take Opu with him, because so he said,
the lad did not get enough to eat at home, whereas if he went
away for a spell he would get milk and butter and other
nourishing foods which he ought to have to make him strong.

This was the first time that Opu had been away from home.
He had walked as far as the bokul tree and seen its white
flowers. He had been to the Gosains' orchard, to the chalte
tree, with its bitter fruit, and to the river bank; and, his longest
journey of all, to the metalled road which, he was told, led
to Nawabganj. He had never been further afield than that.
Sometimes in May and June when it was particularly hot his
mother used to take him in the evening down to the steps by
the river. Across the water lay an open stretch of country where

thatch grass grew, with a few acacia trees here and there , their yellow flowers in full bloom. Cattle used to graze there, and he could see a silk cotton tree hung about with a thick-stemmed creeper, which made it look a very old tree indeed. Herdsmen brought their animals down to the river's edge to water them, and Okrur the boatman who lived in their village was usually out in his little boat setting his baskets for fish. Scattered about the plain too, were clumps of shondali trees, their flowers swinging to and fro in the gentle evening breeze. One day at this time Opu stood staring over the grassy plain to where in the far distance the blue sky came down to earth over a line of trees; and as he looked that peculiar sense of far-awayness came over him again. He had not been able to describe it before, neither could he now. All he could do was to shout to his sister when she came up out of the water. 'Look, Didi! Look right over there!' and point with his finger to where field and horizon met. 'There it is! On the other side of that tree there! It's a long way off, isn't it?'

Durga laughed. 'A long way off? Is that all? What a silly boy you are!'

Today for the first time in his life this same Opu had set foot outside the village. He had been counting the days, one by one, and had been so excited that he could hardly sleep at night. Then at long last the big moment came.

The path veered left some distance short of the main road to Nawabganj, and eventually it joined a rough track which led to Asharhu and Durgapur. As soon as they got on to the track Opu said to his father, 'Daddy, where's the railway line? Which way is it from here?'

'It's straight ahead. We shall come to it soon. We've got to go across it. So hurry up.'

Once the calf of their red cow Rangi had strayed away and got lost. Opu and Durga searched for it for three days without finding it, so they went off to look for it in another direction, through the pasture land to the south of the village. It was December and the peas were ripe, so from time to time as they walked along they bent down and plucked some. The Nawabganj road lay ahead, and as they approached they could hear the creaking of the bullock carts as they carried their loads of date-palm molasses to the market at Asharhu. The children stopped for a while and surveyed the country on the other side of the road. Durga, who was staring hard through the haze at something in the distance, suddenly burst out, 'I know what, Opu! Let's go and have a look at the railway line. What do you think?'

Opu was surprised and did not know what to think. 'The railway line?' he echoed. 'But it's a very long way off, isn't it, Didi? How can we possibly go as far as that?'

'Who said it was a very long way off? It's only just on the other side of the road.'

'If it's as near as all that, we ought to be able to see it from there. Come on, Didi, let's go.'

When they got on to the road they stopped and had another look. Then Durga said, 'It seems an awfully long way from here, doesn't it? I don't think we ought to go.'

'I can't see anything,' said Opu. 'How shall we get back home if we go too far?' But his eyes were peering thirstily into the distance. He was itching to go and yet at the same time he was afraid. Suddenly Durga swallowed her fears. 'What is there to be afraid of?' she exclaimed. 'Come on; let's go, Opu. It can't be all that far. We can get back by midday. And what's more, we might see a train. If we're late we can always tell Mummy that we were looking for the calf.'

But before they left the road they looked carefully this way and that to see if anybody was watching them. Then the brother and sister climbed down the embankment together and made off due south across a patch of marshy land. It was late morning and the sun was hot; but they ran and they ran and they ran. In time the red Nawabganj road was lost to sight behind them. On their left they passed the transplanting field, the tree where water was hung out in a jar for thirsty pilgrims, and then the Thakurjhi Lake; on their right there was nothing but empty distance. A small marsh came into view in front of them. Durga looked at her brother and laughed. 'If Mummy finds out where we've been she'll beat the skin off our backs.' Opu laughed with her, but his laugh had a note of alarm in it. Then once more they ran and they ran and they ran. For the first time in his life he was really free, free of all 'don'ts', free of the restrictions of the small circle which had hitherto imprisoned him; and his young blood thrilled to the joy of release. For the first time there was no need to worry about what was going to happen next.

Nevertheless what did happen next was not so enjoyable. They came to a bog. It lay right in their way. It was full of long coarse grass and cork bushes; and, what is more, Didi did not know where they were. She was quite lost. There was not a house in sight, only rice fields, marshy swamps and clumps of cane. They could not force their way through the canes and their feet sank deep into the mud of the swamp. The sun was high in the sky too, and it was so hot that even though it was the cold season their faces were dripping with perspiration. Didi's dress was torn in a number of places, and Opu had to keep stopping to pull thorns out of his feet. At last the question of how to get to the railway no longer seemed important; their real problem was how to get back home. They had come a long way by now. The main road was too far away to be seen from where they were, and when finally after a seemingly endless walk, they splashed their way through the water in the rice fields and found it, the hour

146

was well past noon. Eventually they reached home. Didi told a long rigmarole of a story and they did not lose the skin from their backs.

This was the same railway line; but today he was going to get to it without any difficulty. There was no need to hurry. There was no chance of losing the way, and there was no fear of being scolded.

A little way on Opu noticed with surprise that there was a road ahead of them. It stood high above the fields and looked like the metalled road to Nawabganj. It cut right through the countryside from far on the left to far on the right. Red-coloured stones were piled up in tiny heaps alongside it and there were pillars of white metal joined one to another by long lines of string. And the pillars went on and on; indeed as far as his eye could see there were white pillars and strings stretched between them.

'Look, child!' said Horihor. 'That's the railway line.'

Opu bounded through the gate on to the line. He looked up and down the track, his eyes wide open with surprise as he took in every detail. Why do those two iron rails run side by side like that? Are they what the train goes on? Why should it? Why should it go along them instead of across the fields? Doesn't it ever come off? What are those things? Are they what are called wires? What is that whispering noise they are making? Is it a message going along them? Whose message can it be and why is he sending it? Where is the station? Is it this way or that?

'I want to see the train, Daddy. What time will it come?'

'How can you see a train now? There isn't one till midday; and that's two hours off.'

'It doesn't matter, Daddy. I want to wait and see it. I've never seen a train. So please let me stay, Daddy, please!'

'Don't make a fuss now. That's why I don't like taking

147

you out with me. How can you see a train now? We will have to stand about in this sun until twelve or one o'clock. Run along now. I'll let you see a train on the way back.'

There were tears in Opu's eyes, but he had to go on after his father.

You are going on a journey. You have no notion what you are likely to see as you travel on. Your childish eyes are big, and they take in the world around you with a hungry appetite that gulps down everything. Just think of the pleasure you are getting, for you too are a world explorer. It is nonsense to suppose that you must roam the whole world to taste the joys of the unknown. You are bathing for the first time in new rivers. You are cooling your body in winds that blow through new villages. What can it matter to you if somebody else has done all this before you? To your eyes it is an undiscovered country, and today for the first time you taste its newness in your heart, and in your mind and with all your senses.

Amdob! It was only a tiny village, but what a pretty name it had! Young women were busy in the yards, chopping straw, or tethering goats or feeding their chickens with rice. There were older people out too: they were drying jute or slicing bamboos or ... but even while Opu's eyes were taking it all in, the village slipped behind and they were out in the open country once more. Low lying places were brimful of water. Cranes stood motionless in fields where wild rice was growing. There were some hollows through which you could not see the water because of the water-lily leaves and their wide-open flowers.

Presently they came to the Kholsemari Lake. They called it Kholsemari because of the kholse fish that lived in it. In the fields nearby the summer rice grew lush and green and overhead was the blue expanse of the September sky. The gorgeous pageantry of the setting sun emblazoned the vault of heaven, and the many-coloured clouds were now like mountains, now like islands, now like the vast sea itself, and now like fairyland seen in a dream. Opu had never before seen the sky as he saw it today. It seemed so friendly. That far-off country beyond the fields had at last drawn aside its veil and disclosed its secrets to an eight-year-old boy.

But it was getting late. His father said to him, 'What a boy you are for gaping at things! Why do you have to stand and stare at everything you see? Walk more quickly.'

It was almost dark when they reached their destination. Their host, Laksman Mahajan, a very prosperous farmer, was one of Horihor's religious clients. He received them with great respect and put a large outhouse at their disposal.

Early the following morning, the wife of Laksman Mahajan's younger brother went down to the tank for her bath. As she stood on the bank her eyes fell on a little boy she had not seen before. He was in the banana orchard close to the water's edge. He had a switch in his hand and was darting in and out among the banana trees in a most odd way; and what is more he was talking to himself, as though he was not quite right in the head. She put down her water pot at once and went to meet him. 'Whose house are you staying at, Khoka?'

Opu was forward enough with his mother but he was extremely shy with strangers. His first impulse was to run away, and when he did answer her it was in a very diffident little voice. 'Over there, in their house.'

'Oh, in Laksman Mahajan's house? Then you must be the son of their Brahmin priest. I see.'

She took him with her to her own house, which stood by itself some little way from Laksman Mahajan's house and on the other side of the tank. Opu's shyness left him as he got used to her. He followed her into the house and began a round of inspection, looking at everything with great interest. And what a lot of things there were to look at! They were quite different from the things they had at home. These must be very rich people. There was a wooden stand inlaid with shells, a hanging bag woven of many colours, a bird made of wool, a glass doll, and a pottery doll, and much else besides. At first he hesitated to touch them, but curiosity overcoming him, he picked one or two of them up and turned them this way and that gingerly so that he could have a good look at them.

Until now the young woman had not had a chance to look at Opu properly, but when she did she realized that he was still very young. His face might have been that of a five-year-old. And his eyes! She had never seen a boy with such beautiful eyes. She noticed too how fair he was, how slenderly shaped, and what a pretty little face he had. But his eyes fascinated her. They were big and innocent, such as an artist might have painted. She quite lost her heart to the little stranger.

Opu sat down and was soon chatting to her about all sorts of things, but the subject uppermost in his mind was the railway line he had seen the day before. She listened to him for quite a long time and then she got up and made him a delicious confection called mohonbhog. The jar she served it in was almost full, and she had put so much butter in the sweets that he got it all over his fingers. He took just a little at first to see what it tasted like, but the first mouthful was enough to make him realize that he had never eaten anything so delicious before. There were raisins in it too. His mother did not put raisins in mohonbhog when she made it. At home he often used to plead with her, 'Mummy, please make me some mohonbhog today.' She used to laugh. 'All right, I'll make you some this evening.' Then she would boil some ordinary ground-wheat, mix a little molasses with it and serve it to him—she loved doing it—on a brass tray. But for all the love that went into the making of it, it tasted just like porridge. Hitherto however Opu had always eaten it with great relish. He did not know then that mohonbhog could taste like this. But today he knew that there was a world of difference between this mohonbhog and what his mother made for him; and as he thought about it his heart was filled with pity and sympathy for his mother. Perhaps she did not even know that mohonbhog could be like this. Yet deep within he knew that the real reason was that his mother was poor. They were a poor family, and that is why they could never have good food like this at home.

One day Opu was invited to the house of a Brahmin family who lived in a neighbouring part of the village. It was midday, and a daughter of the house came to fetch him. She made him feel at home at once and took him into their kitchen. There she placed a low stool for him to sit on, and because he was a Brahmin she sprinkled the floor round his seat with water. Her name was Omola. She was a pretty girl with a fair complexion and she had big eyes. She was about the same age as Durga. Omola's mother sat by Opu as he ate and helped him to food, and as soon as he had finished his rice, she put on his plate some sweets she had made herself. When it was time to go Omola went back home with him and stayed to play. As they were playing Opu caught his toes in the bamboo fence round the garden. It was a new fence, made of freshly sliced stakes, and they had sharp edges. His toes were cut and bleeding; and they might have been even more deeply cut, if Omola had not been there to get his foot out for him. As it was he could not walk, so Omola carried him to a grain shed nearby and wrapped his foot up

151

in some leaves that were lying about there. Opu did not mention the incident to anybody for fear his father should hear about it and scold him.

When he went to bed that night he had a dream, and it was all about Omola. She was carrying him in her arms; she was sitting by his side; she was playing with him; she was bandaging his foot; and they were running together along the railway line. All through the night as he slept Omola's smiling face was with him. Next morning as soon as it was light he went out to wait for her, wondering when she would come. Other children came and began to play; but there was no sign of Omola. The morning wore on and the young wife of the house sent for him to come in and have his food (every day, morning and evening she prepared his food for him and served him with her own hands). He went, but the moment he had finished, even before he got up to go he asked if Omola had come. She had not. In time the games came to an end. It was late then, and his father called him to go for his bath. There was still no Omola. He was very cross with her by now. 'All right,' he said to himself, 'I don't care if she doesn't come. I won't have anything more to do with her. I shan't ever speak to her again.' In the evening the games outside began again. Everybody came except Omola. There were plenty of children to play with, but no Omola. He did join in for a while but his heart was not in what he was doing. And still Omola did not come.

Next morning she did come, but Opu would not speak to her. He did not go anywhere near her, but he kept glancing in her direction to see whether she realized that he was angry and was keeping away from her on purpose. To begin with she did not notice that anything was the matter, but later on she sensed that something must have happened, so she went up to him and asked him what it was. 'What's the matter,

Khoka? Why aren't you talking to me? Has anything happened?'

Opu was too young to handle a situation like this, but he was very cross. He bit his lips to stop them trembling, and then finally he blurted out, 'Of course something's happened. What do you think? Why didn't you come yesterday?'

For a moment Omola did not understand what he meant, but then it dawned on her. 'Do you mean to say it's because I didn't come? Is that why you're cross with me?' Opu nodded, 'Yes, that's why.' Omola started to giggle; then she grabbed him by the hand and dragged him off inside the house. When the young wife heard about it she went into peals of laughter; but presently she restrained herself, though a trace of a smile still lurked on her lips. 'In that case, Omola, you can't go home any more. That is quite clear. There's only one thing for you to do: if Khoka won't let you go, you must stay here. That's only right and proper you know.'

Omola understood quite well what the young wife was getting at, and she was very embarrassed. 'It's not like that at all, Boudi,' she retorted; 'and if you ever talk to me again like that I won't come into your house any more.'

A little later Omola took Opu home with her. She opened her cupboard and showed him a grown-up doll made of glass, a wax bird and a tree and all sorts of other things too. Opu asked her where she had got them from and she told him that they had all been bought at the fair which had been held at Kaliganj during the river festival. Some of the toys were quite new. There was a rubber monkey which followed you round with its eyes no matter where you went; and there was a most amazing doll. If you pressed its stomach it waved its arms about wildly and beat a drum. But the best of Omola's treasures was a tin horse. It had a winding apparatus inside it like the wall clock at Ranu's uncle's house, and if you wound it up and let it go it pranced about the floor, and quite a long way too, just like a real horse. Opu was spellbound. He picked it up and turned it upside down to have a good look at it; and then he questioned Omola about it. 'What a wonderful horse it is, Omola! Where did you get it from? How much did it cost?'

A little later Omola opened a vermilion jar and held it out for him to see. Thee was something inside. It was reddish in colour. He thought it was tin foil. 'What is it?' he asked. 'Is it tin?' Omola laughed. 'Tin? Of course it isn't tin. Haven't you ever seen gold leaf before?' He never had. Could gold be as red as that? He took a piece of it in his fingers and held it up to see.

Soon it was time to go back to the house. Omola took him there but as he walked by her side his thoughts were all about Durga. 'Poor Didi hasn't got toys like these. Poor Didi! She has to play with dry berries and seeds she collects from the jungle; and if she as much as takes somebody else's doll she gets a beating.' He did not know until now that a girl of Didi's age could have so many toys; but today he had seen them and as he compared what Omola had with what Didi had, his heart welled over with sadness for his sister. If he had the money, he told himself, he would buy her a mechanical doll or perhaps a rubber monkey which followed you round with its eyes wherever you went.

The young wife had a pack of cards in her room. It was not a pack really but a collection of odd cards left over from several packs. Opu played with them from time to time. They reminded him of the card games that were played sometimes in the middle of the day at Ranu's house. He had often watched them. Ace, jack, king, queen! What battles they fought with them! It was most exciting. He did not know how to play cards. His mother and sister did not know either, though his mother did try to get into a game now and then. But no one would have her as a partner. They said she did not know anything about the game. On one occasion however—Opu remembered it well—she did manage to persuade them to let her play. She started off by pretending that she knew all about it; but it did not take the others long to find her out. 'Good gracious!' somebody shouted. 'What on earth did you play your ace for, Bouma? (They all called her Bouma.) Didn't you see that they had already played the jack of trumps?' His mother laughed to hide her ignorance. 'Yes, of course,' she said. 'It was stupid of me. I played without thinking.' The game went on; and his mother looked from one player to another and smiled knowingly as if to give the impression that she had some cunning move up her sleeve and that she knew all the cards they had in their hands. It was not long however before she made another blunder. Her partner it was who burst out this time. 'Just look what you've done now, Bouma! You've got a sequence and you didn't show it.' His poor mother did not even know what a sequence was; but she smiled and said in a superior tone. 'Yes, I know I had; but I didn't show it on purpose. I had a plan in mind.' Her partner was furious. 'What nonsense!' she yelled. 'You don't know what you're talking about. It was a wonderful hand and you've ruined it. It's the last time I shall ever have you as a partner. Hand over the cards to Shejbou.' Shorbojoya tried to pass it off with another smile, as if nothing had happened, as if they were only joking and she did not mind. It was very humiliating, and Opu had never forgotten it.

If he had a pack of cards they could play together in the middle of the day after they had had their meal, he, his mother and Didi. They would play by the window which looked out into the forest, the window with leaves that were so worm-eaten that if you shook them a yellow powder

155

rained down, yellow as mustard, and gave out a smell like that of old wood, the window through which the slightly bitter scent of the gondhobhedali creeper wafted in on every breeze that blew; while in the bushes in the yard—they called them black-cloud bushes—Didi's old friend the firefly would fly and settle, fly and settle. There in the middle of the day when nobody was about they would spread a mat by the window and play cards to their heart's content. What did it matter if they did not know what a sequence was. And if they had one and did not want to show it that would not matter either. Nobody would order anybody else away. There would be no humiliation, no hurt laughter, no scorn. They would all play as they wanted to. It would just be a game, and knowing about sequences would not make any difference.

That evening there was a special party at the young wife's house. When Opu sat down to eat he was astounded by the magnificence of the appointments and the number of utensils which had been set out for his use. Why were the limes and the salt on separate dishes by themselves, dishes carved to look like flowers. At home his mother helped him to put salt and lime on his own plate. There were separate dishes too for all the meat and vegetable courses—and how many of them there were! And that big lobster's head! Was that all for him?

And there were luchis! Luchis! They conjured up before his eyes, though he could hardly believe it, that blue shore of fairyland which he and Didi imagined they saw through the mists of desire across the river of their dreams. How many days, how many nights when all they had had to eat was rice and stringy root vegetables or boiled unflavoured pumpkin; how many mornings, how many evenings when there was nothing for them to eat at all, had they sat in the house dull and not caring, when suddenly their imagination had quickened and borne them off in an ecstasy of longing to that fairyland where one day in the year of Biru Ray, the best cook in the village, napkin on shoulder, walked up and down in the heat of the day by the side of an oven he had just built himself, on which stood a huge pan, swimming with butter and filling the air with ambrosial odours of frying luchis! The children of the village, all of them in their best clothes, were buzzing round him; and in the Gangulis' garden, because it was summer and the sun was very hot, the great carpet was spread under the awning of the dance tent and out beyond it as far as the olive trees. Only on one day in the year did they know where to find fairyland, and that day was the Spring Festival in March, the birthday of Ramchandra, when they were invited to the Gangulis' house on the other side of the village. Now as if Ramchandra was having a second birthday, that auspicious day had come again. Opu sat down to eat, but as he did so he kept thinking, 'Poor Didi has never had anything like this to eat'.

Next morning the games began again. Omola came and Opu rushed up to her and seized her by the hand. 'Omola and I are on this side,' he said. 'The rest of you are on that side.' It did not take Opu long to realize however that Omola would rather have had Bishu on her side. The truth was, though he did not know it himself, that Opu was not good at the game, and whoever had him on their side was bound to lose. Bishu on the other hand was very good. He was hard to catch and his side seldom lost. Once Omola indicated quite clearly that she was annoyed. Opu tried to win for all he was worth in order to please Omola, but try as he would they lost again.

The next time they picked sides Omola joined Bishu's team.

Opu's eyes filled with tears. The game no longer had any attraction for him. Omola talked to Bishu all the time, and

157

all her smiles were for him. After a while Bishu said he had to go home to do some work, and Omola asked him more than once to be sure to come again. Opu was very jealous. The morning and all its fun became meaningless and hollow. Suddenly he remembered something that Omola had said. She said that if Bishu went away there might not be enough players left. 'If I go,' he said to himself, 'she will say the same to me and much more besides.' It was easy to find a pretext, so he said aloud, 'It's getting late. I must be off to have my bath.' Omola did not say a single word. The blacksmith's son, Narugopal, said, 'All right then, Opu; come again this afternoon'; but he was the only one who said anything.

Opu went a little way and then looked back. Nobody seemed to miss him. The game was still going on. Omola was standing near the post playing the part of the old woman for all she was worth, and she did not as much as cast a glance in his direction. He was very hurt and jealous. When he got home he would not speak to anybody. He had finished with Omola. If she did not want to look at him, well, what did it matter?

A day or two later Horihor took Opu back home.

They had only been away for a few days, but Shorbojoya felt quite lost without him. Durga's games had not been such fun either. Some days before Opu went away she had quarrelled with him about the dried gourd shells they were using as boats, and for a while they had not spoken to one another. Now she had a lot more gourd shells, but she was not interested in them. She did not even bother to take them down to the water. 'Why did I have to quarrel with him?' she asked herself. 'It was so silly. I pulled his ears too. When he comes back I'll never quarrel with him again. He can have all the shells if he wants them.'

For the first fortnight after getting home Opu did nothing

but tell stories of his wonderful trip. It had been such a short time and yet he had seen so many astonishing things. There was the railway, and real trains ran along it. There were those custard apples, papayas and cucumbers too; they were only made of clay, but at first he thought they were real. Then there was that doll. If you pressed its stomach it waved its arms about all over the place and beat a drum. And of course there was Omola too. He had been such a long way. There was low-lying land full of water and covered with lotuses, villages he had never seen before, and long empty roads across wide open spaces. There was the blacksmith's shop by the side of a road through a village where his father had taken him for a drink of water; and the house where they had spread a mat for him to sit on, and made such a fuss of him and given him milk, parched rice and sugar sweets to eat. He did not know what to tell and what to leave out.

Didi was fascinated by what he said about the railway and kept interrupting to ask questions. 'How long were the rails you saw, Opu? I suppose the wires were hanging down? Did you see a train? Did one go past while you were there?' No! Opu had not seen a train. That was the one thing he had not seen; and it was all his father's fault. They would only have had to wait four or five hours by the railway at the most, and the train would have come. But he just could not get his father to let him wait for it.

A few days had passed. Shorbojoya came into the yard in a great hurry. She had a lot to do and it was late. She rushed through the gate without looking where she was going, and as soon as she got inside she felt something like a thin string catch her across the chest. There was a tearing noise and then a snap. Two loose ends fluttered slowly down to the ground on either side of her. It was all over in an instant before she could know that anything had happened.

Opu came in a little later. The moment he got through the gate and came into the yard he stopped in his tracks. He could not believe his eyes. 'What's this? Who's broken my telegraph wire?' The disaster was so enormous and so unexpected that it was some time before he could take it in. When however he managed to pull himself together he noticed wet footprints on the earth. They had not yet disappeared. Something told him that they were his mother's. They had to be hers. They could not be anybody else's. He went into the house and saw her sitting on the floor. She was washing some jackfruit seeds, quite unaware of the storm that was impending. He stood stock still for a moment, then bending forward dramatically like some character in a play he had once heard, he began to speak in bitter-sweet tones, his voice pitched high like a flute.

'Very nice, to be sure! It was no trouble for me to scour the forest and the orchards for all those silly little things and bring them home with me, was it?'

Shorbojoya looked up in surprise. 'What things? What are you talking about?'

'It was no trouble at all, was it? And I didn't scratch my hands and get thorns into my feet, did I?'

'What's all this mad talk about? What's the matter?'

'What's the matter? I went to all the trouble of putting up a telegraph wire and now it's been torn down. That's the matter.'

'There's never a moment that passes without your being up to some extraordinary nonsense. There was something hanging in the yard, right across the path where everybody walks. How was I to know whether it was a telegraph or a sillygraph or what it was? I was in a hurry, and it got torn. I didn't do it on purpose.'

Thereupon she turned back to what she was doing.

What dreadful heartlessness! There had been a time when he thought his mother loved him, but though he had long since changed his mind about that he never imagined, even in his dreams, that she could be so cruel, so like a stone. He had spent the whole of yesterday in Uncle Nilmoni's deserted compound, in the Palits' vast mango orchard and in teacher Proshonno's bamboo grove. He had made his way alone through the most fearsome jungles and with the greatest difficulty had torn down some gulancha creepers from the tall trees they grew on. And how difficult it had been! Then when he had collected enough he brought them home. At last all his preparations were made and he was ready to start playing railways. And now ...!

He wanted to say something really violent to his mother, something rude, something that would hurt her; but he could not think of the right words. So he stood there for a while and then said with a shriek that was more shrill and piercing than before. 'I won't eat my food today. I won't, and now you know.'

His mother replied, 'Well, if you won't you won't. That's all there is to it. Usually you can't even wait till your food's ready. But if you won't eat, you might as well go away. We shall soon find out who'll feed you when you're hungry.'

That was all there was to it. In the twinkling of an eye it was all over and done with, and Shorbojoya was once more washing the jackfruit seeds. But where was Opu? He had vanished without trace like a piece of evaporated camphor. Durga was coming in at that very moment and he burst past her in the doorway like a cyclone. Taken by surprise she looked after him for a moment and then she called out, 'Where are you going off to like that, Opu? What's happened? Come and tell ...'

Her mother said, 'It's quite beyond me, the two of you and all the extraordinary things you get up to. It's wearing me down to skin and bone. He hung something across the yard, just inside the gate. I came in and it broke. I couldn't help it. Do you think I'd do a thing like that on purpose? But that's why he's in such a rage, "I won't eat my food today," he said. All right, he won't. So what about it? You'd think I was born into this world just to cook for you two.'

Mother and son were both angry and hurt, and it fell to Durga to act as peacemaker. She called all round the house for Opu, but he was not there; so at two o'clock she went out to look for him. She found him in the Ray's orchard at the other end of the village. He was sitting on the trunk of an up-rooted mango tree. He was dry-eyed and grim.

If however you had gone past Opu's house that evening you would never have recognized him as the same Opu, the Opu who had been in such a rage with his mother that he was going to run away from home. All that was changed now; for there was a wire strung right across the yard from one side to the other. He could not take his eyes off it. He inspected it closely but it was right in every detail. It was just like the wire on the real railway.

He went round to Shotu's house, and told him about it. 'I've put up a telegraph wire in our yard. Come home with me and let's play railways. Please come.'

'Who did you say put up the wire?' asked Shotu.

'I put it up myself. Didi was there of course, and she helped me a bit.'

'All right, but I can't come now.'

Opu was never able to get big children to come and play with him. They were not interested. He knew this quite well. He stood about despondently for a minute or so, holding nervously on to the corner of the verandah; and then he plucked up courage to ask him a second time, but he spoke shyly and the tone of his voice suggested that he had little hope of success.

'Do come, Shotu. Didi will be there, and we can all play together.' And he added as an inducement, 'I've collected some pomelo leaves, and we can use them as tickets.' He opened his hand to prove that he had them. 'Do come.'

Shotu refused. Opu never found it easy to talk when he was away from home, so he went back without saying any more. But he was very sad and close to tears. He had said a lot despite his shy nature, but Shotu had taken no notice.

Next morning Opu and his sister built a big shop with some bricks and then went out to collect things to sell in it. Durga was in her element. She knew just where to look in the jungle; so between them they collected a lot of things. There were custard apple leaves they were going to use for betel, and balls which looked just like potatoes, and flowers from the radha creeper which would do for fish. Some trees and bushes grew long seed pods, and these they could sell as potol and shim beans. They found lumps of clay too for rock salt. All these they collected and lots of other things too; and when they had got them home they spent a long time fitting out the shop.

'What are we going to have for sugar, Didi?'

'There's a lovely heap of sand on the way to the bamboo grove. Mummy uses it to bake rice in. We can get some of that. It's quite white, just like sugar.'

While they were out looking for sugar in the bamboo grove they went into the forest that grew down to the side of the path. There were some very tall trees about there, and among them a chotka tree. It was almost enveloped by a creeper, but on a branch at the top of it they saw some fruit hanging. It was bright red and quite round. After a long struggle they succeeded in tearing down part of the creeper and some of the fruit fell to the ground with it. They rushed to pick them up.

Only three of them were ripe, but they would do. They put them in the shop as decorations and they arranged them in such a way that if a customer came in they were bound to catch his eye at once. Then business began and it was very brisk. Durga bought so much betel that stocks almost ran out. The game had been going on for some time when Opu saw Shotu come in through the front gate. He was delighted, and ran to bring him in. 'Shotu, come and see what a lovely shop we've got. Look at all the fruit. Didi and I went out and collected it. Look at this one. What's its name? Do you know?'

'It's called makal. We've got lots of it in our orchard,' Shotu replied.

Shotu's coming made Opu's day. He so seldom came; and moreover he was the ringleader of the big boys' set. Now that he had come their shop became much more than a children's game.

Their buying and selling now became most professional. Durga said, after it had been going on for some time, 'Give me two bags of rice, please. It must be very fine. Tomorrow's my doll's engagement ceremony. We've got a lot of guests coming.'

'You'll invite us, won't you?' Shotu asked.

Durga shook her head. 'No, of course not. You're the bride's party. We shall come in the morning and escort you here as part of the ceremony. And Shotu, ask Ranu to get the sandal paste ready tonight. I'll come and collect it in the ...'

She was not able to finish her sentence. Shotu grabbed something from the sale counter and dashed off towards the gate. Opu went after him. 'Didi, he's taken them!' and shouting at the top of his thin high-pitched little voice he went off in pursuit.

Durga was flabbergasted for a moment, and before she knew what had happened Shotu and Opu were outside the gate. She looked back at the shop and saw that the red makal fruit was gone. He had taken all three of them. It did not take her long to get to the gate. She saw the two of them tearing along the path to the mangosteen tree, Shotu in front and Opu some distance away behind him. Shotu was not only three or four years older than Opu, he was also much more strongly built. He had very powerful arms and legs, quite different from Opu's slender limbs. Ordinarily Opu would have been quite incapable of keeping up with him, but on this occasion it did look as if he might possibly catch him. The only reason for this was that Shotu was only running because he wanted to keep stolen property whereas Opu was running for his very life.

As they ran Durga saw Shotu bend down and then turn round. At the same moment Opu came to a sudden halt, but Shotu continued running and was soon out of sight. When she came up to Opu she saw that he was doubled up. His eyes were closed and he was rubbing them with his hands.

'What happened, Opu?' she asked.

Opu could not see properly and he kept on rubbing his eyes. There was pain in his voice too. 'Shotu threw some dust in my eyes, and I can't see, Didi. I can't see at all.'

Durga quickly pulled his hands away. 'Stop a minute, and let me look. You mustn't rub your eyes like that.'

Opu took his hands away. 'Oh, Didi! It does hurt; and I've gone blind, Didi.' His voice sounded very frightened.

'Let me see, let me see! Don't touch your eyes. Move your hands away.' She spat on the end of her sari and dabbed his eyes with it, and after a while he was able to open them and could see a little. Then she rolled back his eyelids and blew on them several times. 'Can you see all right now? Good, well you go home, and I'll go to their house and tell his mother and grandmother all about it. I'll be back soon.'

Durga actually did go as far as the back door of Ranu's

house, but when she got there she could not summon up the courage to go in. She was afraid of Shejbou; so she waited outside the door for some time trying to make up her mind, but in the end she turned away. When she reached home Opu was standing behind the gate. He had pulled it right back and was hiding there. He was crying silently. He was not a child who was given to crying; in fact he hardly ever cried. He might lose his temper, or be thoroughly upset, but he did not cry. So when she saw him Durga realized how very hurt he was. He was very attached to that fruit, and now it was gone: and on top of that Shotu had humiliated him by throwing dust in his eyes. She could not bear to see him cry. It made her heart ache.

She took him by the hand and tried to console him. 'Don't cry, Opu. Come into the house with me and I'll give you all my cowrie shells. Are your eyes still hurting? ... And look, you've torn your clothes ...'

It was midday. Opu had had his meal but he did not want to go out anywhere. He stayed in his room instead. It was an old room in an old dilapidated house; but it had a lot of furniture in it. There was an old-fashioned wooden chest, a multicoloured cane basket, a very old cupboard which was inlaid with shells, and a bath stool. There were many boxes in the room too, some of which Opu had never seen open; and on the shelf there were a number of pots and jars. He did not know what was in them either.

With so many old things standing together in one room it was not surprising that it smelled of antiquity. Opu did not know what sort of a smell it was, and he certainly could not have described it, but whatever it was it made him think of days long past. He was not in this world as long ago as that, but that cupboard with its cowrie shells was; and so was his grandfather's cane basket, and the big wooden chest. The branches at the top of the shondali tree had towered head and shoulders above all the other trees in the forest; and the derelict land near it, now covered with jungle, had in those days been the site of somebody's rustic shrine, and many children of many families had played round it. But now they had passed into the shadows and all memory of them was lost. It was so long ago.

Shorbojoya had gone out for her bath, and Opu was alone. He felt a strong urge to open the chest and the basket and uncover the secrets they concealed, and have a good look at them in the light of day. A large wooden tray rested on the highest crossbeam, and on it was a pile of palm-leaf manuscripts and sheets of paper. He had noticed them before and asked his father whose they were. They had belonged to his grandfather, Ramchand Tarkalankar, who had been a great scholar in his day. He would have loved to take them down and go through them, but he could not reach. Sometimes in the middle of the day he used to sit by the window which looked out into the forest and read from a torn copy of Kasidas's Mahabharat. He had taught himself to read quite well, so much so that he no longer liked having stories read to him as once he had done. He could read them easily enough for himself; and he understood what they meant too, for he was a clever and intelligent little boy. From time to time the older men of the village used to meet together on the Gangulis' verandah, and sometimes Horihor took Opu along with him. On such occasions he would tell him to read from the Ramayan or from those old narrative poems known as panchalis. 'Read aloud, Khoka. I want them to hear you.' The old men were full of praise. Dinu Chatterji said, 'That grandson of mine—he's about the same age as your little boy—has already worn out two a b c books, but if you heard him read you wouldn't credit it; for even now he doesn't know his letters properly. It's all right as long as I'm alive, I tell them; but once my eyes are closed they'll have to turn to and work as farm labourers.' Horihor's heart swelled with pride. 'This is as it has to be,' he thought to himself. 'You can't expect your children to be like mine. You've always been moneylenders. We may be poor, but we've always been scholars. That's a fact and you can't deny it. My father did not fill those palm-leaf manuscripts of his with nonsense. He received the family tradition and handed it on; and it's not likely to come to an end.'

The wall of their compound was only a few feet away from the window where Opu was sitting, and the forest began the other side of it; indeed the thick tangle of the jungle actually touched the wall. All that the eye could see from the window was a roof of undergrowth, billowing like the waves of a green ocean; pierced here and there by trees, festooned with innumerable creepers, and ancient bamboos, whose spikes now heavy with age drooped over the shondali and bonchalta trees; but beneath it all the bosom of the earth was black and there the wagtail danced. Between the trunks of the tall trees was the dark green war of the thickets, holud, bonkochu and kotuol, which strove one against another, locked in a life and death struggle to break through to the light of the sun; and if in this deadly encounter a thicket gave way it was crushed at once under the triumphant weight of its proud neighbour, where it mouldered and died, leaves and branches, in the sickly pallor of decay. And over this death-stricken scene the chequered light of the late-autumn sun which filtered through every crack and cranny in the earth-bound roof began to fade, and the earth itself, heavy with lush intoxicating odours from plants and creeping flowers, slowly darkened and disappeared from the view with all its vast and secret loveliness.

This jungle of a forest, which began from the wall of their

compound, stretched unbroken to the factory field in one direction and down to the bank of the river in the other. To Opu it seemed endless. He had walked a long way into it with his sister, but he had never come to the end of it. All he knew of it was the path which ran by the side of the tittiraj tree, and of course the clusters of fruit on the bonchalta trees, for they grew everywhere, and the festoons of the gulancha creeper. The narrow path seemed to come to an end in a mango grove, but actually it went on again on the other side, though where and how nobody knew. There was one great open space, and here a cucumber creeper swung free and the eye could just make out a convolvulus twining round the mossy branches of an ancient acacia tree.

This forest, with its freshness and deep green shadows, had laid its fingers on Opu and his sister alike, and had brought peace and consolation into their hearts. They had known it all their lives. Day by day, hour by hour, its silence and its delights poured rich and varied nectars into their thirsting souls. There was a dark green bush freshened by rain and crowned by the long yellow petals which fell from a thorn tree's fragrant flowers, and above, in the higher branches of that thorn tree, veiled in shadow as the sun began to set, squirrels ran to and fro. The wonder and ever-changing joys of the forest filled Opu with emotions which lay too deep for words. There was that little unknown bird which, scorning the rich profusion of leaf, flower and fruit which grew all around, came and sat on the twisted branch of a barren tree. The bird song he heard around him was like something in a dream, something not of this world; and the flower petals floated down silently like soft rain and the light of sunset thickened into dusk.

Somewhere in the middle of this forest there was an old pond. It was quite silted up now. Very near to it were the ruins of a derelict temple. In early days the goddess Bisalaksi had been worshipped in the village as Panchananda was worshipped there today. One of the local families, Mojumdar by name, had installed her; but she became angry with them and told them in a dream that she was going to leave the temple and would never return to it again. It seems that for some reason or other, possibly because a wish had been granted, they performed a human sacrifice in the temple. But all this is old history. No one living today had ever seen ceremonies performed in honour of Bisalaksi. The temple itself had fallen completely into ruins, and the pond in front of it was now no more than a quagmire. The jungle had overgrown the site entirely, and there were no Mojumdars left to light a candle there.

But—and this is an old story too—a man named Shorup Chokroborti was returning home from a neighbouring village where he had been to attend a ceremony. It was getting dark, and as he was walking along the path which led to the river steps he saw a beautiful sixteen-year-old girl standing in the way. He was very startled to see such a young and lovely girl in that lonely part of the forest at so late an hour; but before he could say anything she addressed him. Her voice was musical but it had the ring of authority. 'I am Bisalaksi, the goddess of this village. In a few days' time an epidemic of cholera will break out. Instruct the people to worship Kali in the temple of Panchananda on the fourteenth night and make an offering of one hundred and eight pumpkins.' Her voice stopped, and she faded slowly right before the eyes of the astounded Shorup Chokroborti and disappeared into the winter mist which was already beginning to settle round them. Not long after this incident there actually was a terrible epidemic in the village.

Opu had heard people tell stories about the goddess very

often, and sometimes when he stood by the window he thought about her and wondered whether he too would ever see her, see her just once. Then one day when he was out in the jungle collecting gulancha creepers, it happened.

'Who are you?' the goddess asked.

'I'm Opu.'

'You're a very good little boy. What would you like me to do for you?'

He was lying down on his bed. The bitter-sweet scent of many creepers came floating in on the breath of the whispering wind. It was just noon, and far away, high above even the tallest trees, a fish-hawk called its shrill long-drawn cry. Trilling down the lonely paths of the blue sky, radiant with the mid-day brilliance of the autumn sun, it was like the voice of a goddess, speaking far above the petty joys and sorrows, quarrels and reconciliations, past or present, of their ordinary little village. It was like the voice of a goddess wandering free, and untrammelled by the bonds of home or temple; and the music of it faded from distance to distance until he could hear it no more.

He did not remember falling asleep, but he did; and when he woke up the afternoon was far advanced. Outside his window the shadows of the evening had spread over the whole forest, except for the spikes of the bamboos, which still held the red light of the sun.

Every day at this time, when the afternoon was full of shadows, he looked into the empty forest and his mind stirred with many strange thoughts. He was aware of a deep contentment. It seemed to him that he had known days like this before, days filled with the sweet fragrance of creepers; and the memory of all those past days quickened the present with a vague but happy hope for the future. He felt that something was going to happen and these days he was now

171

enjoying had not come in vain. Some great joy must be awaiting him in the end.

These afternoons and his well-known, life-long friend, the forest, joyous and full of changing forms, were the time and place of the stories of his secret dreamland. Deep in the darkening sky beyond the bamboo grove he could see that persuasive suppliant, the god Indra. He had caught the youthful Karna in a generous mood, and holding out his hands he begged of him his impenetrable armour, thus luring him to his death. He could see that poor wretched little boy, Asvatthama, Dron's son, drink his thin rice gruel and dance with glee before his playmates, exclaiming, 'It's milk, milk! I've been drinking milk.' And under the bel tree in the deserted compound, he saw Arjun pierce the earth with his sharp arrow and bring forth the sacred river Bhagavati so that he could moisten the lips of the mighty Bhishma, who lay mortally wounded on a bed of arrows. King Dasarath, still a young man, went hunting in the flowery woods on the banks of the Sarayu. There he saw a boy who had gone to the river to draw water and mistook him for a deer and killed him. That took place by the tank near the big rose-apple tree in Ranu's orchard.

Opu had a book at home. The pages of it were quite yellow, and part of the binding had been torn off. The name of the book, *The Poem of Brave Women* was still there, but not the name of the author. The first few pages too had been lost. It was Opu's favourite book, and he was especially fond of the canto which contained the lines:

A pool I saw close by, and by that pool
Thigh-smitten, writhing in pain, the royal
Charioteer. I woke and cried, "O God!
What dream is this, what awful, evil dream?"

Kuluichandi was one of Shorbojoya's personal feastdays,

and whenever it came round she used to take Opu with her for a picnic in the open country to the north of the village where there was an old, overgrown pool. Nobody knew that this little pool, now surrounded by the jungle, was the Dvaipayan of the Mahabharat, and that near it, alone and sorely wounded, lay that hero with a broken thigh; and no one ever went to search for him. To the north of it farmers came and went to their fields, where they grew bananas and egg-plants: but here by the Shonadanga plain was an undiscovered country, an unpeopled, unknown land, over which the darkness of a moonless night was now descending. Opu's eager and inquisitive mind was awakened to a deeper sympathy by the pictures he saw there: the sorrows of men of old, thousands of years before, the elation of a silly boy who rejoiced that he had deceived his poor father, or the unhappy prince who lay there alone and helpless. And as he read this book by an author whose name he did not know Opu's eyes were often wet with tears.

Horihor was for the time being away from home; but when he was in the house Opu had to stay in, get out his books and do his lessons. He was not even let off in the late afternoon, and that he found very irksome. How much longer would he have to sit there mugging those arithmetical rhymes? Was he to have no time to play today? There was precious little left of the day as it was. He felt thwarted, and was very angry with his father. But suddenly when he was no longer expecting it his father let him go. He hurriedly piled his books together in one place and danced happily out into the yard, which by now was getting dark with the shadows of evening.

Nevertheless it was a wonderful evening, even more so than the others. His playhouse was under a tree, and it was very dark inside beneath its roof of branches he had torn from

173

a date palm. The wire he had made of gulancha creepers was strung across it. The red light of sunset glowed on the top-most branches of the pomelo tree in the deserted compound which once belonged to his great-uncle; and the brilliant yellow tero bird was hopping about in the bonkolmi bushes with its fledglings. Opu's little world was brimming over with happiness, though he could never have said why.

It was dark. Shorbojoya had started cooking the evening meal. Opu was sitting on a mat in the verandah. It was quite black outside, and the cicadas were blaring their unending, monotonous chant.

Opu asked, 'How many days are left before the big festival, Mummy?'

Durga was chopping vegetables. 'Twenty-two isn't it, Mummy?'

She was right. Their father would be home before then, and he would be bringing something for all three of them, a doll, clothes, and red alta for their feet.

Durga was a big girl now, and her mother would no longer let her go to parties far from home. She had almost forgotten what luchis tasted like. Until a little while ago, when the nights were bright with the full moon of September and the path through the bamboo grove was like a thread woven of light and shade, she used to wander all round the village and come back with her sari full of sweets and dried, pressed and toasted rice for the Lakshmi festival. At this time of the year conches were being blown in every house, and all along the path floated the smell of frying luchis. She always hoped that somebody in the village would send some as part of the festival offering. Whatever sweets she brought back were made to last for two days and her mother had some too. This year however Shejbou had said to her mother, 'It isn't right for a girl of a good family to wander round from house to house collecting sweets as if she were a peasant girl. It doesn't look very nice. I wouldn't let her go any more if I were you.' So from then on she was not allowed to go.

Durga said, 'What about having a game of cards?'

'All right. Go and fetch the cards from the other room and then we can have a game.'

A frightened look came into Durga's face and she turned appealingly to Opu. He laughed and said, 'All right, I'll come with you.'

'I can't for the life of me make out what it is you're so frightened about,' Shorbojoya said peevishly. 'All day long you go wandering about here, there and everywhere, but at night you're too scared to go from one room to another.'

The pack of cards they used was the one which Opu had brought back from the house he visited when he was away with his father. None of them knew very much about playing cards. Opu did not even know all the suits yet. From time to time he used to show his cards to his mother—it did not make any difference that they were supposed to be playing against one another—and ask her, 'What suit is this, Mummy? Diamonds? Do have a look and tell me.'

Durga was particularly happy today. Usually they did not have a cooked meal at night, only the rice and vegetables which were left over from the morning; but tonight some rice had been put on to cook, and the vegetables would be done later. That was why she was so happy. It was just like a festival day.

Opu said to his mother, 'Mummy, please tell me a story while we're playing, the one about Shyamlanka.' When she took no notice he lay back with his hand across her lap and stroked her cheek in an effort to coax her into doing what he wanted. 'Please tell me that story, Mummy. The one about

Shyamlanka grinding the spices, with her hair trailing on the floor.'

'You can't play cards and listen to stories at the same time, Opu,' Durga said. 'Sit up and play properly.'

Shorbojoya said, 'Where did you get those mushrooms from Durga?'

'You know that big orchard which belongs to the Gosains, don't you? They were there. You remember it, Opu. You and I went there once looking for Rangi the cow. There were lots of mushrooms out and nobody seemed to know they were there. The undergrowth is very thick there, otherwise people would have seen them and picked them all.'

'You mean to say you went there by yourself?' said Opu. 'It's quite wild there.'

Shorbojoya kept looking at Opu as they sat there, and as she did a look of tenderness came into her eyes. 'Can it be the same Opu?' she asked herself. 'How grown up he's become! It doesn't seem so long ago since I used to sing, "Come, moon; come, moon! Put your mark on baby's forehead." And how he used to clench his fists and rock backwards and forwards like a clockwork motor, and bang his fists on his forehead which looked just like the moon itself. And now he's big enough to play cards.' Her eyes told her that it was so, but still she could hardly believe it. So if Opu did not know what card to play, or if he tried to win a trick and muffed it, or if he got bad cards and she got good ones, she was sad on his account even though she was playing against him.

Durga interrupted her thoughts. 'Do you know what he did today, Mummy?'

'Don't tell, Durga,' Opu said. 'I'll never speak to you again if you do.'

'I don't care. Listen, Mummy. He didn't know what

176

poppy seeds were. We were at Raji's house today, and they put some poppy seeds to dry in the sun; and he said, "What are these, Raji?" She told him they were sweets and he went and ate some. He didn't even know what poppy seeds were. Isn't he stupid, Mummy?'

Opu had said that he would not speak to her again, but he did not really mean it. His mind went back to that unhappy morning when Shotu ran off with their red makal fruit, and Didi spent the rest of the day in the jungle looking for some more; and when she came back in the evening she had a whole heap of them tied up in her sari, 'What do you think about these?' she said, as she untied her sari and showed them to him. 'Will they be enough for you? You cried such a lot this morning, didn't you?' He was so happy that evening; but it was the look on Didi's face and the happy smile that glowed so tenderly in her big eyes, rather than the makals, which made him happy.

'We're playing sixes now, Opu. So be careful and mind what you do,' said Durga, happily, as she picked up the cards and laid them out.

'How strong the scent of those flowers is, Didi, isn't it?'

'There's a chatim tree behind your old uncle's house,' Shorbojoya told him. 'It's the flowers from there that you can smell.'

'That's the tree you told us about, isn't it?' they both chimed in hopefully. 'The one the tiger came to?'

But as they spoke their mother threw her cards down. 'Oh! the rice is burning. I can smell it from here. Wait a minute while I take it off, and then I'll come back and tell you.'

A little later they sat down to their supper. Durga said, 'What a treat it is to have mushroom curry like this, Mummy'; and her face beamed with satisfaction.

Opu was not to be left out. 'Oooh!' he said. 'They taste

lovely, just like meat, don't they, Didi? There were lots of mushrooms in that place, Mummy; but I didn't pick any of them because I thought they were toadstools.'

Shorbojoya's heart swelled with pride and joy to hear such spontaneous praise from the two of them. 'If only I could get really decent things to cook!' she said to herself with a sigh. 'When there's a special do on they call Shejbou to cook for them. If they'd let me do it just once I'd show them what good cooking is. I certainly would.'

'Durga,' she said aloud, 'pour some water on Opu's hands. Goodness, how tiresome he is! He's going out into the yard to wash his face there. That's what he's taken to doing every night now.'

But Opu would not come back indoors. In front of him was the hole where the wall was broken, and the dark bamboo grove; and the darkness among the bushes was as black as jhinge seeds. That derelict old house was there too, and many other terrifying things. There were so many harmful things in life that he could not understand what harm there was in washing his face out in the yard.

A little later they went to bed. It was a dark night. The air was damp with dew and there was the touch of autumn in it; and it was heavy also with the strong scent of the chatim flowers. Towards midnight the waning moon rose above the tips of the bamboo trees, and its pale light sparkled on the dew which lay so thickly on leaves and branches. There was a strange mysterious magic in the play of light and shade which filled the forest. It looked like fairyland asleep. Suddenly a gust of wind stirred, and the branches of the shondali tree began to sway and the telakucho bushes trembled.

Sometimes at about this time Opu used to wake up, and when he did he thought about the goddess, the divine Bisalaksi, the forgotten foundress of the village; and he wondered if she would come to visit them. Men whose footprints had long, long ago disappeared from the mud and from among the reeds which grew by the Ichamoti, with its many sandbanks and luminous waters; men, on whom the ancient pomegranate which still stood on its bank no longer looked down, once worshipped in the temple of that goddess of olden times with offerings of fruit and flowers. Today nobody remembered her. But she had not forgotten her own village. Often late at night when the whole village lay asleep, she used to wander through it, and at her touch flowers bloomed on all the forest trees, young fledglings were at peace in their nests, and in the last hours of the moon-lit night the hives of the wild bees were filled with honey from the flowers. She knew the bushes where the bashok flowers lay hidden, the secret recesses of the forest where the chatim blossoms slept in the shade of their trees, the clusters of green reeds by a bend in the Ichamoti where the indigo and kolmi huddled together, and the thorn trees where the baby tailor-birds had just woken up in their little nests of straw. The whole forest glowed with the light of her gracious loveliness, for here was that magical beauty which lives in the silence of the moonbeams and in the fragrant mists where light and shade for ever play hide and seek.

Yet before the day dawned she had vanished. Where to no one knew. Nobody, since Shorup Chokroborti, had ever seen her.

SIXTEEN

Things had taken an awkward turn for Onnoda Ray. A land survey was due, and the survey team had already pitched their tents in the open country on the northern side of the village. The head surveyor's office was in the field near the river; and he had a host of junior clerks and officials with him. Most of the local residents had inherited land from their ancestors, and all this time they had been living comfortably on the proceeds of it, without effort, ambition or active occupation of any kind, floating lazily along the uneventful river of their lives like inanimate pieces of flotsam. But now they were all of them in trouble. Ram, for instance, had been enjoying uncontested possession of a field which turned out to be Yodu's property. Yodu for his part had been deriving an income from twelve acres of land for which he was paying only a ten-acre ground rent. The others were also similarly placed. Life which had gone on peacefully for so long was suddenly about to be turned topsy-turvy. Yet though everybody was embarrassed in one way or another, Onnoda Ray's predicament was of a different order and much more uncomfortable. A relative of his, a sort of distant cousin, had been living for many years now in some place in Bihar, and in his absence Onnoda Ray had been enjoying his gardens, orchards and arable land as if they were his own. He had held them so long in fact that he felt sure that when the surveyors came he would be able to get a considerable part of the property, if not all of it, registered in his own name. Somebody however, he did not know who, had written a letter to his cousin, and in consequence some ten or so days ago his cousin's eldest son had turned up in the village to keep an eye on the property during the survey.

There is many a slip, as the proverb has it. It was so near and yet so far. Yet serious though the land situation was, it was by no means all the trouble he was in. Part of the house he lived in, including most of the better rooms, was his cousin's property. Ray had been using these rooms as his own for the last twenty years, and now he was being forced to vacate them. The cousin's son, who was a college student, was used to living in comfort. He required one room to sleep in and another for a study. So all the iron chests, the goods which he held in pawn—for Onnoda Ray was a moneylender— and all his files and account books had to be shifted downstairs. Then there was the matter of the building timber too. He had bought a lot of it cheaply in the locality and had stored it all in one of the lower rooms. He was being asked to vacate that room also.

Late one afternoon several of Onnoda Ray's neighbours had assembled in his sitting room. It was the usual hour for their dice session, but the day's work was not yet finished. Onnoda Ray was still going through the accounts of the people he had advanced money to. He was checking them one by one, both capital and interest. A young peasant woman and her small son—she had a veil over her face—were sitting in the courtyard just below the verandah. They had been there a long time. At last, thinking that her turn had come, she stood up and moved towards Onnoda Ray, who lowered his head and looked at her over the top of his spectacles. 'Who are you and what do you want?' he asked.

She answered in a low voice, untying a knot in her sari as she spoke, 'It's not been easy for me, but I've managed to save some money. Here it is. Take it. And now I should be glad if you'd take the lock off our rice store. We're in great trouble, sir, but there's no need for me to go into all that, is there?'

Onnoda Ray's face lit up. 'Take the money from her, Hori,' he said. 'Count it and check the date in the ledger, and then work out how much interest she still owes.'

The woman took the money out of her sari and put it on the verandah in front of Horihor. He counted it and said, 'Five rupees.'

'Good. Credit it to her account. Now what about the balance?'

'That's all I've got at the moment,' she said. 'I'll pay the rest off later. I shall be able to get a job and settle the interest. So please take the money and unlock my rice store. I've got to live and feed my family, and the house needs repairing too, you know. But after that ...'

She spoke calmly enough as if the key of the rice store was already in her hand; but she did not know Onnoda Ray.

He did not let her finish what she had to say. 'That's quite ridiculous, you foolish woman! You owe me close on forty rupees, taking capital and interest together, and yet you've the cheek to say, "I've brought you five rupees, so open my rice store." There's no end to what low-caste people like you think you can get away with. Go away now; it's late. I can't waste any more of my time on you.'

Some of the visitors in the sitting room knew the peasant woman, but Dinu Bhottacharji could not see very well, so he asked, 'Who is she, Onnoda?'

'She's Tomrej's wife from the other side of the village. Her husband died some four or five days ago. They owed me forty rupees in all, so the day he died I put a lock on their rice store. And now she wants me to open it up for her as if the matter were settled.'

Tomrej's wife could not have been more surprised if the earth had opened under her feet; but she was no longer in any doubt about the position she was in. She moved towards the moneylender and said, 'Don't say that, sir. My baby had a gold locket. His father had it made for him the year before last. I sold it to Bhonda the goldsmith, and he gave me five rupees for it. It was the child's ornament and I didn't want to sell it, but we have to live, and there was no other way I could get money for food. I told myself that I'd have another one made for him if God lets me live long enough. Do please let me have the key, sir.'

'No, no! Be off with you. You can't pay off your debts by just coming here and weeping. Business isn't done that way. You ought to know that. Your son's father would have understood if he'd been alive. Go away now and stop making a fuss. I've credited the five rupees to your account; so go away and get the rest, and then I'll think about it.'

Onnoda Ray took off his spectacles and put them in their case. Then he got up and was just beginning to make a move to go inside the house when Tomrej's wife cried out to him. She

183

was almost frantic at the turn things had taken. 'Don't go away, sir. You must do something for my child. How am I to feed him if you don't. I haven't a pice to buy rice with. If you won't open my rice store then give me my money back.'

Onnoda Ray frowned in irritation. 'Go away,' he said. 'This is no time to make a scene. It's late as it is. Besides it's my money you've wasted, and you don't seem to be making any attempt to get it back for me. All you can say is, "Open my rice store or give me my money back." What have you got in your rice store, in any case? At most a few bushels of grain, and what do you think they'll fetch? You've paid the five rupees and it's credited to your account, as I told you; but when am I going to see the interest on it? "How am I going to feed the child?" How should I know how you're going to feed him? Go away. If you're not satisfied you can take the matter to court.'

Thereupon he went inside the house. Dinu Bhottacharji said to the woman, 'When did Tomrej die? How did it happen?'

'It was last Wednesday. He bought some fish from the market and I cooked it with onions. I gave him some rice too. A healthy man needs a lot of food; but after he had finished it he told me he was feeling cold and asked me to get him a wrap. I went and fetched one. Early next morning, before the morning star had risen, I looked at him and saw that he wasn't moving. By midday he was dead. And I was left with nobody to look after me or my baby.' Her voice choked with sobs. After a while she turned to the men who were sitting there and appealed to them. 'Won't one of you say a word for me? Please ask him to give me the key to the store. That's all I've got to live on. I'll pay him what I owe as soon as I can.'

At this point Onnoda Ray's cousin's son, the one who had just come to the village, walked into the house. His arrival put an end to the conversation. Dinu turned to welcome him. 'Come in, come in, my dear Niren. I suppose you've been out for a walk? This is the place your father lived in, and your grandfather before him. But you know that of course. How do you like it?'

Niren merely smiled. He was not more than twenty-one or twenty-two, well-built and good-looking, and he was reading law at the college in Calcutta; but he was not given to talking very much. He had been sent by his father to look after his property, though he was not particularly interested in estate management; neither did he understand it. He spent all his time reading novels and shooting. He was so keen on shooting that he had brought a gun with him to the village.

Niren went straight past the people who were sitting on the verandah and climbed up the stairs to his room. When he got there he saw Gokul's wife down on her hands and knees sweeping something up from the floor. He could see from the door what it was. His expensive English lamp had been knocked down and the chimney was smashed to pieces. There were bits of glass lying all round the room. Gokul's wife looked round with a start when she heard the sound of his shoes at the door. She was trying to sweep up the broken bits of glass with her sari. She had gone into the room to clean up, as she did every day, and had tried to light the lamp, but somehow or other it had fallen and broken and now she was trying to remove the evidence of her guilt before the owner returned. Unfortunately for her he came back too soon and she was caught in the act. She was most embarrassed. Niren laughed to make her feel less awkward about it. 'Oh, it's you, Boudi!' he said. 'It looks as though you've broken my lamp. I've caught you red-handed. That's what comes of being a law student, you know. But never mind. Run off and get me a cup of tea as quickly as you can, and let me see what an efficient housewife you are. But wait a minute. Just let me light the lamp. Fortunately I've got another chimney in my trunk.'

Gokul's wife said shyly, 'Do you want me to get you a match, Cousin?'

The question gave Niren opportunity to tease her. 'If you hadn't any matches with you when you came into my room what were you doing meddling with my lamp? Don't try and get out of it now, tell me the truth.'

This time she laughed, but when she spoke it was in little more than a whisper. 'There was lamp black all over it, so I thought I'd rub it off; but when I tried to get the glass out, somehow or other—I don't know about English lamps, you see ... I....' She was too embarrassed to finish the sentence; so she laughed and fled down the stairs.

Niren had been in the house for some ten or twelve days, but though Gokul's wife was some sort of connection of his by marriage he had not so far had a real opportunity of talking to her. The accident to the glass that evening broke the ice however and dispelled all the shyness of new acquaintance. Niren was the son of a very well-to-do father. This was his first visit to the Bengal countryside, but the lack of companions and the fact that he had nothing to amuse himself with made his days there drag along very slowly. But now the gateway to friendship with Boudi, who was the same age as himself, had been opened. She brought him tea in the morning and evening and he looked forward to her visits. They were times of great enjoyment to him, the sort of enjoyment that springs from the give-and-take of easy conversation.

One day about noon Durga peeped in through the kitchen door. 'What are you cooking, Auntie?' she asked. 'Oh, it's you, my dear! Come in. You can give me a hand. I can't do all this alone.' Durga used to drop in like this from time to time, and whenever she did she helped with whatever work was going on. On this occasion it was chopping up some fish. 'Where did you get these crabs from, Auntie? They aren't very good crabs, are they?'

'Why aren't they? Don't be silly. Bidhu the fisherwoman told me that everybody's eating this kind of crab.'

'So you bought them from her, did you?'

'Yes, I did. She let me have all these for five pice.'

Durga did not say anything, but she thought to herself. 'Auntie's a lovely woman, but she's not very practical. Who on earth would go and pay five pice for crabs like these? And who would eat them anyway? Bidhu knew she didn't know what was what and she's cheated her.' And as she thought thus about her simple-minded auntie, Durga's affection for her grew even warmer than before.

The other day Uncle Gokul had hit Auntie over the head with a wooden slipper. Shorno the milkwoman brought them the news. When Durga went down to the river for her bath later that day she noticed that her auntie did not dip her head in the water for fear it would smart. It hurt Durga to see it, but she did not say anything because she did not want to upset her, nor make her embarrassed by having to talk about it in front of so many people. The eldest sister of the Ray family however did not keep quiet about it. 'Bouma, aren't you going to have a proper bath?' she asked. The reply came with a smile. 'No, not today. I'm not feeling very well.' The poor soul was under the impression that nobody knew that her husband had beaten her; whereas in fact everybody knew. As soon as she went up the steps out of the water the Ray sister said to the others, 'That was a terrible blow Gokul hit her. Did you notice? Her hair's still matted with blood.' Durga thought that it was most unfair of her to talk like this. The wretched woman knew what had happened to Gokul's wife, so why did she have to ask her questions and draw everybody's attention to it?

Durga finished washing the fish, but before leaving she said to her auntie after some beating about the bush, 'Auntie, have you got any paddy for making baked rice ? Mummy told me that Opu likes baked rice, but we haven't got any of that sort of paddy in the house.' 'Sh!' whispered Gokul's wife, and she pointed towards the built-in verandah. 'Come early this afternoon. They'll all be asleep by then.'

Durga changed the subject. 'There's someone living in your house, isn't there? I haven't met him yet.'

'You haven't met my cousin? He must have gone out somewhere. He isn't in now. Come this afternoon and you'll be able to meet him.' Then she laughed. 'He'd make you an excellent husband.'

Durga blushed. 'Don't be silly,' she said.

Gokul's wife laughed. 'What's so silly about that? You'd make a good wife, wouldn't you? Let me have a look at you.' And she put her hand under Durga's chin and tilted her face up. 'Yes, you've got a pretty little face. It's just like the goddess Durga's. Why should it matter if your father is poor?'

Durga jerked herself free. 'What nonsense you talk, Auntie!' she said and rushed out through the kitchen door. All the way home she kept saying to herself, 'Auntie's such a nice woman, but she's very silly at times. If she weren't, she wouldn't say the things she does. Who ever heard such nonsense!'

Durga had barely left the house when Shorno the milkwoman arrived to milk the cows. Gokul's wife called out to her from inside. 'Shorno, 'I've got my hands full at the moment, but the calf's outside in the yard. It's tied to the pituli tree. Bring it here. And you'll find the milk bucket on the verandah. It's quite clean.'

Shokhithakrun had just finished her morning prayers. She came out of her room and turning to the north towards the temple of Kali she bowed a number of times and droned out a prayer in a slow monotone. 'O Mother Siddhesvari, save me! Take me safely over the ocean of existence. O Mother Kali, keep me and save me.'

Gokul's wife called to her from the kitchen. 'Auntie, I've kept some coconuts sweets for you. You can eat them while you're having your drink of water.'

Shokhi answered abruptly from the verandah. 'Bouma, come and look at this.'

The tone in which the old woman spoke made Gokul's wife shrivel up inside. She was frightened to death of her, and not without reason. God had certainly shown no partiality towards Shokhithakrun when he was distributing love and ordinary human kindness. No one could be in any doubt about that. When Gokul's wife came out she saw her bending accusingly over a pile of pots and pans which were stacked together in a corner of the verandah. She pointed to one of them with her finger. 'Just look at that one now. Haven't you got eyes in your head? It's got water stains on it. And what's more, it's one of these that Shorno has taken for the milk. To begin with, the bucket wasn't cleaned properly; and secondly it's been handled by a low-caste woman. Moreover, it's going to be taken into the kitchen. What's going to happen to the purity of our caste. My ancestors have preserved it for generations, and now it's ruined, I tell you; and all because of you.'

The gesture she made as she seated herself on the verandah was one of utter despair. She could not have looked more tragic if she had just had news of the death of a grown-up son. Then she went on. 'This is what comes of picking a bride from a good-for-nothing, poverty-stricken family. They've no idea how respectable people behave. They don't know what to do themselves and they can't be bothered to learn. You scoured the pans yourself, didn't you? And yet you couldn't take the trouble to see whether all the dirt had been cleaned away or not. I come here to have a drink of water and what do I find? That the vessel's been handled by a low-caste woman. What a mercy it is that I didn't touch it! If I had I should have had to go and bathe all over again.'

Gokul's wife was petrified and the colour drained out of her face. 'Why on earth did I ever tell Shorno to put the vessels away?' she said to herself. 'There would have been none of this trouble if only I'd done it myself.'

Shokhithakrun's face was grim. 'What are you standing there doing nothing for?' she said peevishly. 'Go and throw the earthenware pots away. There's no way of getting them clean now. The pans you'll have to scour again. When you've done that go and clean the kitchen floor with cow-dung, as always has to be done when a place has been defiled. You and your wretched family! You'll be the ruination of all of us yet.' That said, she stamped off to her room, still seething with rage. It was hot out on the verandah and she could not bear it when it was hot.

The young wife did everything she had been told to do, but it took her the whole day to do it. Then she went to the river to have a second bath; and so what with the heat and the fatigue, and the fact that she had had nothing to eat or drink, it was not surprising that her little face looked pinched and pale.

It was evening, and there was plenty of shade down by the water. The sun was sparkling on the shimul tree on the other bank, and a boat came round the curve in the river. It had its sail up and its rudder was pulled well over to get it round the sharp bend. A man was standing in the stern drying a piece of cloth, and as he let one end of it go, it flew straight out in the wind like a flag. In the middle of the channel a tortoise lifted its head out of the water for air and then immediately submerged again with a gurgling splash. From the water itself rose a delightful and cool fragrance. The river was narrow at this point, and on a sandbank near the far side a cormorant was sitting on a bamboo cage that a fisherman had left behind. The sight of the bird took the poor girl's mind back to her childhood and she recalled a song she used to sing then: 'Cormorant, cormorant, fly to me here on the shore.' From the bird of her childhood her mind turned to her mother, and she tried to remember her face as she knew it then. No one but her mother had ever really loved her, and her mother had died young. They had always been a poor family, and now all of them were dead, except herself and one brother; and he was an opium eater. He had no home of his own, and nobody knew where he lived; but last year at the season of the autumn festival he had come to stay with her for four days. He had no money; and as she had a few coins hidden away in her box she gave them to him when nobody was looking. The next day he disappeared. After he had left it came to light that he had bought a warm shawl from a Kabuli's shop and given her husband's name as security. There was a terrible fuss, and everybody made rude remarks about her family. That was the last she had seen or heard of her brother.

In the evening, when her day's work was done, she often thought about her wayward and penniless brother. She looked sadly along the lonely path across the fields, and wondered whether it was along some such road that he was trudging homeless in the empty darkness, without anywhere to lay his head, and with no one to cast him as much as a passing glance. Her heart was very full; and the shadowy water of the river, the open country in the distance, the steps down the bank, the shimul tree on the other side, and the big boat which had now rounded the bend misted over as her eyes grew dim with tears.

SEVENTEEN

❧⟨◉⟩❧

Opu was wandering round the fishermen's sector of the village, looking for somebody to play cowries with. It was about half past two in the afternoon, and the sun was very hot. Bonka, Tinkori's son, was sitting under a guava tree whittling bamboos. Opu asked him if he would like a game of cowries. Bonka said he would very much, but it was time for him to go down to the boat, and his father would be cross with him if he started to play games instead. So Opu went off to the house of the fisherman Ramchoron. Ramchoron was sitting on the verandah smoking.

'Is Hridoy in?' Opu asked him.

'Hridoy? What do you want him for? Oh, I see. You're looking for somebody to play cowries with. No, he's not in. I'm afraid you'll have to look somewhere else.'

By this time Opu's face was very red, but he plodded on in spite of the heat. He called at several other houses without any luck, but when he came to the tamarind tree near the Paruis' place his face lighted up with pleasure; a number of boys were on the point of starting a game. He was just in time. All the players were fishermen's sons except for Potu who lived in the Brahmin sector of the village. Opu did not know Potu very well. Their homes were rather a long way apart. He was a little younger than Opu, but Opu remembered him as the small boy who had been sitting quietly chewing his palm leaf the first day he went to school. Opu went up to him and asked him how many cowries he had. Potu took out a purse and showed him. It was a lovely little purse, woven of red thread, and he was obviously very proud of it. 'I've got seventeen cowries with me,' he said; 'and seven of them are gold-coloured. If I lose, I can always go and fetch some more. Then with a smile he showed Opu the purse once again and said, 'It's a lovely purse, isn't it? It's big enough to hold a hundred.'

The game started. Potu lost to begin with, but he soon began to win. A few days ago he had realized that he was good at cowries—he certainly was a very good shot—and that is why he had come so far afield looking for a game. He wanted to become a champion. He always used heavy cowries to shoot with and whenever he struck one of his opponent's cowries full in the face and sent it with a sharp crack whirring out of the court, a broad grin spread over his face. The cowries he won he picked up and stuffed into his purse, and in the in-between times he examined it greedily to see how many more it would hold. It was easy to see how happy he was.

The fishermen's sons on the other hand were not so happy. They soon began to grumble among themselves, and eventually one of them said, 'You'll have to stand a yard further back. You're too good.'

'Why?' replied Potu. 'Why should I? It's not my fault that I'm a good shot. You would have won if you could. In any case I'm not stopping you.'

He turned and looked round at the others. They were standing in a group together. He thought the matter over and said to himself, 'I've never won so many cowries before. I'd better stop now. If I don't they probably won't let me take my winnings home with me. As for playing a yard back that's too much. I'm bound to lose if I play from there.' So he picked up his purse and said aloud. 'I refuse to play a yard further back. I'm going home.' A nasty look came into their eyes. He noticed it at once and without being conscious of what he was doing he tightened his grip on his purse.

One of them came up to him. 'You can't do that. It isn't fair. You've been winning all our cowries and now you want to go home without giving us a chance to get our own back.' Without waiting for an answer he grabbed hold of Potu's hand, the one which held the purse. Potu tried to wrench it free, but he was not strong enough. 'Let go my hand, I tell you,' he said; and his face went pale. They had gathered round him by this time, and one of them gave him a push from behind. He fell down on his face, but he clutched the purse to his stomach and held it there for all he was worth. He was only a little boy however, and not very strong. He had no chance against them, for they were older than he was, and much more powerfully built. It was not long before the purse was torn from his hand and burst open. The cowrie shells were scattered all over the place.

It would not be entirely true to say that Opu was displeased when things began to turn awkward for Potu. After all he had lost a lot of cowries too; but when he saw him knocked down and being beaten without anybody to help him, he felt sorry for him. He pushed his way into the middle of his assailants and called out to them. 'What are you hitting him for? Let him go. He's only a little boy. Stop it.' He managed to get to Potu and tried to pull him up from the ground, but someone punched him in the back so hard that for a moment or two he could not see. Before he could get his breath back he was on the ground and they were trampling on him too.

There is no doubt that Opu would have been beaten up as well as Potu; his arms and legs were no stronger than a girl's, and he was not able to defend himself; but at that very moment Niren chanced to come along the path. He saw what was happening and drove the rabble away. Potu had been badly mauled, but Niren pulled him up and began to dust his clothes. When the little fellow had got his breath back he began to look around for his cowries, but apart from the odd one which was still lying on the ground they had all vanished, and his purse with them. He then turned to see how Opu was. 'I hope you're not badly hurt, Opu,' he said.

Niren gave them both a good scolding for wandering so far from home in the middle of the day, and for getting involved in a cowrie game with a gang of boys from the fishermen's sector. Then he began to talk to them. He told them that to pass the time away he had opened a small school for boys on the verandah in Onnoda Ray's house, and suggested that they should come on the following day. Potu hardly heard him. He could think of nothing but the cowries and purse he had lost. 'It was such a lovely purse too! I had an awful business to get it from Chibash the other day, and now it's gone. Besides,' he argued with himself, 'if I wanted to stop playing while I was still winning, why shouldn't I? What right had they to stop me? Surely I've a right to do what I want to do.'

As soon as Opu got home he went and had a word with Durga. 'Didi,' he said, 'I left a curved stick leaning against the trunk of the shiuli tree, and somebody's gone and broken it. It was you, I suppose?'

He was right. It was Durga who had broken it. 'What do you want to make such a fuss about a curved stick for? Such silliness! You can get dozens of them in the bamboo grove if you go and look for them. You ought to know that by now. There's no scarcity of sticks round about here.'

Opu was very upset. His face showed it. 'Scarcity?' he shouted. 'Of course there's a scarcity! You go out and try and find me another like the one you broke and you'll soon know. I spend a lot of time looking for things and you come along and take them or break them. It's rotten of you.'

His eyes filled with tears.

Durga said, 'All right, but there's no need to cry about it. I'll get you as many sticks as you want.'

Curved sticks meant so much to Opu, especially if they were long and thin and properly dried out. They had to be thicker at the base and taper off thinly to the other end. It always gave him a thrill of delight when he came across one. He would take it and spend the whole morning or afternoon wandering by himself down the path through the bamboo grove or by the bank of the river. Sometimes he was a prince; sometimes he kept a tobacco shop. Or he would be a traveller, or a general, or even Arjun in the Mahabharat. It was such fun to identify himself with this person or that and make up all sorts of incidents that could happen to them and pretend that they were happening to him. And the incidents he made up really did happen. That was where the curved stick came in. The more slender and curved it was the better he liked it and the greater the play it seemed to provide for his imagination. But it was extremely difficult to find just the right sort of stick. He knew this from experience. He had searched far and wide, and this was the only one he had found so far, at least the only one which was quite right.

Opu made every effort to ensure that nobody knew what he was going to do when he wandered off alone like this with a curved stick in his hand. He was afraid that if they saw him talking to himself they would think he had gone off his head, or something like that. So, as far as possible, he did not go to places where people usually walked about or even where there was a chance of someone's coming along by accident. He went to the river bank, or down the lonely path that ran through the bamboo grove, or to a place behind the house that was hidden by the thickets under the tamarind tree. Even while he was acting these plays of fancy he kept an eye open lest any one should come along and catch him unawares. If however any one did come along and take him by surprise, he would drop the stick immediately and stand there shyly with the tip of his tongue showing—a nervous habit of his when he was embarrassed. He was extremely touchy about these games. After all people might think....

Durga was the only one who knew. She had caught him at it a time or two, so there was no point in trying to hide it from her any longer. That was why he asked her straight out about the curved stick. If it had been anybody else he would never have mentioned the subject, even if they had been completely ignorant of the secret he shared with his curved stick. He had a sneaking feeling that other people did in fact know about his stick, and that if he mentioned it to them they would think him silly and tease him. Who could possibly understand that once he had his curved stick in his hand he was perfectly content to spend the whole day by himself down by the river or on some lonely jungle path, without ever a thought of meal times or food?

He asked Durga to keep quiet about it too. 'Didi,' he said to her, 'don't say a word to Mummy about it.' She did not. She told herself that he was quite mad, but she loved him all the more for it, her silly adorable little brother. She would never have dreamed of telling her mother.

Shorbojoya had a special personal feast day which fell at the end of the year—they called it honey-day. So the day before it she called to Opu and said, 'Go and invite your teacher to come and eat with us tomorrow at midday.'

The meal consisted of coarse rice with papaya figs, banana shoots, prawns and other curries; and there were fried banana fritters and sweet creamed rice.

Shorbojoya asked Durga to see to the serving of the food. She had never done it before and was very nervous. When it came to placing a bowl of daal before their guest she did it so slowly and timidly that you would have thought someone was going to scold her for it. Niren was not used to such coarse rice, and it had never crossed his mind that anybody ever ate their vegetables cooked with so little oil and butter. The creamed rice was thin too. It had been made with watered milk, and once he had had a mouthful of it he did not feel like eating any more. Opu on the other hand was delighted. He ate with great gusto. Only once or twice before had they had such wonderful food; so today was a memorable occasion for him. 'Have some more creamed rice, sir,' he said; and he kept asking his sister for further helpings of everything for himself.

When Niren got home, Gokul's wife asked him about his visit. 'What did you think of Durga? She's a pretty little thing, isn't she? And she's got such a nice voice. It's a pity they're so poor. Her father has absolutely no money at all. I wonder who'll marry her. Niren! She's the right caste for you, you know, and she'd make you such a nice bride. Both brother and sister are just like little dolls, aren't they? They're so pretty.'

Some few days later Niren was walking back from the surveyor's office along a path which cut through the mango orchards just outside the village. The trees grew close to the path, so there was not much room to walk on. Suddenly a girl jumped out from among the trees on to the path just in front of him. He recognized her at once. It was Opu's sister, Durga. 'Hello, little girl,' he said. 'This is your mango orchard I suppose.'

Durga looked back to see who it was but she was too shy to speak to him. She merely stood to one side so that he might go ahead. 'No, no, child. You keep in front. It's a good job for me that I've met you. I missed the way near the tank and I'm completely tired out trying to find it again. I'd no idea the jungle was so thick in your part of the world.'

So they walked along together. Suddenly Durga stopped and looked back at Niren over her shoulder, but as she did so some fruit that she was carrying in her sari fell out on to the path.

'You've dropped something,' Niren told her. 'It's some kind of fruit, isn't it? What fruit is it?'

Durga bent down to pick them up, but she was very embarrassed. 'They're nothing much,' she said; 'only wild potatoes.'

'Wild potatoes? What are they like? Are they good to eat?'

The question astonished Durga. A five-year-old child would have known the answer to it, yet a clever man like Niren— he was wearing spectacles, so he had to be clever—did not know. 'No, they're not good to eat,' she said. 'They're bitter.'

'Then why are you ...?'

'I collect things like this to play with,' Durga answered shyly. She had not forgotten that her auntie had teased her

200

the other day and suggested that she ought to marry this bespectacled young man. She would have given a lot to be able to have a good look at him. She had not had an opportunity of seeing him properly on the day of the feast, and she could not today either.

'Tell Opu to bring his books early tomorrow morning. You won't forget, will you?'

Durga nodded, and then started to walk on ahead. A little further on they came to a fork in the path. Durga pointed and said, 'That's your road. Go down there and keep straight on.'

Niren said, 'I know where I am now, thank you. But you can't go on alone. Let me come a little way with you.'

Durga pointed down the other path. 'That's our house,' she said, 'just over there. I ... I can do this little bit alone. There's no need for you...'

Niren had not seen her properly before. She had very lovely eyes. He had not before seen such a beautiful expression in any one's eyes, except perhaps those of her brother Opu. They were big and sleepy. They had that same drowsy quality which was hidden in the deep fresh greenness of the mango and bokul trees that lined the paths in the village. The dawn that would quicken them had not yet come; and the heavy sleep that precedes waking still brooded over them. Yes, it was dawn they made him think of; dawn, when sleeping eyes first open, dawn when maidens walk down to the river's edge, and every window gives forth the odour of incense; dawn, that ambrosial hour when the waters of awakening flow cool and fresh through house after house.

Durga stood still but she was not at ease. Niren felt that she wanted to say something but could not. So he spoke instead, 'No, little one. May I not go a little further with you? Do let me take you as far as your house.'

She hesitated, and then she smiled. Niren felt sure now

that she was going to speak; but she did not. She merely shook her head to let him know that there was no need for him to go with her, and went off down the path alone.

It was early afternoon. Gokul's wife had gone on to the roof to bring in the clothes she had hung out to dry, and on the way she peeped in at the door of Niren's room. Niren had lain down to sleep, but after tossing about for some time in the heat he finally gave it up. He had spread his mat on the floor and was sitting there writing home.

Gokul's wife laughed. 'Couldn't you sleep, Niren? I thought you would have been asleep by now. You didn't eat much of that banana curry today. You left most of it on your plate. The other day you finished it all off.'

'Come in, Boudi. How could I eat the banana curry? It must be your country cooking. You make things far too hot. I can hardly see out of my eyes when I eat them, and that goes for all your curries, not only the banana.'

Gokul's wife stood with her head leaning against the door-post, but she kept the lower part of her face hidden behind her sari.

'Don't be silly. You're just making a fuss. It wasn't all that hot. Don't you ever have hot things to eat at home?'

'Forgive me if I seem to contradict you, Boudi,' he said with mock humility, 'but if that's not what you call hot, I must try something really hot one day before I go. I'm in for it any way, so I might as well go the whole hog. There's no need for you to be shy about it. You can put as many chillies in it as you like.'

'Goodness! What do you take me for? Do you think I put my curry stone away and stopped giving you hot food because I was shy. What a thing to say, Niren! And then you talk about going the whole hog.' She laughed so hard that the tears streamed down her cheeks; but after a while she pulled herself together and changed the subject. 'What's it like where you live, Niren? Is it hot?'

'Where do you mean? Calcutta or Bihar? People who live here have no idea how hot it gets in Bihar. Bengalis don't know what heat is. The nights are so hot in the summer that we can't possibly sleep indoors. We go out on the roof, but even there we have to sprinkle water before we can lie down.'

'Is it far away from here?'

'By rail, it's about a two-day journey. If I caught the early morning train from Majherpara station today I should be home tomorrow at midnight.'

'Somebody once told me that they had to cut holes in the mountains to get the line through to Gaya and Benares. Is it true?'

'Yes, it's quite true. Many of the hills round about there are very high. They are covered with forests, and the railway goes under them. It's pitch black in the tunnels too. You can't see a thing without the lights on.'

Her curiosity was not yet satisfied. 'Yes I can understand that,' she said, 'but don't the tunnels ever fall in?'

'Fall in? How can they? They spent a lot of money on these tunnels, Boudi. They were built by expert engineers. They are not like those steps of yours at Raypara Ghat that fall down twice a day.'

Gokul's wife did not know what sort of a thing an engineer was, but she had not run out of questions. 'Those mountains, are they made of earth or stones.'

'Of both, silly. Goodness me, Boudi, what a country cousin you are! What's the furthest you've ever been by train?'

She laughed again, impishly; then she screwed up her eyes and stared at the ceiling. 'Oh, a very long way,' she said childishly. 'Let me think now. I've been to Benares, and to Gaya, and I've been to Mecca too.' She laughed again. 'No,

I'm teasing. The other year I went with my aunt and Shotu's mother to see the statue of Krishna and Balaram at Aronghata. That's the only time I've been in a train.'

She was like that. Even the most trivial things she could weave into a net of fun and laughter. Niren found it fascinating. She was one of those rare people who seem to possess an endless store of happiness, whose hearts cannot contain the fountain of joy that springs within. Her laughter was most infectious. Yet she was only a country bride. Niren used to look forward to her coming; and when she did not come he was disappointed, perhaps a little hurt, though he did not show it.

'In that case, Boudi, why don't you all come and visit us? I'll take you with me when I go back from here.'

'All of us go away at the same time, Niren? What on earth are you thinking of? Who would be here to look after the vegetables in that garden of ours outside the village?'

She laughed again, but this time her laughter carried a note of ridicule as well as amusement that he could make such an absurd suggestion. The next moment however she became serious. 'Niren, will you promise me something?'

'Tell me what it is first, and then I'll see.'

'No, you must promise first.'

'No, Boudi. You're not going to get me to sign a blank piece of paper. I'm not a law student for nothing, you know. Tell me what it is first, and then I'll give you my answer.'

Gokul's wife moved away from the doorpost and came into the room. Then she took a paper package from inside her dress and said, 'Will you lend me five rupees against this pair of earrings?'

Niren was surprised. 'Won't you tell me why?'

'No, I can't do that. Will you lend it to me?'

'What do you want five rupees for? Tell me that first. Otherwise...'

She answered very quietly. 'I want to send it somewhere. Here's the address. It's written in English on this letter.'

'It's your brother, isn't it, Boudi?'

'Sh! You mustn't let the people in the house know. He wrote and asked me for five rupees. How can I get hold of five rupees? You know how completely dependent I am, don't you? So I thought about these earrings. Do let me have five rupees. The poor boy has nobody else to help him, nobody in the world.' Her voice thickened to a sob, and there were tears in her eyes.

'Of course,' Niren said. 'Of course I'll give you five rupees, Boudi. Five or ten, whatever you say, and you can pay me back when you can. But I couldn't possibly take the earrings.'

Gokul's wife's smile showed how pleased she was, but she shook her head. 'No, Niren! I couldn't do that. It's very nice of you; supposing I died before I could pay the money back. You must take them; you must. But I can't stay here any longer. There's a lot of work waiting for me downstairs.'

She hurried out of the room, but when she got to the top of the stairs she came back and said in a whisper, 'You won't tell anybody about the money, will you? Nobody.'

Durga was still in bed. She was very happy. 'Opu, O Opu!' she called.

Opu had not spoken yet, though he had been awake for some time. 'Didi, please close the window. There's a cold wind.'

Durga got up and closed the window. 'Do you know when the marriage is going to take place at Ranu's house,' she asked him. 'It can't be very far off now. It's going to be a very big affair. They're getting an English band. Have you ever seen an English band?'

'Yes. They all play with hats on, and they've got lots of big 'phulots'—that was the nearest he could get to 'flute'—

'and enormous drums. They play another kind of phulot too; it's black and not so big. They call them phulot, you know. They sound lovely. Have you ever seen one?'

But Durga was thinking of something else.

Last evening she had been to the other side of the village to see her auntie. They talked about all sorts of things, but suddenly her auntie said, 'Durga, where was it that you met Niren yesterday?'

'Why, Auntie?' Durga asked, but then she went on to tell her all about it. She laughed as she explained how it happened. 'He was lost. He had lost his way in the jungle, somewhere near the fort pond.'

Her auntie laughed too. 'I was talking to him about you, yesterday. What I said was, "They're very poor, cousin. Her father will never be able to pay any dowry for her. But she's a very nice girl, not like so many girls nowadays. Why don't you marry her?" That's why he was asking about you. He told me he had missed the way and was wandering about when he met you on the path that leads to the pond. I've been thinking about it for the past three days, and wondering whether I should get my father-in-law to speak to your father about it. I think my cousin would be prepared to consider it. He seems to like you.'

Ordinarily Durga did whatever chores there were to do at home, but today the very thought of housework was distasteful to her, though she did not forget to take the calf out of the shed and tie it up in the sun. There were days when she felt like this, days when she could not bear to stay indoors. The house seemed like a prison. Something seemed to be dragging her outside, into the village, along the jungle paths, anywhere. And today the breeze was very gentle. It was neither hot nor cold, and there was a delicious scent from the lime blossoms. She did not know why she felt restless, but she did.

So she went outside and walked over to Ranu's house. Bhubon Mukherji was a rich man, and it was his eldest daughter who was getting married. The preparations for the wedding were most elaborate. When Durga arrived a man who sold fireworks was haggling about the price. Sitanath, the most famous flute player in the district, had already been paid a retaining fee and relatives from all over the place had begun to pour in for the ceremony. The yard was crowded with children. Durga was terribly excited. In a few days they would be letting off a lot of fireworks. She had never seen any before, except for one day during the Swing festival at the Gangulis', when they had let off one firework. It went off with a loud sizzle right up into the sky. Then it actually bumped into a cloud and came down again. It was a wonderful sight. Opu called it a sky firework.

In the afternoon Shorbojoya went into the covered part of the verandah. She draped her sari round her and settled down for a nap, so Durga slipped out again. It was February, and you could feel the heat in the sun. The wind was warm and steady, and the yellow leaves from the neem tree in Ranu's orchard were spiralling down to the ground. There was no one in sight, though near Nera's house someone, she could not see who, was beating a drum. She could hear its muffled boom. Then she heard something else. What was it? Was it a crystal beetle? Almost automatically Durga scrabbled up the end of her sari in her fist and looked round to see what it was, her big eyes wide open. But it was not a crystal beetle, it was what they called a shudorshon, a good-luck beetle.

She was thrilled. She let her sari fall free and began to tiptoe towards it as noiselessly as she could. It was sitting on the path just ahead of her, and she could make out the round marks on its wings. They looked like little dabs of white and red sandal paste.

The shudorshon was not really a beetle at all, it was a god. Her mother had told her, and many other people had too, that it was very lucky to see one. She sat down on the path as gently as she could, so as not to disturb it, and raised her hands to her forehead in respectful salutation. Then she began to say a prayer to it. She spoke quickly and repeated the prayer time and time again. 'Shudorshon, be kind to us!' (She had often heard people say this kind of prayer.) Then she introduced a personal note into her intercessions. 'Keep Opu safe! Keep Mummy safe! Keep Daddy safe! Keep my auntie safe!' Here she paused a little nervously, and then went on. 'Keep Niren safe! And, O Shudorshon, let him marry me; and let us have a wedding with fireworks and music like Ranu's sister's!'

So intense was her devotion that the shudorshon was powerless to fly away; it could only move round in a little circle. She poured forth her heart to it, and then, when she had finished her prayers, she respectfully moved away. She walked on through the village, now taking one path, now another; and overhead she could see the blue of the February sky between the gaps in the trees. It was deep blue like the neck feathers of a peacock, Krishna's bird.

The narrow path to the river steps ran through a jungle of wild bushes and behind them on both sides were the trees of a mango orchard. The breeze was warm and heavy with the scent of blossoms, and bees and crystal beetles murmured among the branches; while from the shade beneath the trees came the song of the kokil. Durga's heart felt very warm.

She passed through the orchards to the open ground where the Shiva festival was celebrated. The shade was already beginning to creep across the grass as she pushed her way through some thickets looking for senyakul fruit; but there were very few left. They fall off at the end of the cold

208

weather. There was a tree growing on a little mound and a few days ago it had had a lot of fruit on it, some of which she had eaten; but today there was none. It had all fallen off and lay scattered about among the undergrowth like dried pepper pods. A swarm of jackdaws chattered in the trees but they flew away as she approached.

A wave of gladness broke over her heart. The wedding was so near now. There would be the night watch in Ranu's sister's room, and there would be songs which she hoped they would let her stay to hear. She was so happy she felt like running right across the open fields, from one end to the other. She could not of course, but she did run round in a wide circle flailing her arms up and down like wings. If only she could fly! Her body was light enough. If only she could spread her arms like wings and breast the wind with the birds.

She marched up and down over the thick carpet of dry leaves kicking them before her for the sheer joy of making a noise. The brittle leaves powdered beneath her feet, and mingling with the dust they rose to fill the air with a dry aromatic smell. Ahead of her, not far away, a bullock cart creaked its way along a rough track which led across the plain in the direction of Shonadanga. The cart was roofed with a framework of split bamboo over which was stretched a red-patterned cloth, patched and torn in places. Inside a little girl was crying with a thin high-pitched wail. It was probably some peasant's daughter being taken from home to live in her father-in-law's house.

Durga stared at the cart for a long time.

If she got married it would be like that with her. She would have to leave her mother and father, and Opu, and go and live a long way off. She wondered whether they would let her come home from time to time. The thought had never occurred to her before. All the places she loved, the orchards, the bushes where the basok flowers grew, the red cow and the jackfruit tree in the yard, and this smell of dried leaves, and the path down to the river, all these she would have to leave for ever, for ever. That was probably why the little girl in the cart was crying.

On the other side of the track there was a small field, which was no longer cultivated, and beyond that the river. Some fishermen were at work on the opposite bank, and she wondered what they were catching. Perhaps it was khoyra fish. If they had been on this bank she would have bought two pice worth. Opu was very fond of khoyra.

It was already dark when she got home so she settled down to tidying her doll's box. Her mother had spilt some kerosene oil on the floor, and the room was full of the smell of it. It was hot indoors and very stuffy. She had just managed to get the box in order when Opu came in. 'Didi,' he said, 'did you take a mirror from my box? It must have been you.'

'Yes, I did. But it's my mirror not yours. It was lying under the bed and I saw it first. So go away, I'm going to keep it in my box. Besides, what does a boy want with a mirror?'

'Your mirror? How can it be your mirror? Mummy went to that party at auntie's house and they gave it to her as a present. I asked her for it first. So it's mine. Give it to me.' With that he squatted down by the doll's box and began to rummage around in it.

Durga gave him a hard slap on the cheek. 'You horrid little boy! Here I am getting my box all tidied up and you come along as if you owned it and turn everything upside down. Go away and leave my box alone. I'm not going to give you the mirror.'

Opu jumped on to her back. He grabbed hold of her dry hair and began to bite and scratch her. It was pandemonium. He spluttered with tears and rage. 'What did you hit me for?

You hurt me. Give me the mirror. If you don't I'll tell Mummy that you stole some alta from her Lakshmi basket.'

The mention of the alta infuriated Durga. She caught hold of his ears and began to pull them hard; and she slapped him again and again. 'What do you mean, you miserable little monkey? I stole the alta? Do you think I didn't see you tear those cowrie shells off the Lakshmi basket? You wait till Mummy hears about that!'

Shorbojoya heard the noise they were making and came rushing in to see what had happened. Durga was pulling Opu's ears and holding him down on the floor. Opu had a firm hold on Durga's hair and was dragging at it so hard that she could not raise her head. But he was more hurt than she was. As his mother came in he started to cry. 'Look what she's doing to me, Mummy. She took my mirror out of my box and she won't give it back; and when I asked her for it she gave me a slap on my cheek.'

'No, Mummy,' Durga said. 'I was tidying my doll's box, and he came in and upset it all.'

Shorbojoya turned on Durga and slapped her several times on the back. 'You're no longer a child now. What are you always hitting him for? You know you're much older than he is. And what's this about a mirror? What on earth would you be wanting a mirror for, unless you're keeping it for your funeral? You're getting vain. That's what it is, and so you try to take it out of him. As for your doll's box, I'll show you.' Whereupon she seized hold of the box, which Durga had made so neat and tidy, and pitched it out into the yard. 'You're grown up now, and it's about time you started to do some work. But not you! All you do is to sit about waiting to be fed or go wandering round the village like a vagabond. And when you come back you do nothing but play with your doll's box. Your precious doll's box! I'm going to take it and throw it out into the bamboo grove. That'll put an end to all your nonsense.

Durga was speechless. The doll's box was her life. Ten times a day she tidied it; and now all the treasures it contained were scattered about the yard. Her doll, a few bits of tin foil, some pieces of printed cloth, her alta, the nataphol she had been at such pains to collect, her mirror which was mounted on a piece of tin, and a bird's nest; and they were all lying out there in the dark. How could her mother be so cruel as to throw them all away, her box and all the precious things in it, things she had wandered all over the place to collect. She could hardly believe it; but she was too frightened to say anything.

Opu thought the punishment very severe too; but he did not say anything either. He just got up and went to bed.

It was late. The room still reeked of kerosene oil, and the mosquitoes could be heard buzzing about in the bamboo clump outside. Durga sat there stunned; but eventually she too got up and went to bed. She did not utter a word.

The bedroom window was broken; and the February moon shone in through the gap and fell on the bed, and waves of scent wafted in from the lime blossoms in the neglected compound next door. Durga was contemplating going out for her doll's box. She knew that if she did not get her things now they would not be there in the morning. And they meant so much to her. But she dare not. She felt that her mother would beat her again if she did.

Some time passed. Then a hand moved over timidly and touched her body. It was Opu's. He whispered to her to find out if she was awake, but before she could answer he buried his face in the pillow and began to weep bitterly. 'I won't do it again, Didi. Don't be angry with me.' He could not say any more. His voice choked with sobbing.

Durga was surprised, but she sat up and tried to pacify him. 'Sh! Stop crying. Be quiet. If Mummy hears you she'll be cross with me again. There's no need to cry. I'm not angry with you. Do stop it.' She had very good reason to be afraid that her mother would beat her again if she heard Opu crying.

Eventually she managed to quieten him. Then she lay down again and began to chatter to him. She told him all about Ranu's sister's wedding. Opu listened for a while, and then he blurted out, 'Didi, shall I tell you something? You're going to marry my teacher.'

Durga was embarrassed but she could not help being curious. Nevertheless she did not say anything because it was not something she wanted to talk about to her little brother. Opu however did not stop. 'Auntie was talking about it to Ranu's mother yesterday afternoon. She said she thought teacher was not unwilling.'

Durga could not keep quiet any longer. 'Nonsense!' she said as if she were not interested. 'What can you know about things like this?'

Opu bounced straight up in bed. 'But it's true, Didi. It is, I promise you. I was standing right beside them. It was because I was there that they started to talk about it. They're going to get Daddy to write a letter to teacher's father.'

'Does Mummy know?'

'I don't know. I meant to go and tell her, but I forgot. Shall I ask her, Didi? She probably hasn't heard about it. Auntie said she'd come and speak to her about it tomorrow.' After a short pause he went on. 'You'll have to ride in lots of trains, you know, Didi. Teacher's home's a long way from here and you'll have to go by train.'

Durga did not say anything.

She had seen pictures of a train in one of Opu's books. It was very long and had a lot of wheels. There was an engine in front. It has a fire inside it and smoke came out. The train was made of iron, all of it, and so were the wheels, quite unlike the wheels of a bullock cart which were made of wood. There were no thatched cottages near the railway line. How could there have been? They would have caught fire, because when the train moved fire came out of its pipes. She patted Opu with her hand and said to him, 'I'll take you with me, Opu.' With that they stopped talking and tried to go to sleep. One thought kept recurring to her as she fell asleep: 'The god Shudorshon has heard my prayer. I only asked him today. What a god he is! What Mummy said about him was quite right.'

But Opu was not asleep. He still wanted to talk. 'They've bought some lovely saris for Lila to wear at her wedding. Her uncle got them in Ranaghat. Auntie said they were made in Baluchor.'

The name made Durga laugh. 'Do you remember that funny song Auntie Indir used to sing to us?

"A marvellous thing I saw, my friend, on the
    sands of Baluchor.
A buffalo swallowed a peachick as it scratched
    for food on the shore".'

EIGHTEEN

❧

There was one piece of information which Opu had not passed on to anybody yet, not even to his sister.

One day at about noon he had opened a wooden chest which belonged to his father. He had done it very quietly and nobody had seen him. The chest was crammed with books, and it was in one of them that he had come across this amazing piece of information.

He knew it was about midday because the shadow of the bamboo clump was not lying across the yard in a long line between east and west—village folk still tell the time of day by the length of shadows of that ancient banyan tree which grows in the vast Shonadanga plain.

On this particular day his father was out. Opu went into the room, quietly closing the door behind him, and managed to open the wooden chest without being detected. He was very excited. He opened the books one by one, and turned over the pages to see whether there were any pictures to look at or a good story. One book had a title on the cover, *An Anthology of Ancient Philosophical Works.* He had not the slightest notion what the title meant or what the book was about, but the cover was faded and mottled like marble, and as he turned it back a swarm of silverfish darted all over the page and disappeared as fast as they could. Opu raised the book to his nose. It had a peculiar old smell. The pages were thick and dust-coloured, and he loved the smell of them. There was something about the smell which made him think of his father. He did not know why it did, but it did, always.

It was the book in the damaged board cover and the mottled marble jacket which attracted him most, so he hid it under his bolster and put all the other books back in the box. He read it when he was alone, and one day he came across an amazing statement. If somebody had told him about it he would have been astonished, so would anyone else; but this was not hearsay, it was in cold print. The writer was describing the properties of mercury. If you put some mercury in a vulture's egg and leave it in the sun for a few days, and then hold it in the mouth, you can fly high up in the sky.

Opu could not believe his eyes. He read the passage again and again.

He hid the book in his own broken box, and went outside to think; and the more he thought the more surprised he was.

He said to his sister, 'Didi, do you know where vultures build their nests?'

She did not know. So he asked the boys in the village, Shotu, Nilu, Kinu, Potol, Nera, all of them. One of them said, 'Not anywhere here. They build at the top of big trees in the open country.' His mother was cross with him. 'Where have you been wandering in this heat?' He moved into his room and pretended to lie down. He opened the book and found the place again. There it was! Astonishing! It was so easy to fly and yet nobody knew about it. Perhaps nobody had a copy of this book except his father. Or it might be that all this time nobody's eye except his own had come upon this particular place in the book.

He thrust his nose into the book again, and smelt it. That same old smell! It never occurred to him to question the truth of what was written in such a book.

There was no problem about mercury. He knew that mercury was quicksilver, and that it was quicksilver that was used on the back of mirrors. There was a broken mirror in the house, and he would be able to get some from there. The problem was where to get vulture's eggs.

One day after their midday meal his sister called out to him. 'Come here, Opu. Come and see the fun.' She had saved a handful of rice from her meal and gone out to the bamboos near the back door. From there she called, 'Bhulo ... o ...'. She called only once and then stood in silence, looking at Opu with a smile on her face. Her smile seemed to say that the gate of an unknown fairy city was going to open before their very eyes. Suddenly a dog appeared from somewhere. Durga pointed, 'Look, he's come,' she said. 'Did you see where he came from?' And she giggled happily.

This business of feeding the dog was apparently a daily routine for her, and she got great pleasure from it. 'You call: there's nobody in sight. Everywhere's quiet,' she told herself. She put the rice down on the ground and stood with her eyes shut, but in her heart there was great excitement, as hope that he would come fought with the fear that he might not; and she always talked to herself about it. 'I don't suppose

Bhulo will come today. I must watch to see where he comes from. He's probably not heard me.'

Then suddenly there was a noise in the bushes, and there in the twinkling of an eye was Bhulo, panting hard, and tearing aside the leaves and creepers.

A shiver of excitement thrilled through Durga's body. Her eyes were bright with surprise and curiosity. She said to herself, 'He heard me all right. But where does he come from? Tomorrow I'll call softly and see if he hears me then.

So every day at mealtimes, in spite of her mother's scolding, she saved a little of her food to feed the dog with. It was such fun; and she did enjoy doing it.

Opu however could not see what fun there was in calling a dog. It was one of Durga's girl's games, and he was not interested. It gave him no particular pleasure to see a hungry dog eating his food. Besides, he had something else on his mind, vultures' eggs.

At last he got on to the track of them. The cowherd boys used to tie their cattle to the jackfruit tree that belonged to Hiru the barber, and go into the village to get oil and tobacco. Opu knew one of them. He lived in their part of the village. So he broached his problem to him. 'You go all over the countryside. Have you ever seen a vulture's nest? If you can get me some vultures' eggs I'll give you two pice.'

A few days later the cowherd boy turned up at the house and called Opu. When he came out he produced two small black eggs from a bag in his waistband. 'Look at what I've brought for you, sir,' he said—it was usual for low-caste people to use the word 'sir' when addressing a Brahmin— Opu stretched out an eager hand to take them. He turned them this way and that in high glee, and murmured, 'Vultures' eggs!' Then he said to the boy, 'They are real, aren't they?' The boy produced his evidence. It was most impressive! They must be vultures' eggs. 'There's no doubt about that. I got them from the top branch of a very high tree, and a very risky job it was too. But,' he added, 'I can't let you have them for less than two annas.'

Opu's face fell when he heard how much they would cost. 'I'll give you two pice,' he said, 'and you can have my cowries. I'll let you have all of them, and the tin box I keep them in. There are lots of golden coloured ones. Shall I show them to you?'

. The cowherd boy was, it seemed, much more experienced in worldly matters than Opu. He was not prepared to sell the eggs except for cash. He haggled for a long time and eventually the price was fixed at four pice. Opu managed to get two pice from his sister, and completed the deal. Then he got the eggs, but the cowherd took some of his cowries as well. These cowries were Opu's life. At any other time he would not have parted with them for half a kingdom and a princess thrown in. But playing with cowries seemed poor sport in comparison with flying in the sky.

He had the eggs in his hand and his mind felt as light as a balloon when it is first blown up. Then slowly a little shadow of doubt rose in his mind to darken his joy. So far he had been quite sure; but once he had really got the eggs in his hand, he began to wonder. It was not a serious doubt however, just a suspicion of uncertainty. That evening before dark he was in Nera's orchard, sitting on a branch that had been cut off a rose-apple tree. His mind was busy with questions. 'Shall I really be able to fly now? Where shall I fly to? To my uncle's house? Or to where Daddy has gone to? Or shall I fly across the river? Or shall I fly to where the stars rise in the sky, as the sparrows or the mynas do? Shall I do it today or tomorrow?'

Later that same evening Durga was looking for an old

piece of cloth to use as a wick. While she was rummaging among some torn rags which were bundled together between the pots and pans, something rolled from the back of the shelf and fell on to the floor. It was dark indoors, and she could not see clearly, so she picked it up and took it outside to see what it was. 'Goodness, Mummy,' she exclaimed, 'there are two big eggs here. They fell and broke. I wonder what bird came into the house and laid its eggs here.'

It is best to pass over what happened later on. Opu refused to touch his food for a whole day. He cried and made a terrific to-do. Shorbojoya talked about it when she went down to the pond for her bath. 'Opu's making an enormous fuss. I've never heard the like of it. Do you know, Shejbou? He says that if you have a vulture's egg you can fly. That cowherd boy's a proper scoundrel. He collected a couple of eggs from a crow's nest or somewhere, and said they were vultures' eggs. And he made Opu pay four pice for them. I can't tell you what a simpleton the lad is, Shejbou. I don't know what I'm going to do with him.'

How could poor Shorbojoya know? Everybody had not read the *Anthology of Ancient Philosophical Works*, and not everybody knew the properties of mercury either.

It is as well they did not, because in that case everybody would be able to fly.

NINETEEN

Some time ago now Opu had made friends with Norottom Das, an aged Vaisnava teacher who lived in a little thatched cottage right over on the other side of the village, near where the Gangulis lived. The old man had a kind face, and when Opu met him he noticed at once how unusually fair his skin was. He was a happy-natured person too, but he did not like noise, so he mostly kept to himself and seldom went out, except that now and then in the late evening he would go to the Gangulis' and sit with them for a while on their verandah. But even this he did not do very often. As soon as Horihor thought that Opu was big enough to walk all the way across the village he took him with him to call on the old teacher; and the two of them, young boy and old man, were drawn to one another from the start. Norottom

Das soon began calling Opu 'Little Sir'; and Opu addressed him as 'Grandpa'. In time Opu was allowed to walk there on his own. 'Are you at home, Grandpa?' he used to call out as soon as he got into the yard, and the old man came running from inside the house to greet him; and he always brought a grass mat with him. 'Come in, Little Sir. Come in and sit down.' And the grass mat would be unrolled and spread out on the floor for Opu to sit on. It was quite a little ceremony. In other people's houses Opu was awkward and silent; but he was completely at ease with his kindly old friend. He chattered away to him as naturally as he did to the children he played with. He felt he could say anything to him.

Norottom Das had no living relative. He was quite alone in the house, except for a Vaisnava girl of his own caste who came in every day and did the housework for him. This was just what Opu liked. He would not have felt nearly so much at home if he had thought that other people might drop in; but they hardly ever did. So, as he was practically certain that he would have the old man to himself, he often used to walk over and spend whole afternoons with him, listening to his stories and telling some of his own. It did not matter in the least that Norottom Das was a very old man, much older than his father, and older too than Onnoda Ray. Perhaps it was this difference in their ages which brought them so close together. Yet whatever the cause, when Opu was there he forgot to be tongue-tied and his shyness left him completely. He laughed when he felt like laughing, and said anything that came into his mind. He would never have dared to talk so freely anywhere else; the grown-ups would have thought him forward, and have scolded him.

One day Norottom Das said to Opu, 'Little Sir, you remind me very much of the saint Gouranga. His face was fair, almost white, like yours.' He spoke so seriously that Opu laughed. 'No, don't laugh,' he said; 'I mean it. You always make me think of him. At your age he would have been just like you, happy, innocent and very pretty. His eyes too must have been glowing and affectionate as yours are now.' If anybody else had spoken to him like this Opu would have blushed and been most embarrassed, but because it was his grandpa he laughed again and went on talking. 'Grandpa,' he said,' 'please show me the picture of Gouranga in that book of yours. I should like to see it again.'

The old man was delighted. He jumped up at once and ran inside the house; and in a minute he came back with the book in his hand. It was called *The Moon of Heavenly Love.* It was his greatest treasure and he used it when he was at his prayers. It seemed to lift him out of himself and let him glimpse something of the bliss of heaven. Very few people knew what it meant to him, for ordinarily he never took it down from the shelf unless he was alone. There were only two pictures in it, and one of them was a portrait of Gouranga. He was delighted that Opu had asked to look at it again. 'When I die, Little Sir,' he exclaimed, 'I shall leave this book to you. You will know how to treat it.'

Norottom Das had a few disciples who came to him for religious instruction. One of them was a self-opinionated young man who fancied himself as a poet. From time to time he tried his hand at writing hymns in praise of Gouranga, and when they were finished he brought them to the house to read to his teacher. The youth's insensitivity upset the old man and made him angry. It seemed to him like sacrilege. 'I suppose,' he said, 'there's no harm in your dabbling with poetry, but for heaven's sake don't come and read your wretched verses to me. You should know by now what I feel about them. Apart from Vidyapati and Chandidas nobody has been able to compose hymns that are worthy of the name;

223

and that includes you too. So if you must read this awful stuff aloud, go and do it somewhere else.'

There was something about his warm-hearted old friend and the simple, unpretentious way he lived that stirred Opu deeply. Often as he sat there listening to him talk or read he felt as though his soul was like a boat which the strong current of a deep river was sweeping on and on, out of this life into a nobler world, where there was no unkindness and no pain. The happy intimacy that had sprung up between the two of them was now a part of Opu's innermost being, like the communion he had with the fresh earth and the birds and the trees when the leaves were on them.

One evening as Opu was leaving his friend's house he plucked a bunch of flowers from the golden champak tree in the yard, and as soon as he reached home he went and laid them on his bed. By now it was getting dark and the lamp had already been lit. This was the time his father expected him to settle down to his lessons. He was required to work for only one hour, but today it seemed an eternity, dragging on its slow minutes far into the night. At long last however his labours did come to an end, and he was free. He bundled up his books without an instant's delay and ran to his room, jumped on to the bed and buried his face in his precious flowers, breathing in their fragrance and murmuring their lovely name, champak, golden champak. They were only flowers of course, flowers he had brought home and put on his bed; but they were much more than that to him. Their scent was full of memories, happy memories of the games he had played and all the fun he had had. It made him sad to think that happy things could have an end, and that Time could snatch away the hours of gold. The wonderful thing about the champak flowers today was that they seemed able to make Time recoil upon itself and to cancel the sense of loss which so often grieved him. The past became present again, and he was out at his play once more. It was late, but he still lay on, his face buried deep on his posy and his heart warm with the joys he had plucked back from the thieving hand of Time.

The next day was one of the festivals of the goddess Chandi. From early morning women and children had been streaming along the path in front of Opu's house to join in the picnic which was being held as usual in a meadow to the north of the village. Shorbojoya had been gone some time, but she had gone alone. She did so because they had very little food in the house and she did not want to distress Opu by exposing him to what she knew was bound to happen. The custom was for every family to take its own food; and some of the women used the occasion to show off to their neighbours by making a public display of what they had brought, the finest rice, a great variety of pulses, butter, milk, sweetmeats, and so on. All the unhappy Shorbojoya could scrape together was some coarse rice, and not much of that, a little very ordinary pulse and a couple of eggplants. Shejbou of course was there with all the Mukherji children; and their banquet, which was spread out for all to see, included milk thickened with a syrup made from fresh sugar cane and a delicious confection of bananas and rice. Shorbojoya saw it all, as she was intended to do, and she thought bitterly of the meagre fare which was all her own children ever had to eat. She was so mortified she could have screamed; for her Opu liked cream syrup and banana sweets too.

Evening was falling as she made her way home. The golden rays of sunset still glowed warm through the trees; but she had eyes for none of its beauty. She could not get Opu's face out of her mind.

That same morning however, shortly after their mother

225

had left the house, Durga came up to Opu and said, 'Opu, what about you and me having a picnic on our own instead?'

Now Nilmoni Ray's compound, next door to their house, had for years been nothing but a patch of jungle in which long grass and tangled bushes were slowly being submerged beneath a sea of creepers; but Durga went to work on it with a sickle, and soon she had cut a clearing large enough for the two of them to have their picnic in. 'Opu,' she said breathlessly when it was done, 'go and stand under the tamarind tree and shout out if you see Mummy coming, I'm going back to the house to get some rice.'

That was not the only trip she made. She had to go back and forth a number of times. Each time she searched different parts of the house, and whatever food she found and thought her mother would not miss she brought out with her and left in Opu's charge. 'Keep it over there,' she said, pointing to a place that seemed safe; 'but mind the cows don't come and eat it.' From one of her trips she returned very slowly indeed, picking her way through the undergrowth with much more than usual care. When she got near enough for Opu to see, he noticed that she had something tucked away under her sari. It was a coconut shell, and she was holding on to it with both hands for all she was worth. It contained very precious cargo, a few drops of oil from a bottle she had ferreted out from one of her mother's many hiding places. The shell was duly deposited with Opu, and she went back to the house; but as she was crossing the yard for the last time she suddenly stopped with a start. Somebody was coming in through the gate. It turned out to be Mato's mother, with Mato just behind her.

'Oh!' Durga gasped with relief. 'It's you, Tomrej's wife. How did you get here?'

Mato's mother was still a young woman, and she was not

bad-looking either; but since her husband's death life had been hard for her, and she looked pinched and drawn. 'I've been out in the factory field gathering firewood,' she replied. 'I came to see if you would like a bunch of boinchi berries.'

Durga shook her head. What would she want with boinchis? The forest was full of them. She was always coming across them. 'No thanks,' she said. 'I don't want any.'

'Do take just one bunch, little mistress. They're ever so sweet, these ones are. I got them near the flood water in the Modhukhali meadows.' And she pulled a bunch of them out from under her sari to show her. 'Look how big they are.' Then pausing for a moment, she went on, 'It's going to take me a long time to carry this wood all the way to the market and sell it; and I must try and get a pice worth of rice for Mato before I go there. He's had nothing to eat for a long time. Do take some, please. I'll let you have two bunches for a pice.'

Durga had no money so she had to refuse again, but she turned and called out to her brother, 'Opu, there's a little rice left over in the pot. Go and give it to Mato's mother.' Opu went and got it, and presently the visitors went away.

It was an excellent place that Durga had chosen. There were bushes and trees all round it, so there was little likelihood of their being seen from outside. The first thing Durga did was to put the rice on to cook. The pan she was using however was no bigger than the little earthenware pot in her doll's box. 'Look, Opu!' she called out. 'Look, what big wild potatoes I've got! I came across them near Punti's place. You know the thicket near the big palm tree, don't you? Well, that's where I found them. There were lots of them. I'm going to boil them with the rice.'

Opu was not idle either. His job was to collect dry twigs for the fire. This was his first proper picnic. He found it hard to believe that they were going to have real rice and real vegetables, and that it was not a make-believe game as it had always been before, with sand for rice, bits of broken earthenware for fried potatoes and jackfruit leaves for luchis.

It was a happy time for both of them, and such a beautiful place too, with bushes all round and long creepers swinging to and fro in the light breeze. There were still a few berries on the seora bush under the bel tree, and they could see some longtailed birds hopping about in the thick grass which was just beginning to turn brown in the sun. It was all very lovely, and they felt so private sitting there behind the bushes. Spring had come, and the fresh, young leaves were already showing. The old derelict garden was brightened here and there by long fronds of ghentu flowers, and some of the white blossom still gleamed on the pomelo tree, though most of it had fallen to the ground.

Trees! Yes. Durga loved her trees! She loved the village too, every stick and stone in it, and the river, and the path that led down to it. She had known them all her life so naturally and intimately that they had become a part of her. Yet now she was beginning to learn that love could hurt. Something seemed to be telling her that she was going to lose them, and she longed to be able to gather them all in her arms and hold them close for ever. How could she live without them? They were her own dear friends, her lifelong companions, and as she sat there she tried to picture them to herself, one by one: that dear path under the mangosteen tree; the bamboo grove behind the house; the river steps with the evening shadows creeping along them. Shadows! The thought stayed with her, for today the shadows were black and frightening under that cloud of separation which she felt thickening overhead. And there was Opu too, her darling little brother, whom she could not bear out of her sight even for an hour. The thought that she might have to leave him behind and go far away made her heart very heavy. And supposing she did not come back! Like her Auntie Nitom who once lived in this very house! She had married many years ago and had never come back home again. It all happened long before Durga was born, but people were always telling her about it. The marriage they said took place in Murshidabad, which to Durga was the other end of the world. And where was Nitom now? Nobody seemed to know. They did not know whether she was alive or dead. All they could tell her was that she never came back to see her father and mother or her sisters and brothers. And now it was too late. They were all dead. How sad it all was, and how wrong! Surely someone could have gone to find out how she was! Durga often used to think of her Auntie Nitom, and she could never do so without wanting to cry. What would her poor auntie think if she came and saw her father's house as it was now, just a heap of rubble buried beneath the jungle?

Was this, she wondered, to be her fate too? Would she have to leave her father and her mother and Opu, and never see them again? Never? Never see this home of theirs, or the mangosteen tree, or the path down to the river? The horror of it shivered through her like an ague. Yet, deep within, she knew with a certainty which increased from day to day that something was going to happen to her, and that it was going to happen soon. The fear like a dreadful, savage beast dogged her, wherever she went and whatever she did. There seemed no escaping it. Something was going to happen to her, and it was going to happen soon.

A voice from beyond the bushes interrupted Durga's gloomy probing into the future.

'That sounds like Bini's voice, doesn't it, Opu? Go and have a look.'

Opu came back with a dark-skinned girl of about Durga's age. It was Bini. She was tall, thin and plain. Her sari was old and not very clean. The general impression she gave was one of drabness, and this was accentuated rather than relieved by the cheap glass bangles she was wearing on her arm. When she caught sight of Durga, she gave a shy, apologetic little laugh which seemed to convey that she was not sure whether she was going to be welcome or not.

'Hello, Didi! What are you doing?'

'Oh, it's you, Bini. We're having a picnic. Come and sit down.'

Bini's father, Kalinath Chokroborti, was by birth a high-ranking Brahmin, but he had come down in the world. He had, so it was said, consorted with low-caste yogis; and in consequence no Brahmin of his own status would have anything to do with him. He and his family were forced to keep to themselves, and they were never invited to any of the social gatherings in the village. They were poor too, and that did not help. The depressed condition of her family was obvious in everything Bini said or did. She was pathetically eager to please. She had come on a visit and was delighted that she had not been repulsed, but she did not want them to think that she was pushing herself forward. After all they might be doing something important; and she was by no means sure that they were going to invite her to join in their picnic.

But Durga's welcome was real. 'Bini,' she said, 'would you see if you can find some dry wood. The fire's not going very well.'

Bini rushed off at once to do her bidding, and in a few minutes she came back with an enormous armful of sticks she had picked up under the bel tree. 'Are these enough, Didi?' she asked happily, 'or would you like me to get some more?'

'Opu,' said Durga, turning to her brother, 'we shall need some more rice now that Bini's come. Go back to the house and get some.'

Bini's face lit up with joy. She was sure of her welcome now; but they would want some more water to boil the rice in, and she ran off all smiles to get it. When she got back, she was so excited she could hardly speak. 'W-what things are you going to c-cook, Didi?' she stammered.

As soon as the rice was done Durga took it off and began to fry the egg-plants in the oil she had brought out from the house with such care. This was the critical moment, and she kept her eyes glued to the pan. Then, suddenly, they almost popped out of her head. 'Look, Opu,' she cried in amazement as if she could not believe what her eyes were looking at. 'Look what colours they are. They look just like real fried eggplants, don't they? Just like they do when Mummy cooks them.'

Opu peered into the pan. He was surprised too. So far he had not been altogether convinced that this was going to be a proper picnic with real rice and real eggplants, but here was proof beyond doubt. They spread banana leaves to eat from, and squatted down beside them with unconcealed glee. Never had rice and eggplant made so rich a feast. Opu, being a boy, had of course to take the first mouthful; and Durga trembled with excitement as she watched him.

'What's it like?' she blurted out as soon as he had swallowed it.'

'Wonderful!' was the reply. 'Wonderful! ... BUT ... didn't you forget to put the salt in?'

She had forgotten, it is true, but that was the only mistake she had made: and in any case what did it matter? A little thing like salt was nothing when they were having such fun. They did not give it another thought as they settled down in earnest to gobble up all that delicious food, rice with wild potatoes and fried eggplants. They did not even notice that the potatoes had not been peeled or that the eggplants were a bit burned and had not much taste. Durga had never cooked anything before, and how she enjoyed eating it now that she had! though she was more than a little surprised that she had been able to do so. To think that they were out together sitting under a date-palm tree with leaves from a custard apple tree lying like a carpet all round them, and that it was real rice and real vegetables that they were eating! How wonderful it all was! Durga looked at Opu, and Opu looked at her; and they laughed, as only happy and carefree children can laugh. And once they had started they could not stop, until Durga got a lump of rice stuck in her throat.

Bini, who was eating just as hard as they were, said in her nervous little way, 'Don't you think it would be a good thing if we had a drop more oil, Didi? It would be nice with the rice and potatoes, wouldn't it?' Opu was despatched to get some.

This indeed was life, and they were only at the beginning of it, just opening the door of a vast treasure house filled with countless delights, which glinted as the forest does when the fireflies' lamps are lit. They were journeying towards an unknown horizon along a road that twisted on its long unending way like the serpent of the world; and at every bend there was something waiting to welcome them, fruit or flowers, laughter or sympathy, with a welcome that was always new. How happy life was! And what joys went to the making of it: the joy of going somewhere; the joy of the unexpected that lay round the next bend in the road or beyond the mist that lay in thick white layers across the fields; joy in the things of today, the ordinary things, the simple trivialities of life.

'Are you going to tell Mummy about our picnic, Didi? I think you'd better, because I shall never be able to eat another meal tonight.'

232

'Of course I'm not going to tell her. Don't be so silly. You'll be hungry enough when she gets back this evening. Just wait and see.'

Bini was in a dilemma: she was very thirsty, but there was no glass for her to drink from, and it would have been most improper to ask to use one of theirs. The rules about drinking from other people's glasses are very strict, particularly among Brahmins. If a Brahmin who has for any reason lost caste goes into an orthodox Brahmin house and asks for a drink of water, they will give him one; but the glass he drinks from immediately becomes unclean and has to be scoured and washed before anyone in the family can use it. Bini knew this, and in consequence though she was very thirsty she was reluctant to ask. At last however she plucked up sufficient courage to point to Opu's glass and say to him, 'Opu, I'm thirsty. Would you mind pouring some water into my mouth.'

'Here!' said Opu, holding out the glass to her. 'Drink from the glass yourself. I don't mind.'

Bini was pleased, but she still hesitated, so Durga came to the rescue. 'Go on, Bini, take it. What's the harm?'

The meal was over at last and they had to clean up. 'What shall we do with the cooking pan, Opu?' Durga said, when they had finished. 'I don't want to throw it away. We shall need it again if we have another picnic later on. What do you think? Shall I hang it on a tree somewhere?'

'It won't be there when you come back if you do,' he replied. 'Mato's mother often comes round here gathering sticks, and she's bound to see it; and if she does she'll take it. She takes everything.'

Durga nodded, and looked round for somewhere else. Presently her eye fell on the broken-down wall nearby, and she began to feel along it to see if there was a hole large enough to hide the pan in. It did not take her long to find one, but while she was groping in and out of the bricks and rubble Opu's heart was in his mouth; for a little further along the wall there was a small crevice which only he knew about. It contained a packet of cigarettes, and he was sure that his sister was going to find them.

It happened some days before. Opu had gone to Nera's house to play. The brother-in-law of the family and a friend of his from Calcutta were staying there at the time. They were very smart young men. They smoked all the time. As soon as they had finished one cigarette they lit another. Opu was most impressed, and thought it must be a wonderful thing to smoke like that. He and Nera talked about it, and when the chance came they sneaked off to Horish Jugi's shop and bought ten cigarettes in a red paper wrapper. They cost one pice. Opu took his five and went by himself into the jungle. He did not tell even Nera where he was going. There he lit up and drew the smoke into his mouth as he had seen Nera's brother-in-law do, but he did not like it at all. It tasted very bitter, and what is more it burned his mouth. He took a second puff to see if that would taste any better, but it did not, and he decided that he did not like smoking. Nevertheless he could not bring himself to throw the other cigarettes away. He had in his pocket an empty packet he had brought away from Nera's house, so he put the four cigarettes in that and hid it in a crevice in the broken wall. He dare not go home yet though, for fear his mother would detect the smell in his breath; so he hunted round for some bitter fruit, and when he had found some he chewed and swallowed it and then blew into his hands to see if the smell was still there. He could not smell anything, but he ate some more to make sure. This apparently worked the trick, for when he got home some time later his mother did not discover his secret. But now ... there was Durga groping along his wall! He knew what keen eyes she had, and he was certain that any minute now she was going to find him out. No wonder his heart almost stopped beating.

He need not have worried however. Durga found the sort of hole she was looking for before she got as far as Opu's hiding place; and it was all right.

TWENTY

❦

The village was agog with the latest news from Onnoda Ray's house. Everybody was talking about it except apparently Shorbojoya, who did not hear what had happened until she went down to the river that morning for her bath. The women at the water's edge were full of it, and as soon as they saw Shorbojoya they clustered round her eagerly to bring her up to date; but as they all tried to talk at once it took her some time to understand what they were talking about.

'Have you heard the news, my dear? About Niren and Onnoda Ray, I mean...'

'Yes, they've been quarrelling for some time now, but yesterday...'

'And Niren and Gokul can't meet without almost coming to blows...'

'No, let me tell it. It happened yesterday about noon...'

'Yes, there was an awful shindy...'

'They yelled and screamed at one another for a long time and then Niren packed his bags and went away.'

'Utter pandemonium it was, and now Niren's gone...'

Eventually however Horimoti, Jogyeshwar Dighri's wife, took over. She lived next door to Onnoda Ray, so naturally she could claim to know more about it than anybody else.

'I've no idea whether it's true or not, my dear. Though it's an amazing story all the same. But I'm not the one to be uncharitable, as you know, and in my heart of hearts I don't believe it. Gokul's wife isn't that sort of girl, is she? Nevertheless one can't get away from the facts, can one? It's quite certain that Niren gave her some money and that she sent it off by money order. That's how it all came out. The money order receipt came back and Gokul got hold of it. It was in Niren's handwriting. And that's all there is to it, my dear. But it isn't our business, is it? And what I say is that it's quite wrong for other people to make a scandal out of it. Nevertheless it is true that there was an awful row in the house. I heard it myself. And do you know what brought it to a head? It was something Niren said. He said, "It's all your fault for plaguing the girl as you do and making her life such a misery. I've a good mind to take her away with me. She's only to say the word and I will, and there's nothing you could say which would stop me. And I would have you know that if I do take her she'll be treated with proper respect. We shall treat her as we did my own mother when she was alive." That was a bit much, wasn't it, my dear? You can understand why they were so angry and shouted so much, can't you? And they did shout too, all of them; and in the end Niren sent for a cart, put all his luggage on it, and left the house.'

'Niren gone!' Shorbojoya stood stunned and silent. Her

hopes lay in ashes at her feet. She had for a long time been urging her husband to get Ononoda Ray to write to Niren's father and broach the subject of marriage. Twice Niren had accepted her invitation and come to the house; and she had come to like him very much. Horihor had been reluctant to do as she asked, and tried to talk her out of the idea, arguing that Niren's father was a rich man and that it was unlikely that he would let his son marry a bride from so poor a family as theirs. It was all of no avail, Shorbojoya was not to be dissuaded by any argument. Something within her, intuition, instinct, whatever it was, made her keep on. It told her that the marriage could and would happen, and that it was quite wrong of Horihor to suggest that what she said was wishful thinking. Horihor was not convinced, but he yielded to her importunity and did raise the subject with Onnoda Ray a time or two. Shorbojoya's hopes ran higher and higher; and now this terrible thing had happened.

A few days later Gokul's wife met Durga on the road and in broken whispers told her the whole unhappy story. When the poor woman came to tell her of Niren's final departure, she broke down. Tears streamed down her cheeks, but she was far too distressed to try to restrain them, or even to wipe them away. 'It's hits, kicks, and scolding all the time,' she sobbed. 'They're all against me, and I've no one of my own left, except my brother, and he's no man. My home's gone now; and if I could run away there's nowhere for me to run to.'

Durga was all sympathy. She searched her little brain for the right words to say, something that would console her poor auntie and make her feel less sad. She wanted to say how wicked she thought they all were. But the words would not come. When she did manage to speak, all she could get out was nothing more than a few disjointed sentences, and not at all what she wanted to be able to say. 'That Shokhithakrun is a wretch! But don't bother about her, my dear; she can't really do anything ... I'll come and see you every day, Auntie, so don't cry.'

Shorbojoya was very excited when she heard that the two of them had had a talk, and she poured out questions in a spate. 'Did she talk to you about what's happened, Durga? What did she actually say? Did she give you any news about Niren?'

Durga was too shy to tell her mother all she wanted to know. 'I don't know,' she said at last. 'You'd better ask her yourself tomorrow when you go down for your bath.'

Opu was curious too. 'Did she tell you that my teacher would not be coming any more?'

'How should I know?' Durga snapped. 'You be quiet.'

Recently Durga had been subject to occasional fits of depression, and they were getting more frequent as time went by. They most often came on in the evening when the last light had gone out of the sky and the path in front of the house was dark. Darkness unquestionably had something to do with her moods, but the real cause of them was fear. She was afraid for Opu. If he was out of the house for any length of time, or sometimes even if he was in and she could not see him, she worried about him and began to imagine all sorts of unpleasant things which might be happening to him. None of them ever did happen to him, but still she worried. Tonight however he was in and she could see him. He was sitting near the gate playing cowries all by himself. His hands and face were dirty and his clothes were patched and torn, but in her eyes he was like cream and roses and as pretty as a doll. 'How I wish I had some money to buy him toys with,' she sighed; but she had none, and her heart ached with longing for what could not be.

Ranu's sister's wedding was over, but a number of the relatives who had come to Bhubon Mukherji's house for the ceremony stayed on for a while afterwards. There seemed to be children everywhere, and one of them, a little girl called Tuni, had made friends with Durga. Tuni's father had stayed on too, but that morning he went back to work leaving his wife and daughter behind. Shejbou was busy in one of the outer rooms when she heard Tuni's mother call out, and she went to see what was the matter was. 'What is it, Hashi my dear? Is anything wrong?' Tuni's mother looked worried. She was feeling under the bedclothes and pillows, and then she started to turn the mattress over. 'It's my little golden jar,' she explained. 'You know the one I mean. It's the one I keep my vermilion in. I had it here on the bed; but what with my husband leaving and baby beginning to cry, I forgot to put it away. It isn't here now, and I can't find it anywhere.'

'Are you sure you didn't take it out of the room with you?' Shejbou asked.

'No, I'm sure I didn't. I left it here. I remember quite clearly. It was just here on the bed.'

Shejbou helped her to look for it, and between them they searched everywhere; but the jar was not to be found. Shejbou asked the others in the house if any of them had been into the room. Apparently none of them had, except for some of the children, and they did not know anything about the jar. Tempi was the only one who could throw any light on its disappearance. 'Mummy,' she said in a whisper, 'just as we were going in to have our food I saw Durga sneaking out of the back door. Oh, look! Here she is again. She's just come back.'

Shejbou asked a few questions which none of the others could hear, and then turned abruptly on Durga and shouted, 'What have you done with that jar, Durga? I know you've taken it. Go and bring it back at once.'

Durga went pale. Her face seemed to shrivel up. Her tongue went dry and stuck to the roof of her mouth, and for a moment or two she could not utter a word. When she did manage to speak it was in such a hoarse whisper that nobody could hear what she was saying, let alone understand.

So far Tuni's mother had not said anything. She was shocked to hear such a respectable girl being accused outright of thieving. She had come to know the family quite well during the last few days and had taken a liking to Durga. 'She has such a pretty little face,' she murmured more to herself than to anybody else. 'She can't possibly be a thief.' But Shejbou heard. 'What do you know about her?' she asked harshly. 'You keep out of this and leave it to me. I know when she's been stealing and when she hasn't.'

At this point one of the other women spoke up. 'Be a good girl now, Durga. If you've got it, go and get it; and that'll be the end of it. We only want the jar back, dear; that's all. Why should you try to lie about it?'

Durga was frantic by this time. She was trembling so violently that she had to lean against the wall to prevent herself from falling. 'I don't know anything about it, Auntie, I didn't...'

Shejbou did not let her finish. 'Do you expect me to believe a lie like that?' she shouted. 'Just look at her face,' she said, turning to the others. 'Of course she took it. I can always tell by looking at her. And don't you think that I don't mean what I say,' she said, shouting at Durga again. 'I do. So go and get it wherever it is, and hand it over. I promise you I won't say anything more if you do. So go and get it at once. I ... want ... it ... back!'

Durga was incapable of saying anything, but the woman who had spoken before was ready enough to let her views be known. 'She comes of such a respectable family too. To think of a girl like her being a thief. I never heard the like

241

of it before. I never did. And they live next door, don't they?'

'Respectable indeed,' Shejboy echoed, her eyes still on Durga. 'There's nothing respectable about her. I suppose she thinks it's a joke, and that she can come into this house and take anything she likes the look of; and that nobody will mind. Well, we do mind. And now I'm going to show you that we do mind. This is no ordinary thing you've stolen this time.'

So saying, she seized Durga by the hands, dragged her away from the wall out into the middle of the room, and began to shake her violently. 'Now will you tell me where it is...?' The pause produced no reply ... 'Oh, you won't, won't you? You're only a little girl and you don't know anything about it. Do you think I'm likely to believe that? Tell me where it is at once. I'll knock your teeth down your throat for you if you don't. Where is it? Tell me at once ... Where is it? ... Where is it?'

Tuni's mother rushed forward and tried to pull Shejbou back; but one of the others said, 'Don't interfere. Can't you see that she's stolen it. There's only one way to treat a thief and that's to beat her.' Then the same speaker addressed Durga. 'Why don't you go and get it? That's all you've got to do. Lying about it won't do any good.'

Durga's head was throbbing. She looked round helplessly and then with a great effort she forced her dry tongue to speak. 'I don't know anything about it, Auntie. They all went away, so I went away too.' She cowered down against the wall, petrified with fear; though her eyes remained fixed on Shejbou.

The others tried to make her own up, but all she could say was, 'I don't know'. Then Tempi chipped in. 'It isn't only this, Mummy, is it? There are our mangoes too. She's always stealing them. She won't even wait till they fall off the tree.'

Mangoes to Shejbou were like a red rag to a bull, and she lost control of herself completely. 'You wretch!' she yelled at the top of her voice. 'You good-for-nothing, you! You spawn of a thief. You won't give it back, will you? Well, I'll really show you.' As she spoke she sprang savagely upon Durga and started banging her head on the wall as hard as she could. 'Tell me where you've put it,' she screamed. 'Tell me at once ... tell me ... tell me.'

Tuni's mother ran to them and seized Shejbou by the hands. 'What are you doing? What are you doing?' she sobbed. 'Stop it. What do you have to hurt her like this for? Forget about the jar. Let her go. Stop it.' She was weeping bitterly now. She could not bear to see a child savaged like that. One of the others, the woman who had spoken before, said, 'Poor little thing! Look, she's bleeding.'

Until then nobody had noticed that blood was dripping from Durga's nose. Her blouse was stained with it.

'Run, Tempi,' said Tuni's mother, 'and get me some water. There's a bucket out there on the verandah.'

Ranu's mother was not in the house while all this was going on. She had gone to talk to the womenfolk in the blacksmith's house next door; but when she heard the screaming and sobbing she came hurrying back to see what was happening; and the other women came with her.

Durga's head by this time had been hurt so badly that it was almost numb to pain, and she was burning hot. Her eyes were wide open, but there seemed to be no sight in them; and it was obvious that she was no longer fully conscious of where she was. Ranu's mother went to her at once, took her by the hand and made her sit down; and as soon as the water came she began to sponge her eyes and face with it. But the vacant look did not go out of Durga's eyes, and her head was still spinning. Ranu's mother could not keep quiet any longer. 'You ought to be ashamed of yourself, Shejbou, beating her like that. You know she's a delicate child. What's came over you?'

243

'You don't know what sort of a girl she is,' Shejbou shouted wildly. 'She's a thief, I tell you. A dirty little thief! And there's only one cure for the likes of her and that's a thrashing. And don't get the idea that I've finished with her. I haven't. I shall keep on beating her till I get that jar back, even if Horihor Ray sends me to prison for it.'

'You've done more than enough as it is,' retorted Ranu's mother. 'Get a hold of yourself. This is outrageous.'

'And all over a jar,' said Tuni's mother. 'I'd never have mentioned the wretched thing if I'd known it was going to lead to this. In any case I don't want it back now. So stop it and let her go, Shejbou.'

Shejbou was not the sort of woman to give in to anybody, and it is doubtful if she would have done so even now had it not become clear to her that public opinion had turned against her. It was this and not what Ranu's mother and Tuni's mother had said that finally made her back down and let Durga go.

Ranu's mother put her arm round the child and led her out through the door into the backyard. 'How unfortunate it was that you happened to come in just when you did!' she said to her. 'But never mind. It's all over now. But you will have to walk slowly. Don't forget. Tempi, go and open the gate for her.'

The children clustered round to watch her go, but Durga was still in a haze and did not appear aware that they were there. She walked as if she hardly knew where she was or where she was going.

'How brave she was!' one of the children said. 'Did you notice? She didn't admit anything even after all that, did she? And she didn't cry either. Her eyes were quite dry.'

'Dry?' echoed Ranu's mother. 'I should think they were. She was too dried up with fear and pain to have any tears left to cry with. What a cruel way to beat her, Shejbou!'

TWENTY ONE

The Chorok season was approaching. Chorok is an annual festival in honour of the god Shiva. It is held at the end of the Bengali year and lasts for several days. In Nishchindipur it was a village affair and every household was expected to make some contribution towards expenses. Boidyonath Mukherji, the festival treasurer, had already started to go round from house to house with his subscription book. Horihor had been put down for one rupee; but when Boidyonath told him so, he demurred, 'It's not fair,' he said, 'to put me down for a rupee. I can't afford as much as that this year.' Boidyonath was not in the least put out. 'Don't worry. It doesn't matter,' he assured him. 'Give as much as you can. But you know, don't you, that Nilmoni Hajra's troupe of actors are coming this year. They're absolutely first

245

class. Far better than anything we've ever had before. And it's a good job we've managed to get them too, because Mohesh Shekra's boys are going to give a kirtan recital in Palpara Bazar; and whatever we do we mustn't let them get the better of us.' Boidyonath had much to say on this subject, and from the way he talked you might have thought that the life and health of the whole Nishchindipur village depended on their winning the competition with Palpara.

Opu came in just after Boidyonath had left. He was dragging a bamboo branch behind him. 'Just look what I've got, Daddy,' he called out to Horihor. 'It's just what you've been wanting, isn't it? You'll be able to cut a lovely pen out of it. (Horihor always wrote with a bamboo pen.) It was in the bamboo grove by the pond, and I brought it home for you.' His face was covered with smiles as he lifted the branch up for his father to see. 'It will give you a lovely pen, won't it, Daddy? It's absolutely ripe for cutting.'

The days went by, and Chorok drew nearer. It began with the arrival of a party of religious mendicants, sannyasis as they are called, about a fortnight before the date of the main festival. They went round the village, house by house, performing the gajon, a wild ecstatic dance which commemorated the ancient dance of the deity himself. It was a most excisting time for Opu and Durga. They were hardly ever at home. They followed the dancers round wherever they went, and stayed with them until the last dance was over, even though it meant missing their meals and not getting home till long after bedtime. The householders gave the sannyasis presents: clothes, water vessels, food and money too. Horihor had no money to give them. All he could spare was a small handful of coarse rice, and the sannyasis thought this was not good enough, so they passed his house by.

246

Some ten days after the gajon dance came Blue-Worship Day, so named after Shiva, one of whose many epithets was God of the Blue Throat. The day after that was Chorok itself.

The principal rite of the Blue-Worship ceremonies took place in the evening. The sannyasis first performed a dance round a date-palm tree and then broke off the spikes from its trunk. Usually they went to one particular tree, but Durga came back with the news that this year they had decided to go to another tree, a small one by the river. The procession to the tree was followed by a swarm of children, Durga and Opu among them, who clustered round to watch. The spike-breaking dance over, the sannyasis led the way to the Chorok tree, the huge chatim in the village cremation ground. Nearby stood a hut, walled in with palm branches where the Blue-Throated God would be venerated by the people. The ground round about the Chorok tree had already been cleared of jungle weeds and grasses. Here Durga and Opu were joined by three of the Mukherji girls, Ranu, Punti and Tunu. There were very strict rules in the Mukherji household about the girls going out. They were not allowed to wander here, there and everywhere, as Durga did, and they had had to beg very hard before they got permission to go to the Chorok tree.

Tunu said, 'Tonight the sannyasis—she pronounced it 'shonnishi'—will spend the whole night in the cremation grounds.'

'Of course they will,' retorted Ranu. 'Did you think we didn't know? One of them will pretend to be a corpse, and the others will bind him up in funeral clothes and carry him to the chatim tree, where they burn dead people. When they've taken him there they'll bring him back to life again; and they'll hunt round for a dead man's skull—there are lots of skulls lying about there, you know—and when they've got one they'll march round with it in a procession, singing songs and reciting holy texts. They recite lots of holy texts as they go round and round with the skull.'

'I know some of the songs they sing,' Durga informed them. 'Would you like to hear one?' And she started to sing.

'From heaven there came a chariot, down to earth's
wide plain;
the Lord God Shiva was in it, and his arrows fell
like rain.
A corpse from the age of Satya and mud from the
age of old;
Sing Shiva, Shiva, brothers all, and their drums
like thunder rolled.'

She smiled shyly as she finished, and changed the subject immediately. 'They've got some lovely Krishna dolls this year, Nilu, I went to the potter's shop to look at them. Have you seen them yet, Ranu?'

'Is it a real dead man's skull they take round with them, Ranu?' asked Punti.

'Yes, it is. You'd be able to see it for yourself if you stayed out here till late tonight. But you can't. None of us can. We're not allowed to. Tonight's not a good night for people to be out. And it's getting dark already; so come on, let's go. Come on, Opu; and you too, Durga.'

'Why isn't tonight a good night to stay out, Ranu?' Opu asked. 'What's going to happen tonight?'

'I daren't tell you. We're not supposed to talk about it,' Ranu replied. 'So come on; let's go home.' The four girls moved off; but Opu did not go with them. He wanted to find out what there was about tonight that made it different from any other night.

As he stood there by himself, a cloud swept swiftly across the sky, and suddenly it was dark. There was no one in the

248

field by the tree, and he could not see anyone on the road either. All evening he had been listening to stories about the cremation ground and dead men's skulls; and he was afraid. He turned to go home, but as he approached the bend in the road near the bamboo grove he became aware of a peculiar smell. It was an unpleasant sickly smell, and he did not know what it was. He broke into a run to get away from it, when round the bend came Nera's old grandmother. She was going down to the hut in the Chorok field to make an offering to the Blue-Throated God. Opu stood still. At first he could not make out who it was; it was too dark to see. But as soon as he recognized her he spoke to her and said, 'What is that smell, Granny?'

'They're out on the prowl tonight. That's what the smell is.'

'They? Who are they, Granny?'

'You shouldn't be asking that,' she whispered. 'It's Shiva's soldiers out on the prowl. It's very unlucky to mention them after dark.' Then to protect herself from harm because she had done so, she started to ejaculate an auspicious name, 'Ram, Ram: Ram, Ram!'

A cold shudder ran through Opu's body. There was the dark night all round him, and the sky above was black with clouds; in the bamboo grove was the smell of corpses, and their ghosts were on the prowl. He was sure that Shiva's soldiers were dead men's ghosts. He was face to face with an unknown, gruesome horror; and he was terrified. 'How am I going to get home, Granny?' he said in an anguish of fear.

'What are you doing out as late as this tonight of all nights?' she snapped. 'You'd better come with me, and when I've made my offering I'll take you home. I hope to goodness no harm comes of it.'

The place where the village festivities were to be held was under another tree. The open ground in which it stood had been cleared of grass and a number of men were busy erecting the bamboo framework for a large marquee: for it was there that Nilmoni Hajra's company of actors were going to perform their jatra plays. The players had not actually arrived yet, but they were due any time now. Each evening people said they were coming by the morning train; and in the morning they said they were bound to arrive that afternoon. Opu was beside himself with excitement. He could no more contain it than a broken bank can hold back the raging waters of a river in flood. He had almost given up eating and washing, and at night he could not sleep. He spent the whole night tossing this way and that all over his bed; for the jatra, the jatra, the jatra was coming.

Durga's mother had told her that she was a big girl now, and that she was not to go wandering very far from the house; but Durga took no notice, and when she thought her mother was not looking she slipped out and went to see what was going on in the festival field. When she got back she described it all to Opu, the stage decorations and the red and blue paper streamers which they had hung in festoons from the poles of the marquee. Opu was fascinated but at the same time he was puzzled. He could not understand why such an ordinary place, one he knew so well, for he often went to play cowries there, should have been chosen for something so extraordinary as the theatre in which Nilmoni Hajra's players were going to perform their jatra. Such a thing had never happened before, and he could not make it out at all. It seemed incredible.

Then suddenly, when people were least expecting it, news came that the actors were due to arrive that very afternoon. The blood rushed to Opu's head, he was so excited. In spite of the heat—it was just after midday—he ran all the way across the village as fast as he could until he came across a number of boys who had congregated at the bend in the road near where the potters' houses were. He joined them and watched. Presently, away in the distance, he was able to make out a bullock cart. It was stacked high with boxes—they were costume boxes, though he did not know that till later—and behind it came other carts, one, two, three, four, five of them. Potu, whose voice showed how excited he was, counted them one by one on his fingers. Behind the carts came the members of the troupe, walking. Opu noticed that all of them wore partings in their hair, and that many of them were carrying their shoes in their hands. Potu pointed to a man with a bread. 'That must be the king, Opu. Don't you think so?' he exclaimed.

Nothing could ever be the same again. Even the sky and the air changed colour; and Opu went home in high glee. His father was sitting on the verandah writing and humming a tune to himself. Opu at once concluded that he had heard about the arrival of the jatra party and that that was why he was so happy. 'There were five cartloads of costumes, Daddy,' he burst out, waving his hands about in his excitement. 'It's a huge party.'

Horihor was writting out some texts on rough handmade paper for distribution to his religious clients. He raised his head when he heard Opu speak. 'What costumes, child?' he asked with surprise. Opu was dumbfounded. To think that such an important event was taking place and his father did not know about it! He could not help feeling very sorry for him.

When he got up next morning Opu had another shock. His father told him to take out his books and do his lessons. 'Must I stay in the house doing lessons today, Daddy? I want to go to the jatra field. Everyody else's going. It'll be starting any minute now.'

'No, it won't,' replied his father. 'They'll beat a drum when it's due to start, and then you can go. So get on with your work.' Horihor was not a young man and he liked having the boy with him, particularly nowadays when he spent so much of his time away from home; but Opu was tearful and resentful. He recited his arithmetic tables but there were sobs in his voice as he did so: if a man gets paid so much a month, how much does he get each day?

The jatra did not begin in the morning. It was timed to start some time in the afternoon. Opu went and wept to his mother, and told her how cruel his father was being to him. She lost no time in speaking to Horihor about it. 'Why won't you let the lad go? You can see how upset he is. This is a big day for him, the biggest day in the year. What do you hope to gain by keeping him here? You're away nine months in the year. Do you think one more day of class is going to make all that difference to him?'

Horihor gave way and Opu was allowed to go. He spent the whole afternoon in and out of the jatra tent; but when it began to get dark and the performance had not yet begun he went home for his meal. The hour after supper was lesson time, and on any other day he would have had to sit by his father's side and read one of his books; but Horihor was in a mood to humour him. So he said in a voice that clearly indicated that he was not serious, 'Sit down here and write something for me. I want to see how well you can write. I'm going to give you a dictation. "Shiver, shiver, the bogeyman's waiting."' Opu burst out laughing. He had never been asked to write anything as funny as that before; and he grabbed his slate and began to take it down. Then he paused as a doubt crossed his mind. 'You will let me go when I've done it, won't you, Daddy?' 'Yes, of course. So write quickly and let me see it.' Thus assured Opu wrote it out. He did one or two more lines too. As he did so a curious feeling came over him. He felt as if some power from outside had come between him and his father. He looked at the house. It was empty, dark and hemmed in by bamboos. And then he looked at his father. He was sitting there alone in the dark, writing and writing; and he seemed to have lost the authority to demand that Opu should stay in the house with him. Opu knew that he was powerless to say, 'Child, come here and do your lessons'; because if he had, Shiva's army which was prowling round outside would have screamed in protest: 'No, no! We won't let you keep him in. The jatra's about to start.' The exultant demon horde had overpowered his father, and left him ineffectual and very lonely. Opu felt that his father could not now even so much as utter a word of command; and he was sad at heart for him.

'Opu!' It was Durga. 'Please ask Mummy to let me go too,' she asked.

Opu did. 'Why can't Didi come with me, Mummy? There's a screen in the tent, and she can sit behind that.'

'No, not yet. I shall be going there with the other women later on. She can come with me then.'

He was going out alone when Durga called after him again. 'Just a minute, Opu!' she said smiling. 'Hold out your hand.' Opu held out his hand at once, and she put two pice into it and folded his fingers tightly over them. 'Buy yourself some baked rice,' she said, 'or some lichies if there are any.'

About a week ago Opu had crept up to Durga when she was alone and whispered, 'Didi, have you got any money in your doll's box? If you have please give me a pice.'

'A pice? What do you want a pice for?'

He laughed a little guiltily. 'I want to buy some lichies,' he explained. 'They've put up a platform in the tree in the Bostoms' garden, and they've gathered lots of lichies from it. Two baskets full. And they're selling them at six for a pice. They're ever so big, Didi, and as red as vermilion. Shotu bought some, and Shadhon did too. Have you got any money, Didi?' She had not, and he was bitterly disappointed. It made her very sad to see him walk away so despondently; so last evening she had asked her father for two pice for the festival, and this she gave to him now. He was as dear to her as gold, and it hurt her intensely if she could not give him something when he asked for it.

Shorbojoya came in from her bath just after Opu had left. 'Durga, do something for me,' she said. 'Go into Ranu's orchard and find me some white gondhobhedali leaves. Be as quick as you can. I don't think Opu's very well, and I want to make him some broth.'

Durga was off like a shot, and very happily too. The orchard was thick with bushes as high as a man's head, and as she pushed through in search of the leaves she sang a song her old auntie had taught her and nodded her head as she sang.

'When I saw the yellow gleam in the forest my
heart was glad;
But I lost the ring from my nose and now I'm sad.'

TWENTY TWO

❧

The jatra at last began; and from that moment the earth
for Opu ceased to exist, and all the people on it, except for
himself and the actors on the stage in front of him. The stage
was all his world, and the players its entire population. The
atmosphere of the play was set by the violinists who opened
the performance just before dark with a tone poem in a
traditional mode known as Imon. How beautiful it was, but
how melancholy! Opu was deeply moved. He was only a
village boy and beauty such as this had not come into his life
before. It made him happy and sad at the same time. His mind
went back to his father, sitting alone on the verandah writing,
and to Didi, who wanted so much to come but had not been
allowed to. The stage was lit with lights which hung in
clusters from the wooden structure above. The king and his

ministers came in, dressed in robes that glistened with gold thread. And to think that his father was not going to see all these lovely things! Everybody in their locality, indeed everybody in the village was there, except his father. Why should he have to stay at home writing? Then the action began, and moved rapidly from scene to scene. Some time ago he had heard a party of boys sing kirtan songs; but how could you compare a performance like that with this? What magnificent dresses! And how handsome the players looked in them!

Suddenly a voice spoke to him over his shoulder. 'Can you see properly, child?' He had not noticed his father come into the theatre and take a seat just behind him.

'Has Didi come, Daddy?' he said, turning round for a moment.

'Yes. She must be at the back of that screen.'

The king, who had lost his throne as the result of a conspiracy organized by his ministers, was going into the forest with his wife and children. One had only to listen to the violins to know what an occasion it was for tears. The scene dragged out its intolerable grief, as the unhappy monarch, holding his wife and children by the hand, walked slowly across the stage, pausing after each step. It did not matter that this sort of thing could not have happened in real life, that no king who was seeking safety in the forest would, unless he was out of his senses, have behaved in this way before such a crowd of people. Then in came a loyal general, trembling more violently with rage than any epileptic could possibly have done. Opu's eyes were bulging. He was too absorbed even to blink.

Eventually the king and queen reached the forest and disappeared from view, one going one way, the other another. The next scene, showed the royal children, Prince Ajoy and

Princess Indulekha, wandering about alone among the trees. They were quite lost, and there was no one to show them the way. In time they became separated. Indulekha strayed off into the depths of the jungle to find some fruit for her little brother; but she did not return. Ajoy searched for her all over; but when he did find her beside a little stream, she was dead. She was hungry and had eaten some poisonous berries. Ajoy sang such a pathetic song over her body.

'My life's friend dear, what dost thou here,
Leaving me lone in this forest drear?'

Opu could not take his eyes off him; but presently he could bear it no longer, and burst into tears.

Then came the fight between the king of Kalinga and Bichitraketu. What brilliant sword-play it was! The warriors were so engrossed in their violent combat that they did not notice that they had smashed a number of the hanging lamps, or that one of the spectators—unhappy fellow!—was nearly blinded by the flying splinters of glass. The audience had to call out to them: 'Mind the lamps, mind the lamps!' What incredible skill! It's a wonder they both weren't killed. But in the end Bichitraketu won. Wonderful Bichitraketu!

After the fight the chorus launched into a long drawn out song with violin accompaniment. It went on and on interminably, and after some time Horihor called out to Opu, 'You're beginning to look sleepy, child. Wouldn't you like to go home?' Of course he wasn't sleepy. The very idea! And he certainly did not want to go home. So his father called him aside, and whispered to him, 'Here are two pice. Go and buy yourself something. I'm going home.'

Opu went off to buy himself a pice worth of betel nut, but when he got outside there was a crowd of people round the stall, including some of the actors. General Bichitraketu was there. He was still wearing his sword belt; and he was just lighting up a home-made cigarette. A dense throng of people were milling round him. Then, wonderful to relate, Prince Ajoy came out too. He went up to Bichitraketu and nudged his elbow. 'What about buying me some betel nut?' he said. The general's behaviour exhibited none of the loyalty he owed to his royal master's son. He pushed the child away and said roughly, 'Do you think I'm made of money? What's more, I haven't forgotten what you said to me when I caught you and the other boy using my soap this afternoon.' The prince did not go away. 'Please buy me some,' he said. 'I've given you things before now.' But Bichitraketu shook him off again and walked away.

Ajoy must have been about the same age as Opu. He was a good-looking lad, with a ruddy complexion; and he had a very musical voice. Opu looked at him fascinated and he longed to talk to him. For some time he hesitated, but then plucking up courage he went up to him. 'Would you really like some betel?' he asked shyly.

Ajoy turned and looked at him. 'Why?' he asked. 'Do you mean that you want to give me some?'

'Yes,' said Opu, 'I've got some here. You can have it if you want.' From then on they were friends, though friendship as far as Opu was concerned might have seemed too weak a term. He was enchanted, for if there was one person he had been longing to meet all his life it was Prince Ajoy. His mother had told him hundreds of stories about him, and he had pictured him in all the imaginary situations that a young and romantic boy can fashion for himself and dream about. And here he was in the flesh, with the same eyes, the same face and the same voice, that he had seen and heard in his dreams.

'Where do you live?' Ajoy asked him. 'I've been invited

to somebody's house for my meals, but they eat very late. Have you got any of our party eating at your house?'

Opu was thrilled. 'There is somebody coming to us,' he said. 'I saw him a little while ago. He was playing a drum. But that doesn't matter. You come instead. He can go to the house you were supposed to be going to. I'll come and fetch you.'

The two of them strolled around talking for a while and then Ajoy had to go. 'I'm singing a song in the last scene,' he said. 'So I must go now. What did you think of my part so far?'

The jatra dragged on into the early hours of the morning, but it did not occur to Opu to go home until it was all over; and even when he did at last force himself to leave the tent he did not leave the play behind. His eyes saw nothing, his ears heard nothing but the actions and voices of the players in their parts. The chatter of other spectators who were going his way seemed to be coming from the mouths of the men and boys on the stage. Durga was waiting up to talk to him when he got back, but when she spoke to him it was not his sister's voice he heard but Indulekha's, calling to him from the darkness of the lonely forest. Nevertheless he did not forget to tell his mother about Ajoy. 'Mummy,' he said, his voice quivering with excitement, 'do you remember the boy who took the part of Ajoy? He's coming to eat with us.'

'What another of them?' exclaimed Shorbojoya in dismay, 'I've got one already. How can they expect me to feed two of them?'

'No, there won't be two, Mummy. There'll only be Ajoy. The other one's going somewhere else.'

'What did you think of the jatra, Opu,' Durga asked him when they got to bed.

'It was wonderful, Didi. The most wonderful thing I've

ever seen! And the loveliest thing of all was the song Ajoy sang when the princess died.'

Opu had never been out of bed so late before. Nevertheless it took him a long time to go to sleep, and when he finally did fall off the wailing of the fiddles, the clash of the cymbals and the beating of the drums were still ringing in his ears. He slept well on into the morning, and it was the glare of the sun which woke him eventually, stabbing through his eyelids like hot needles. His eyes were dry and burning, and they burned even more when he washed them; but his ears, and his eyes too when he could see again, were full of the sounds and sights of the jatra, as though it was still going on and he was still seated in the tent.

The women of the village chattered as they went past the house down to the bathing steps, but their voices were not their own: one spoke like Dhirabati, another like the queen of Kalinga, and a third like Prince Ajoy's mother, Basumati. And then Opu looked at his sister. She was in every inflection of her speech, in every gesture of her hand or movement of her feet, the true Princess Indulekha. The boy who played the part the night before had not portrayed her badly, but Opu's fancy had fashioned another and truer image of the princess, and that image was Durga. She had the same colouring, the same big eyes, the same lovely face and beautiful hair. Indulekha with all her tender love and sweetness had come from a far-off land, from a country of bygone years, to be born again as his sister. She spoke with Durga's voice and moved with her limbs. When in the depths of the forest she wrapped her arms round the little frightened Ajoy, and when she went out alone to find fruit for him to eat and lost her way among the trees, Opu relived every minute of that sad day when his makal fruit had been stolen and Durga had comforted him and gone into the thickest part of the jungle to find him some more.

260

Children Make Their Own Toys

At midday he went to call for Ajoy. Shorbojoya sat them both down side by side, and soon she was asking Ajoy to tell them about himself and how he came to be here. He told them he was the son of a Brahmin, but his father and mother had died when he was very small, and an aunt had brought him up. She died too, and then he had no one to look after him. He had been working for the jatra party for about a year. Shorbojoya's heart went out to him with a mother's yearning; but though she kept on asking him questions she did not stop plying him generously with food. It was not an exciting meal, but Ajoy ate contentedly enough. When he had finished, Durga whispered to her mother, 'Mummy, ask him to sing the song he sang yesterday. You know the one I mean: "My life's friend dear, what dost thou here...?"'

Ajoy cleared his throat and began to sing. Opu was delighted, and Shorbojoya's eyes were wet with tears to think that such a pretty, delicate-looking boy had no mother to look after him. He sang some other songs too. In time he got up to go, and Shorbojoya, anxious that he should come again, said, 'I shall be baking some rice this evening, and I'll keep some for you; so you will come, won't you? Don't be shy. I want you to treat our house as your home and come whenever you want to.'

Opu went out with him and they turned in the direction of the river bank. When they reached it Ajoy said, 'You've got a nice voice, Opu. Why don't you sing me a song?' Opu wanted to very much. He had been thinking about it for some time, but had been too shy to suggest it. After all Ajoy was in a jatra party! How could he possibly sing for him? Presently they found a place away from the path where a clump of bamboos grew under a silk-cotton tree, and there they sat down and Opu began to sing. 'Lay your burden at his holy feet, Ananta....' It was from Dashu Ray's ballads. He had

261

heard his father sing it and had written the words down. Ajoy was surprised. He had not expected him to be so good. 'You've got a very good voice,' he said. 'You ought to take up singing. Why don't you? Sing me another.' Opu needed little encouragement to sing again. 'My soul sat waiting for the ferry, but night fell fast and no boat came.' It was a song Durga had learned somewhere and she used to sing it to him. Opu liked the melody and learned to sing it himself. Sometimes when there was no one else in the house he and his sister sang it together.

Ajoy let him sing the song right through to the end and he was obviously sincere when he said how much he liked it. 'With a voice like yours, Opu, you should join a jatra party. They would pay you fifteen rupees a month, I'm quite sure; though of course they'd expect you to practise a lot.'

When he was alone with his sister Opu often used to sing to her and ask her what she thought of his voice and whether he would make a good singer. She always said he had a wonderful voice, and Opu was very pleased to hear her say so; but to be congratulated by a famous and much lauded member of a real jatra party raised him to the seventh heaven of delight. He could not speak he was so happy.

When he found his tongue again, he said, 'Please teach me that song of yours.' Ajoy did and the two of them sang it together.

The hours went by. A country boat splashed past and they saw a man on the river bank looking for something. 'What's he looking for, Opu?' asked Ajoy. 'Baby frogs, to go fishing with,' Opu replied. For a while they were silent, then Opu said, 'Why don't you stay with us, Ajoy? You don't have to go away, do you? Why not stay here?' Ajoy had such beautiful eyes and such a sweet voice. To Opu he was a real prince whom he had chanced to meet in the forest. Prince Ajoy, the pretty young son of a forlorn king; and they had to be friends for ever. How could he let him go?

Ajoy in reply told Opu the plans he had in mind for the future. He had never had a friend like Opu, and he was able to speak from his heart. He told him that he had saved forty rupees, and when he was a bit older he was going to leave his present troupe—the manager used to beat him—and join Ashutosh Pal's. He would be happy there. They used to provide luchis for supper every evening! And if anybody did not like the food, he could draw an allowance of three annas a day instead. When he left the troupe he would come to Opu's house and stay with them for a few days.

In time it began to get dark and Ajoy said, 'Come on, Opu; I've got to be getting back. I come on early this evening. They'll probably be doing *The Humiliation of Parasuram* and I've to play the part of Destiny. It's got a lovely song in it. I'll sing it for you.'

The jatra went on for three more days. The village could talk and think of nothing else. People walking along the paths, by the river or across the fields, boatmen rowing their boats, boys out with their goats, were all singing the new songs they had learned. The women of the village invited the boys of the troupe to their homes and asked them to sing the songs they liked best. Opu learned three or four more songs. On one occasion he went with Ajoy into the theatre tent, and the other actors, who had heard from Ajoy what a good voice he had, gathered round him and asked him to sing. Opu as usual was shy and made all sorts of excuses, but eventually they prevailed on him to let them hear one of his songs. In his heart of hearts he knew this was just what he wanted to do, for in spite of his protests and shy reluctance he really did want them to know how well he could sing. When he had finished his song they whisked him off to the manager, and he had to sing it again. The manager was a fat, potbellied man, with a very dark skin. He sang in the chorus. Opu remembered seeing him there. He was pleased with Opu's performance. 'Why don't you join us, my boy?' he asked; and Opu's breast swelled with happiness and pride. They all urged him to join them, and wanted him to start at once. Opu was ready enough to agree. There could be no more exciting work for a boy to do than to sing in a jatra party. He could not understand why he had not thought of it before.

'If I do join you,' he asked Ajoy when they were alone together, 'what sort of part do you think they'll give me?'

'Oh, to begin with, a juvenile part, perhaps a female attendant; and then when you've learned how to act...'

Opu did not want to be a female attendant. He wanted to be a general with a golden helmet on his head, and learn how to swing a sword and fight battles. When he was big, he told himself, he would certainly join a jatra party. Nothing could make him change his mind now.

Ajoy pointed out a youth with a jet black complexion. 'Do you see that fellow over there, Opu?' he whispered. 'His name's Bishto Teli, and I don't like him at all. I buy matches— and with my own money too—and when I go to bed I put them under my pillow; and he comes and pinches them and won't give them back to me. The other day I asked him for them. I said, "Give me my matches back, It's dark and I want them." I am very frightened of the dark, you know. He refused and slapped me instead. It's no good complaining about him, because he's a good dancer, and a great favourite of the manager's.'

The jatra performance came to an end and the five-day visit was over. Ever since the day Opu went and fetched him, Ajoy had been coming and going as if he were one of the family; and indeed he and Opu had come to regard one another as brothers. Shorbojoya soon began to treat him like a son. He was the same age as Opu, and being moved to pity because he was alone in the world she lavished on him the same fondness as she did on Opu. Durga treated him like a brother too. She learned songs from him and in return told him lots of stories, including some her old auntie had taught her. The three of them drew a large hopscotch court in the yard and played Ganges and Jamuna together; and at meal-times they all watched Ajoy to see that he had enough to eat. As soon as he finished one helping they pressed him to have another. This was the first experience of real home life that Ajoy had ever had. He lived with the jatra party, but there was no one to look after him. Nobody bothered where he slept or what he ate; they just left him to get on as best as he could. He had managed, it is true; but now that he had had this unexpected taste of family love and care he was greedy for more, and was very loath to leave.

Nevertheless he had to go; and when the moment to say goodbye came he stood there awkwardly for a moment, and then he plunged his hand abruptly into his bag and produced five rupees which he proffered to Shorbojoya. They were part of his hard-earned savings. 'Buy Didi a sari when she gets married,' he said.

'No, no, my dear,' said Shorbojoya. 'I couldn't take any money from you. It's good of you to offer it, and I appreciate your offer; but I couldn't possibly take it. Besides you'll need every penny you've got when your own marriage comes along and you have to set up house.'

He tried to insist; but she overbore him and finally got him to put the money back in his bag.

They went to the gate with him and saw him off down the path. In the last moments of conversation he asked them to be sure to write and tell him when Durga was going to be married. Then he turned away. His slender young figure passed into the shadows under the mangosteen tree and was lost to sight as the path took him round a corner behind some bushes. 'How grownup he is!' Shorbojoya thought to herself. 'Yet how sad it is that at his age he should have to go away and work for his living! Supposing it had been Opu.'

TWENTY THREE

When Horihor first returned home from Benares—he was a young man then—people said he had a very bright future before him. Nobody had ever come into their district who knew as much as he did. The fame of his learning was on everybody's tongue and they all said that he would do something outstanding one of these days. As for Shorbojoya, she lived in a golden haze. She was sure that it would not be long now before they sent for her husband and offered him a good post, though her ideas about who 'they' were were no clearer than the surface of the sea in a dense fog. Meanwhile time moved on. Month after month, year after year went by, but no horseman clad in gold braid came galloping up to the house at midnight with a letter appointing him head pundit; nor did any spirit from the Arabian Nights

fly down through the air to change their broken-down house
into a gem-encrusted dream palace. None of this happened;
but day by day the worm-eaten doors creaked more noisily
on their hinges and the ceiling beams sagged lower and lower.
Hope was not as strong now as it had been, but she did not
abandon it altogether. When Horihor was at home he said
something most days to help her keep it alive. 'It'll be all
right,' he would tell her; or 'It won't be very long now'; or
'Things are bound to change soon'. But still nothing happened.

Life can be very sweet, when it is made up of dreams and
fond imaginings. The dreams may be false, the imaginings
carry no promise that they will come to pass; but if none of
them are ever realized they are still life's greatest, its only
treasure. So let them come. Let them live on in our lives for
ever. For in comparison with our dreams, realization may
prove a thing of nought, and its profit an insubstantial trifle.

Horihor had been away from home for three or four
months, and it was many weeks since he had sent them any
money. Durga was not well. She had been having bouts of
vomiting from time to time, and they seemed to be getting
more frequent. Her food upset her. For a day or two she
would be all right, and then quite suddenly the vomiting
would start again.

Shorbojoya was always on at her husband to do something
about getting Durga married. She even nagged him into
writing a line or two to Rajyeshwar Babu, Niren's father, for
her earlier hopes were not yet dead. 'You must be mad,'
Horihor protested, 'to think of worrying rich people like
them. Rajyeshwar Babu will never even consider it.' 'You
never know,' she said. 'In any case it's worth a try. Write one
more letter and let's see what happens. After all Niren was
fond of the child.' When after a month or so no reply came,
she started her nagging all over again.

This time when Horihor left home he said he would make arrangements for them to leave Nishchindipur and go and live somewhere else.

But Shorbojoya's dream home was in Nishchindipur. She had such a clear picture of it in her mind. At one end of the village there were two or three thatched cottages, well-tended and spotlessly clean. Fat milking cows lowed in the shed. The stack was piled high with hay, and the storehouse filled with rice. In the field nearby peas were in flower, and every gust of wind brought their fresh clean scent into the yard. The birds were in full voice too, the blue-throated jay, the tailor bird and the nightingale. Early every morning Opu came in for his breakfast, toasted rice and a glass of foaming milk fresh drawn from the black cow; and then he settled down to do his lessons. Durga was well too; she never had fever. And what is more, everybody knew them; everybody respected them. People from the village came in to take the dust from their feet; and nobody ever passed by because they were poor.

It was only a dream, but it was with her day and night. She was confident that it would come true eventually. Deep within, a voice kept telling her it would. But when? When? Why was it taking so long? Ever since she was a child, when she used to wander about under the rose-apple and the sojne tree, or when she lit the evening lamp and drew patterned words of welcome in their little courtyard, the longing had always been with her that Lakshmi, the goddess of bounty, would leave the print of her red-lacquered foot on the floor and bless her with prosperity in her husband's home. But what was there in this broken-down house and bamboo grove to draw even so much as a glance from the goddess?

Durga had just come into the kitchen. She had in her hand a wild yam she had found somewhere; and she stood there forlornly, hoping against hope that her mother would cook it for her. 'What are you standing there like that for, Durga?' Shorbojoya asked when she saw her. 'You know I can't give you anything to eat today. You had fever again last evening. You know that.'

'That was nothing. Mummy,' Durga replied. 'It wasn't a real fever; it was only a slight cold. Please cook this yam for me, and let me have some rice with it.'

'No,' said her mother firmly. 'You're hungry because you've had fever. You know fever always makes you want to eat. If the fever doesn't come back today and tomorrow. I'll give you something to eat the day after.'

Durga pleaded and coaxed, but her mother would not give way; so finally she dropped the yam and went and sat down. There she tried to argue the matter out with herself. 'I'm quite well today, and the fever won't come back again. If it doesn't and it won't, she may perhaps give me some bread and fried potatoes this evening.' But even as she was reassuring herself she began to yawn. She knew that when she yawned like that it meant that the fever was about to come back. Nevertheless she continued her efforts to argue it away. 'It's only a yawn after all, and a yawn doesn't have to mean anything. I'm not going to have fever; I'm not, I'm not!' Her body was not convinced and she began to feel cold. Ordinarily she would have gone out into the sun, but as that would have seemed like admitting defeat she stayed where she was. 'Feeling cold,' she told herself, 'is something that can happen to anybody. It's nothing to do with fever.' These comforting arguments may have brought some consolation to her mind, but they did not deter the fever. That evening well before sunset it was back with her again, and she went outside and sat in the sun so that her mother would not notice. She felt very despondent, but she did not give up the struggle. 'The fever wouldn't have come if I hadn't spent so much time thinking about it. It's not really fever. I'm just imagining it.' So she went on. The declining sun glowed for a time on the weeds that covered the broken wall, but presently it set and the shadows of evening began to thicken into night. Durga remained where she was, resolutely trying to convince herself that she had not really got fever, or that if she had it would leave her if she stopped thinking about it. Opu's arrival gave her the opportunity to practise not thinking about it. 'Come here and let's talk for a bit,' she said.

They talked of many things. First they recalled a night about a year ago. It was during the monsoon and the rain was pouring down. The two of them sneaked out after dark to steal some tal fruit from Shejbou's garden. While they were walking along the path Durga got a thorn in her foot, and the pain was so sharp that she stepped back and immediately got a thorn in the other foot. Next morning they found out that Shotu had been scattering thorns along the path deliberately, suspecting that they might go after the tal fruit during the night.

Another day, they remembered, an astonishing thing had happened. An old Muslim from East Bengal came to the village, with a large tin box which contained various kinds of coloured glass. He opened it up in front of Jibon Choudhuri's house at the other end of the village. Anyone could have a look, he said, for one pice. Durga was there, standing quite close in fact; but she had no money. All the other children had, and when they paid him a pice he let them look through a long tube which had a sort of crystal in it. They apparently saw wonderful things through the crystal. While some of them were peering into the tin the old Muslim was beating its metal sides rhythmically and talking to encourage others to have a go. 'Come and see Taj Bibi's fast,' he shouted; 'and a fight between a tiger and an elephant.'

271

One by one they all put their eyes to the tube, and when they stepped back Durga asked them what they had seen, and whether they were real things or not. Their answers did not make much sense, and she was left to assume that what they had seen was so strange and wonderful that they could not describe it. When they had all had their look, Durga turned to come away: but the old man called after her, 'Don't you want to have a look, little girl?'

Durga shook her head. 'No, thank you,' she said; 'I haven't any money.'

'Never mind. Come and have a look free. I won't charge you anything,' said the old man.

Durga was shy. Her lips repeated her 'No, thank you', but the eager look in her eyes showed how much she longed to say 'Yes'.

'Come on, come on. There's no harm in it. Why shouldn't you have a look when you can?'

Durga's face lit up, and she went and stood near the box; but she was afraid to touch it. 'Pick up that tube and look down it,' said the man. She brushed back the hair that was hanging over her eyes and tucked it behind her ears so that it would not get in the way, and then she had a look. What she saw she could never describe or even understand. How did those real men get inside that box? There were lots of sahibs and memsahibs; there were houses, and battles, and many things she could not now recall. What an astonishing box it was! She wished that Opu could have had a look at it; but she never saw the man again.

So the two of them talked on happily enough, but nothing could stave off Durga's fever which in time made her feel so ill that she had to get into bed and pull the quilt over her.

Horihor was away from home and taking advantage of his absence, Opu was hardly ever to be seen either. His room looked as if a cyclone had struck it. There were books all over the place. He went out in the early morning with all his cowries in a bag and he did not show up again until it was time for his midday meal. At last Shorbojoya lost patience. 'What a naughty boy you are! You haven't done your lessons once since your father went away. You wait till he comes back and I'll tell him all about it.' This frightened Opu and he went into his room at once. He sat down on the floor and arranged his books in piles all round him. Then he thought he had better do some writing, so he asked his mother for some ground khoyer to put in his inkwell. She always had khoyer by her; it was an astringent powder she used to eat with betel nut. She did not know why it was necessary to mix khoyer with ink, but as she was in a mood to humour him she let him take some. He did a lot of writing, and when he had finished he put his book out in the sun to dry. The ink dried with a brilliant gloss, and Opu was delighted. It had never done that before. 'I'll put some more khoyer in tomorrow and see whether that makes it more glossy,' he said to himself. This time he took the khoyer without saying anything to his mother. Once more he put his book out in the sun, and once more the ink dried with a brilliant gloss, a little brighter in fact that it had been the day before.

Thus began a regular series of raids on his mother's betel nut box, until inevitably one day she caught him at it. 'What on earth can you be doing with lumps of khoyer every day? I don't believe you need it for your writing. Leave it alone.'

Opu was put out at being caught, but he argued back. 'You don't understand,' he said. 'You can't have ink without khoyer. It's absolutely necessary, I tell you. Children here don't do any writing, that's why there's so much khoyer unsold in the shop.'

All this time Opu had been writing a play. He had written

so much that his exercise book was almost full. It was the story of a king who had lost his throne and been banished to the forest by a treacherous minister. His children, Prince Nilambar and Princess Amba, fell into the hands of some bandits and there was a terrific battle. Shortly afterwards the body of the princess was found on the bank of a river. There was an odd character in the play who had the name Shotu. He was condemned to death and executed, though there was no mention of a crime sufficiently heinous as to warrant such a heavy punishment. At the end of the play, by the grace of Narad, the princess was restored to life and married to the faithful general Jibonketu. The cynical critic might have said that, apart from the names of the characters, this play did not differ in any important respect from one of the jatra plays Opu had seen last April. Indeed he might have said that it was a copy of it. Such superficial criticism would however have been quite misleading. Long ago on a still starlit night an ancient poet was lying alone in his hut with a dim light beside him, dreaming of a distant forest where peacocks which resembled blue clouds were singing. If this dream had not come to Kalidas and inspired him to describe clouds in motion, the whole course of literature might have been changed. The lovely words he sang in praise of that forgotten night have passed into the heritage of all succeeding generations, and poets throughout the ages have unwittingly used them as their own.

Fire is born of fire. You cannot light a torch by thrusting it into a heap of cold ashes.

There was a very old book in Opu's study named *Biographies*. It was by Ishwarchandra Vidyasagar. Horihor made it a practice to collect books for the boy from the various places he went to. That is how Opu came by this one. He used to dip into it from time to time, and whenever he did so he was possessed by a longing to grow up like the people whose lives it described. There was Roscoe for instance. On his way to market to sell potatoes he used to sit in a hedgerow studying algebra; and not being able to afford to buy paper he did his sums by scratching on a skin with a blunt stick. Next there was the poor shepherd boy, Duval. He was always out with his sheep, and when he reached the grazing ground he let them wander at will while he sat under a tree poring over maps. Opu wanted to be like them. He did not know what algebra was, but he wanted to study it like Roscoe. Why should he have to go on with handwriting, and tables, and arithmetic problems? He wanted to sit under a lonely tree in a forest in the shade of a hedgerow and spread out his maps, whatever maps were. He made up his mind that he was going to read big books and become a scholar like the men who wrote them. But where was he going to get the big books from? Where could he find maps, or an algebra book, or a Latin grammar? All he had of his own was a book of rhyming tables and a *Third Multiplication Book*.

It did not matter if his mother scolded him. What did matter was where to get the books he wanted to read.

TWENTY FOUR

❧◈❧

The monsoon had already broken. Each evening, as was the custom in this part of the village during the rains, a number of people, men of course, assembled on Onnoda Ray's verandah for a gossip. They talked about anything and everything; but this particular evening the conversation took a more fanciful turn than was usual, even for them. It began with an entirely fictitious story about the local indigo factory, though nobody worried that it did not contain a word of truth; and then went on to a description of a huge lodestone, which was said to stand on the roof of a temple at Puri. It weighed over four hundred pounds, and was so magnetic that it jerked sea-going ships off their course and dashed them against the rocks on the shore. Marvellous fairy tales followed, some of which would not have been out of place in the

276

Arabian Nights. The company were fascinated, and it never occurred to any of them that it was time to go home. Eventually after exploring the wonders of geography they got onto astrology. At this stage Dinu Choudhuri held the floor. He was expounding the contents of an amazing book called *The Anthology of Bhrigu.* 'Look at it yourselves if you don't believe me,' he said. 'All you need to know is the date of your birth, and it will tell you your father's name, your family history, and anything you want to know about the past and the future. It's a wonderful book. There's nothing about the planets and the zodiac you won't find in it somewhere. It will even tell you about your previous births...'

You could have heard a pin drop; until suddenly Rammoy happened to glance outside. 'Goodness!' he exclaimed. 'Look at that storm coming up. We must be off at once, If we don't go home now we shall never get there. I shouldn't be surprised if it's a cyclone. It's black enough. Look at it. Come on. We've got to hurry.'

There was no break in the rain. There was a lull now and then; but not for long. In a few minutes it was pouring heaven's hard again, till the air was grey with it like smoke.

There was not a word from Horihor. A long time ago he had sent them five rupees. That was all; and since then he had neither written nor sent any money. But Shorbojoya still went on hoping. Day after day, as soon as she got up, she told herself that a money-order was bound to come today; but no money-order came. Then one morning, her patience wearing thin, she turned on Opu as if it were his fault. 'It's play, play, play all the time with you. You never do anything else. It doesn't seem to cross your mind to keep an eye open for the postman. Go and sit by the postbox, and when the man comes ask him if there's anything for us.'

Opu was very indignant. 'It's not right of you to say I

don't watch out for him. I do. Ask Punti if you don't believe me. Yesterday the man left some letters at Punti's and a newspaper for us. How do you think the newspaper got here if I didn't bring it? Of course I look out for him.'

The monsoon had really set in now; but the rain did not worry Opu. His mother had told him to look out for the postman, and that is what he was doing. Every day he squatted down on the Rays' verandah and watched; but there was nothing for him to see beyond a few rain-bedraggled pigeons which now and then took off from the roof of Shadhu the blacksmith's thatched cottage and flew across to the parapet above his head. He did not like the thunder though. 'God must be very angry to keep on flashing his eyes like that,' he told himself when the lightning came. 'It'll thunder any minute now.' And he closed his eyes and put his fingers in his ears.

When he got home the verandah was piled high with wild yam leaves. His mother and Durga had been out in the rain all morning collecting them.

'Where did you get all these from, Mummy?' he asked. 'You have got a lot.'

Durga laughed. 'Yes, we have, haven't we? And you were nice and dry indoors while we were out in the rain getting them. They were in the pool near the rose-apple tree next door. There's ever such a lot of water in it. It was right up to my knees. Why don't you go and have a look.'

Next morning Shorbojoya got up very early and went down to the bathing steps. There was no one at the steps except the barber's wife. As soon as Shorbojoya was sure that they were alone, she pulled out a brass tray she had been carrying under her sari. 'Here it is,' she said. 'Have a good look at it. It isn't cheap metal, you know; it's solid brass. You were talking about trays the other day, so I thought I'd bring you one to see. I got it as a wedding present. You can see it's solid brass, can't you? They don't make trays like this nowadays.'

For a while they haggled, but eventually a price was agreed on, and the barber's wife untied the knot in her sari and pulled out an eight-anna piece, which she gave to Shorbojoya. She tucked the tray out of sight under her clothes, and the two of them began to move away. 'You'll be sure not to tell anybody where you got it from, won't you,' pleaded Shorbojoya. She asked her several times to make sure that she understood that nobody else was to hear about it.

Meanwhile the east wind had strengthened and the monsoon was getting heavier. Ditches and ponds were full to overflowing, and water lay knee-deep on some of the paths and in other places too. Day and night the wind screamed through the bamboo grove, at times so violently that it brought the topmost branches swishing down to the ground. There was no break anywhere in the clouds. They changed only to get darker. Massive piles of them, like huge black mountains, tore wildly across the sky from east to west. It was as if the demons of the air and sky were assaulting the citadels of heaven; as if their vast hordes, overspreading land and all space, were advancing battalion after battalion, host upon host, on the wings of the storm, behind an invisible force of chariots; until suddenly the countless army of the gods, faster than human eye could follow, began to launch its cannonade of fiery thunderbolts against them, and the whole sky was ablaze from end to end. The clouds were rent asunder; the great column of the demons split and scattered to the uttermost parts of space; and then the dreadful artillery ceased. Yet the battle was not over; for soon the immortal powers once again shrouded the earth and the heavens with dense, impenetrable blackness.

For four or five days it went on. The hurricane howled with demonic force day and night. The water climbed higher and higher up the river banks; creeks and gullies were awash; houses were already collapsing; and under the trees where the village cattle were tied, in the bamboo groves and the forest, and from the eaves of their homes, the torrent poured down incessantly. There was no bird song, and even the insects were still. The only sound was the roar of the wind and the lashing and hammering of the rain.

Opu was standing on the verandah. He was trying to dry his hair. 'The water's come right up into the bamboo grove, Didi,' he shouted. 'Come and have a look.'

Durga would have loved to; but she could not. She was too weak to get up. She was lying in bed with a quilt over her. 'How much water?' she asked faintly.

'It's knee-deep under the tamarind tree,' he told her. 'But you'll be able to see it for yourself tomorrow when your fever's better.' Suddenly Opu began to cry. Even the excitement of the storm could not make him forget that he was hungry. 'Where's Mummy?' he sobbed. There was not a grain of rice in the house, except for a small scraping in the pan which had already been baked and was now quite stale. 'I can't bear it, Mummy. I'm so hungry, Mummy. Do give me something to eat.'

'Don't go on like that, darling,' Shorbojoya replied. 'I'll do the best I can to soften what baked rice there is and you can have that. But I can't do any cooking. Everything's sopping wet; and the fireplace is flooded.' Presently however she smiled and produced a curious looking creature from under her sari. 'What do you think I've got here?' she said, showing it to Opu. 'It's a koi fish. I caught it in the bamboo grove. It was walking on its ears. The river's so high that the fish are coming out. You know that low-lying piece of land where

280

the betel grows? It's joined up with the river, and the fish are coming out that way.'

Weak though she was, Durga threw off her quilt and sat straight up in bed. 'Let me have a look too, Mummy. Did you really mean it when you said it was walking on its ears? I wonder if there are any more of them.' This gave Opu an idea, and he wanted to dash off and find out, rain or no rain; and it was all Shorbojoya could do to prevent him.

'Never mind,' said Durga. 'We can go and have a look tomorrow when my fever's gone down a bit. We might catch a fish in the bamboo grove.... A fish in the bamboo grove! I wonder how on earth it got there,' she thought to herself. 'How extraordinary! And walking on its ears too! I've never seen fish walking on their ears. And there might be another one! I don't suppose Mummy looked very carefully. If there are any more I'll catch them tomorrow. My fever's bound to be better by then.'

It was very dark outside. There was no moon; and night and cloud had coalesced into an undifferentiated blackness which was so dense that even the bamboo clump near the house and the trees in the orchard next door for all their nearness, were completely hidden from view. Opu and his mother were sitting on the edge of Durga's bed; but Shorbojoya was lost in thought. 'I don't suppose it can possibly happen now,' she was saying to herself, 'though he did seem to have become fond of her before he had to go away. I wonder if he'll ever write us a letter. No, he won't now. I'm just one of those unlucky ones; and things like that don't happen to me. And the child's like me, unfortunately. But it would be wonderful if he did.'

Meanwhile Durga and Opu had got into a noisy argument. Opu moved along the bed and sat closer to his mother. The wind had made him very cold, but he was laughing in spite of his discomfort. 'How does that poem go, Mummy?' he asked her. 'You remember it, don't you? It begins, "She was grinding black spices, her hair on the ground..."'

Durga chimed in, 'Her mother had left her and couldn't be found.'

'Don't be so silly. "Her mother had left her and couldn't be found." It doesn't go like that at all, Mummy; does it?' But the line sounded so funny as he said it that he burst out laughing again.

His childish laughter hurt Shorbojoya. 'I haven't got five sons, or even four,' she said to herself. 'He's the only one I've got. Yet when he asks me for food I can't give him any. What an ill-fated creature I am! I can't give him ghee or luchies or sweets; I haven't got any rice for him either except for that stale stuff that's left over in the pan. And the house is in ruins too; but how can we ever hope to repair it when we haven't got enough money to keep body and soul together! Good God,' she prayed, 'grant that he may live to be a man and that all this misery may end for him then.'

Presently she pulled herself together. 'Enough of that!' she said to herself, and began to tell them stories. She talked about the year she and their father had first come to live in Nishchindipur. There was a very heavy monsoon then too, and the river rose so high that a big cargo boat ran aground on the path near the Mukherji's house.

'How big was the boat, Mummy?' Opu asked.

'It was a very big boat. You've seen those up-country boats that come here with lime and cement, haven't you? It was as big as one of them.'

Durga's mind was wandering. 'Mummy,' she said, 'do you know how to do your hair in four plaits?'

Late that night Shorbojoya woke up. Opu was calling her. 'Come quickly, Mummy. It's raining on me.' She got up and lit a lamp. The rain was hammering down, and the broken roof was leaking in several places at once. She pulled his bedding to one side. Durga was sleeping heavily. Shorbojoya leaned over and felt her body with her hand. It was very hot. Her quilt was saturated. 'Durga!' she called. 'Durga, Durga! Listen to me, darling. Sit up a minute. I want to move your bedding. Do sit up, my pet. You're absolutely wet through.'

Durga and Opu fell off to sleep again at once; but sleep would not come to Shorbojoya. The night was pitch black; the rain was teeming down, and she was sick with fear. She was sure that something terrible was going to happen. Horihor was away, and she was worried about him too. 'Why doesn't he write?' she asked herself again and again. Even if he can't send any money he might write. He's never left me so long without a letter before. Heaven grant that he's not ill. Mother Siddhesvari, bring me news of him soon. I'll make you an offering of anything I have if you will.'

Next morning the rain abated just a little, though it was still very wet. When Shorbojoya looked outside she saw that the ditch in the bamboo grove was full of water. Nevertheless she decided to risk going down to the bathing steps. On the way she caught sight of Nibaron's mother and called out after her. 'Just a minute, Nibaron's mother,' she shouted, and began to hurry after her; but when she caught her up she found it was very difficult to broach the subject she had on her mind. 'A few weeks ago,' she blurted out nervously, 'you said something, didn't you, about taking my Brindabon wrap for your little boy. I wonder ... I mean to say ... do you still want it by any chance?' It was not easy for her to plead with a low-caste woman.

'I might do,' was the reply. 'You've still got it, have you? Good! But of course, you know, I'd have to have a look at it first. Just let this storm stop and I'll bring my son round to see whether it is really what we want. What sort of a wrap is it? Is it new or only second-hand?'

'Yes, I've still got it. It's at home in the house. Why not come and look at it now? It's not absolutely new, but it's never been worn. I just washed it once and put it away. But ... there's another thing....' She paused again. 'Didn't I hear that you were husking some rice in your house?'

The other did not answer her question directly. 'Rice!' she said. 'How can anyone keep rice dry in weather like this? Yes, I've got some, but only enough to tide us over. That's all.'

'Please,' said Shorbojoya, 'do you think you could possibly let me have a little. The weather's so bad and I haven't got anybody to go to the bazar for me. I don't want much. I've been round to our neighbours, but they can't let me have any, even though I offered to buy it from them. I don't like to worry you ... but I don't know where to turn to for help.'

'Yes,' said Nibaron's mother, 'I'll go and get you some. I think I can spare a little. But I don't know whether people like you will be able to eat our kind of rice. It's terribly coarse.'

Shorbojoya had boiled some neem bark for Durga, but the child could not stomach it. Her fever would not come down, and there was no medicine to give her, nor special food. Neither was there a doctor to treat her, not even a village doctor. 'Let me have some biscuits please,' she begged. 'Some of those salted ones. I feel I could eat them.' But there were no biscuits in the house. Not even sago.

Heavy rain set in again that evening, and the storm became even more violent than before. It was a terrible night, and they were completely cut off. Nobody could have got to the house even if they had wanted to. The only sound Shorbojoya could hear was the din of the storm and the rain on the roof. The floods were spreading, and the fury of the east wind increased as night approached. Black strands of clouds writhed across the sky like infuriated serpents, until they disappeared from sight in the all-pervading blackness of the dark. It was terrifying. She could not hear herself speak because of the rain and the howling of the wind, every gust of which drove streams of water through cracks in the broken doors and windows; and hard though she worked to stuff the holes with rags and torn sacking, the rain still came in. There was no shelter for them against the onslaught of the storm.

She fell asleep in time, out of sheer fatigue; but not for long. The rain got heavier and heavier. It woke her again, and she got up and sat on the edge of the bed. Still the same hammering on the roof! And the hurricane as it pounded against the walls screamed like a horde of raging demons. With every blast the house shuddered as though the next moment it would crash down and bury them in its ruins. She was panic-stricken, frenzied in her powerlessness. What could a lone woman do to save the children; and there was no one to whom she could turn for help, or even to hear if she called. The house was at the far end of the village, cut off from the other houses and hemmed in by the bamboo grove and the forest. 'O God,' she prayed, 'let me die if I must, but save them. What can I do on a night like this?' The prayer seemed to calm her nerves for a moment, and she began to think out a plan, something she could do to save them. 'If the house does fall,' she told herself, 'the walls will give way first; and that will make a noise and give me time to drag them out into the shed.' Drag them indeed! How could she? She was not strong enough even to sit up for long at a time. She was exhausted physically and mentally. For days now a few boiled leaves were all she had had to eat. The meagre scraps of food she had been able to acquire she had given to the children. She was starving; and that, with all her worry and terror, had

285

brought her to the end of her strength. Her head throbbed with pain, and she could do no more.

Yet the storm raged on, mounting from fury to fury, and torturing time stood still. Suddenly outside there was a long drawn-out sound of something being torn in two, and then a crash. What could it be? The great hammer seemed to be beating against the house more violently than before. Beside herself with fear, and trembling in every limb, she wrenched open the front door and peered into the darkness, as if by looking she could know what the wind would do next. In an instant she was saturated from head to foot, hair, clothes, everything; and for a moment even the thunder of the rain on the roof became inaudible in the orgiastic ululation of the gale. She looked, but saw nothing. There was nothing to see: no sky, no tree, no cloud, no movement, no night even, only black nothingness, opaque and impenetrable; blackness peopled by hordes of demons, who snarled about her like beasts of prey and gnashed at her with their teeth, invisibly. Who could they be but the minions and precursors of the Ultimate Destroyer, as they rushed inexorably on with terror and diabolical speed to consummate their task of universal destruction, involving earth and sky in a bestial cacophony, now hissing, now roaring, now stridently shrieking, now thundering forth the deep dull boom of death? The earth shuddered beneath her feet, its rocky foundation grated and groaned in the almighty churn. Then once more, as she stood there, the hurricane's blast! Surely this must be the end! It ripped through the bamboos and hurled itself against the battered house with sickening explosive thuds. This must be the voice of the Destroyer himself, Shiva, whom nothing, neither pity nor drunken intoxication, could deflect from his purpose, or turn aside from his duty, predestined before the beginning of time, to descend upon the earth in utter annihilation, leaving no more of the smiling land than remains of a star which disintegrates in endless space and hurtles down to the depth of chaos below.

Numb with horror for an endless moment, the poor woman at last with a despairing spasm dragged the door shut, and cowered beside it. What could she do? Nothing! If a wild beast broke in for shelter, or a thief, what could she do? Nothing! She was alone with disaster, for outside was only the bamboo grove and the forest where nobody lived.

Yet the children slept on. The rain was pouring into the room; it was already lapping about her feet as she stood there. She slowly groped her way to Opu's bed and put her hand on his sleeping body. He was wet through, his coverlet no more than a sopping rag. Would the night never end? There were some matches under her mattress. They at least were dry and she managed to get a lamp lit. Then she called to the children 'Opu, sit up. You must listen to me, my darling. Do sit up... Durga, turn on to your side and move over. The rain's pouring on you. Move over to the other side of the bed.'

Opu sat up and peered round sleepily; but almost at once he lay down and was asleep again. There was a loud crash, this time in the house itself. Shorbojoya opened the back door to see what had happened. There was nothing between her and the darkness outside. The kitchen wall had fallen. 'It will be the house next, I suppose,' she told herself. 'And if it is there's nothing I can do about it.' There was no one to hear her, except God; so she prayed. 'Good Lord, please bring us safely through this night, and guard the children.'

It was not fully day yet. The storm had passed, though a light rain was still falling. Nilmoni Mukherji's wife was just going out to the shed to see how the cows were when she heard some one banging on the back door. She opened it, and there to her surprise was Shorbojoya. 'Please call your husband,' she panted. 'Ask him to come to the house at once. It's Durga, she's ill.'

'Durga? Why, what's the matter with her?'

'She's had fever now for several days running. It comes and goes. It's malaria. But last night her temperature went very high, and you know what a terrible night it was. Do call him at once, dear.'

Shorbojoya's hair was tangled and soaking wet. Her eyes were red with sleeplessness and fatigue; and she looked completely distraught. 'Don't worry, my dear,' said Nilmoni Mukherji's wife kindly. 'Just wait here, and I'll go and call him straight away. Then I'll come back to the house with you. The roof of the cattle shed came down in the storm. What a night it was, to be sure! I've never known one like it. My husband was out until very late looking after the cows. I expect he's in bed now. But just wait. I'll go and call him.'

She did not take long, and soon the whole family, Nilmoni Mukherji, his wife, their son Phoni and their two daughters, were on their way to Opu's house. The demons, who through-out the night had rocked, battered and almost overwhelmed the entire village, had vanished down the paths of the sky, but the earth was littered with the havoc they had caused, broken branches, leaves, roof thatching and bamboo fronds. In one place an entire clump of bamboos had been levelled to the ground and blocked the path they were going along.

'Goodness, Daddy! What a mess the place is in!' said Phoni. 'Look, those leaves came from that English tree on the main road to Nawabganj!' And as he kicked his way through the debris he pulled out the body of a dead sparrow from under some bamboo leaves.

Opu was sitting by Durga's side when Nilmoni Mukherji

entered the house. One had only to look at his face to know how worried he was.

'How is she?' Nilmoni asked.

'Oh, Uncle! She's talking nonsense.'

'Move to one side, and let me feel her pulse. Yes, her temperature is high; but I'm sure there's nothing to be alarmed about. Phoni, hurry off to Nawabganj and call Doctor Shorot. See that he comes back with you.' Phoni went at once, and Nilmoni turned and said something to Durga; but she did not reply. She was unconscious.

'What a mess the house is in!' he said looking round. 'It's still flooded after last night's rain. No, my dear,' he said to Shorbojoya, 'it's not your fault; but don't you think it would be better if you all moved over to our house for a while? Just look at the condition the house is in. That wretched husband of yours is a most unpractical man; though I can't imagine why he should let the house get into this state. But that's the sort of man he is, I suppose.'

'Repair the house you say,' his wife blurted out. 'How could he? He's got other things to think about. They haven't got any food to eat. That's why he's had to go away. He wouldn't have left them like this if he'd had any money. But it's Durga I'm worried about. To think that she was lying in wet clothes all night. Go and put on some hot water, and get the window open.'

In due course the doctor arrived. He examined Durga and prescribed some medicine. 'She's had a high temperature,' he said; 'but she'll be all right now. Just give her this medicine and keep wet compresses on her head.' Nobody knew where Horihor was, so they sent a letter to the only address they had.

Next day the rain stopped, and there was no trace of the storm. The clouds lifted and cleared away. Nilmoni Mukherji came over twice during the day to see how things were; but

Durga's fever went still higher, and though the doctor was sent for a second time he could do nothing to bring it down. Another letter was sent to Horihor.

Opu sat by Durga's side putting wet cloths to her head. Now and then he spoke to her. 'Didi, can you hear me? Oh, Didi, do say something to me. Tell me how you are.' It was as though there was a veil between them. She seemed to be talking. He could see her lips move; but when he bent down to listen he could not hear anything, at least nothing he could understand.

In the evening the fever left her, and for the first time after many hours she opened her eyes and looked round. She was extremely weak; and when she spoke it was in such a faint whisper that they could barely make out what she was trying to say. Shorbojoya was doing something about the house, but Opu remained sitting by her, when she suddenly looked at him and said, 'What time is it?'

'It's late now; but the sun's been out today. It's still shining on the coconut tree. Can you see it?'

She did not reply, nor did she say anything more for some time, so Opu went to look out of the window. He was happy to see the sun again, and stood there watching the last rays in the tree-tops.

'Opu, come here a minute.'

'What is it, Didi?' Opu asked, and he put his ear very close to her lips.

'Will you take me to see a train one day?'

'Of course I will,' he replied. 'But I'll do more than that. As soon as you're better I'll ask Daddy to let us both have a ride in a train and go and bathe in the Ganges.'

The next day and night passed. There might never have been a storm. Everything was bright in the August sun. Nilmoni Mukherji was sitting at home massaging his body with oil before going down to the river for a bath. He had not been there for several days. Suddenly his wife rushed into the room. 'Come quickly,' she said breathlessly. 'They're crying at Opu's house. I can hear them.'

They ran together. Shorbojoya was bending over Durga. 'Look at me, Durga,' she was screaming. 'Oh, my darling, open your eyes and look at me.'

'What's happened?' said Nilmoni as soon as he got inside. 'Move away from her. You're keeping the air from her. Move away and let me have a look.' Shorbojoya might not have heard him. She only went on screaming. 'What's happened to her? Tell me. Why won't she look at me?'

Durga did not open her eyes again.

From time to time the hand of eternity breaks through the blue veil of the heavens and beckons to a child, and the little one, no longer willing to wait, tears itself away from the breast of Mother Earth and is lost for ever down a road that knows no returning. In that dark evening hour of her sick and restless life Durga had heard those summons, and leaving the paths she loved so well, she commenced a new journey, down a highway her feet had not trodden before.

Doctor Shorot was sent for again. 'Yes,' he said, 'this sometimes happens during a severe attack of malaria. If the temperature comes down too quickly it can cause heart-failure. I had a similar case a few days ago in Dasghara.'

Within half an hour the people of the village were crowding into the yard.

TWENTY FIVE

❦

Horihor did not receive either of Shorbojoya's letters. The first place he went to when he left home was Krishnagar. He did not know anybody there, but he told himself that as it was a large market town something or other was bound to turn up. To begin with his hopes ran high, for a man he met in the street told him that some of the lawyers and landlords in the vicinity used to employ scholars to read the poems of the Chandi saga in their homes, on a daily or monthly contract. He was elated by such a fine prospect and stayed on in the town for a fortnight; but no appointment came his way, and the little money he had brought with him was by then exhausted.

He was now in dire straits. It was a strange place, and there was no one to whom he could turn for help; and what is more he could no longer pay the rent of his lodging and had to vacate it. In the afternoon however he heard by chance that there was a Krishna temple nearby where wandering Brahmins who could not afford rented accommodation were given free board and lodging. He went there at once and explained his circumstances to the secretary who agreed to take him in and allotted him a corner in a poky little room in the temple. It was a squalid, sordid place. Opium addicts and other riffraff flocked there at night and made such a din that sleep was impossible; and what was worse than the place was, he soon discovered, the rendezvous of a number of women who certainly did not go there to worship Krishna. He was most unhappy. The whole of the next day he spent going round from house to house calling upon senior lawyers and rich citizens, but when he got back to the temple in the evening he found that his bedding had been pushed to one side and that some low-caste fellow was asleep and snoring in the corner that had been allotted to him. He had to go outside and find room for himself on the verandah. Night after night it was the same, until at last he lost his temper and had words with the opium smokers who were lying about in his room. They were furious, and next morning they went and reported him to the secretary. The secretary sent for Horihor and told him that according to the temple rules no one was permitted to live there for more than three days, and that as he had already been there longer than that he would have to leave and find lodging elsewhere. Horihor collected his things and left the temple that afternoon. He had nowhere to go and wandered about aimlessly, until eventually he came across a quiet spot on the bank of the River Khore. Here he laid out his bedding and went down into the water to wash. He had had nothing to eat all day.

Next day, tired and hungry, he sat down to rest in an open shed. It was a wood-merchant's store. Presently he began to chant a hymn or two in praise of Krishna, and the wood-merchant, who was a pious man, was pleased and gave him a rupee. Horihor went off at once to the market to change the coin and when he had done so he bought himself a few pice worth of baked rice and curds. When however it came to eating he could hardly get the food down: he was so troubled at heart about Shorbojoya and the children. He had left them only enough money for ten days, and that was two months ago, How were they managing? he kept asking himself. They must be starving; and all because he, their father, had not been able to send them anything. He remembered Opu saying goodbye to him at the gate, and begging him to bring a copy of the *Padmapuran* back with him. How fond the lad was of reading! Whenever he was alone in the house he used to delve into the box in his father's room for some book or other. Horihor could always tell that somebody had been at the box from the untidy condition it was left in. Opu did not know how the books were arranged, so he had to rummage about until he found what he was looking for. No, indeed, it was not hard for Horihor to know who the thief was, or how fond of reading that particular thief was.

Some time ago, before he left home on this trip, Horihor managed to borrow a printed copy of *Padmapuran* from someone he knew in Jugipara and Opu appropriated it at once. He read it every day. Horihor remembered how thrilled he was by the episode which tells of Shiva going fishing at Kuchuri, and how disappointed he had been when just after he had finished that part of the story, his father had to take the book from him, to return it to its owner who was asking for it. At first Opu flatly refused to part with it. 'You can't have it till I've finished reading it,' he said passionately; and

294

Horihor had to insist. 'You must let me have it,' he said. 'It's their book and they want it back.' Even so Opu was not for giving way; and it was not until Horihor had promised to bring him a copy for himself when he came back from his next trip that he finally handed the book over. The promise once given could not be forgotten. Opu reminded him too frequently. And he could see him now, standing at the gate and shouting after him, 'You won't forget to bring me that book, will you, Daddy? You promised that you would; so you must, you must!' Durga's requests were not at all intellectual. She wanted a pale green sari and some nice bright lac to put on her feet. He would get them all if he could, but there were more important things to do first. They must have food to eat. The merchant allowed him to spend the night in the wood shed, but he could not sleep. He tossed about all night, worrying how he was to get some money to send them.

Another day dawned, and he went out on to the road again, going he knew not where; until presently he found himself outside the iron gate of a large red-bricked house. He looked at the house for some time, trying to make up his mind to go in and wondering whether it would do any good if he did. At last he opened the gates and walked up the drive mechanically, and without hope. He could see a well-furnished verandah room with marble steps leading up to it. On either side of the steps were flower tubs, some stone statues and a palm tree or two; and on the top step lay a door mat. In the sitting room a middle-aged gentleman was reading a newspaper, and when he heard steps on the drive, he put down his paper and sat up straight to see who it was. It was nobody he knew. 'Who are you?' he shouted roughly, and in language which is only used to low-caste people. 'What do you want?'

Horihor replied politely, 'I am a Brahmin and a Sanskrit

scholar. I sing the *Chandi* poems and the holy *Bhagavat* and the *Gita*.'

The lordly gentleman was not in the least interested in Horihor's qualifications, but when he heard that he was a Brahmin, he adopted a more respectful form of address. Nevertheless he made him understand clearly that his time was valuable and that he was not disposed to waste it on such idle frivolities. 'No,' he said finally, 'there are no arrangements here for the sort of entertainment you mention. I suggest you go somewhere else.'

Horihor was desperate. 'Please, sir! I'm a stranger here and absolutely destitute. I'm in great trouble and for many days ...'

The man did not let him finish; but with a gesture which made it clear that he wanted to get rid of him as quickly as possible, he lifted up the cushion on which he had been reclining and took something out from under it. 'Here you are then, take this,' he said, stretching out his hand. 'This is all I can let you have. Take it.'

If the offer had been expressed differently Horihor would have taken the coin which was proffered to him. He had often done so before. But he could not this time. 'Please keep it, sir,' he said courteously. 'I do not accept money in this way from anybody. I'm a reader of holy books, and for that I accept a fee. So please keep your money; I can't take it.'

Horihor's luck changed after this encounter. When he got back to the wood-merchant's shed where he had spent the night, he met a man who told him about a possible opening for him. 'A prosperous moneylender,' the man said, 'is looking for a Brahmin to conduct the domestic rites for his family. He lives in a village just outside Krishnagar; and it's likely to be a permanent appointment.' The wood-merchant, who heard what was said, thought the report was worth investigating, so Horihor went off at once. The master of the house took a liking to him and gave him the post. He provided him with a room to live in, and treated him with hospitality and kindness.

The Durga Puja, the great autumnal festival, came a few days after Horihor had taken up his new post. The master of the house allowed him to go home for it, and as he was leaving gave him ten rupees as his fee and his return train fare. On his way to the station at Krishnagar he dropped in to say goodbye to the wood-merchant, who gave him another five rupees. It was a beautiful day. The fragrance of warm sunshine was in the air, and only to look at the blue cloudless sky was enough to make the heart glad. The monsoon was over, and the fresh green plants and trees filled the traveller with joy and lightened him every step. Shrubs bright with flowers swayed to and fro on either side of the line as the train rushed by; but Horihor's thoughts were only of the home the train was rushing him to. In the market at Ranaghat, where he had to change, he bought some clothes for his wife and daughter. Durga loved red-bordered saris, so he got her one and some leaves of lac: but search as he would he could not find a copy of *Padmapuran* for Opu, and so instead he bought the poem about Kalketu and the goddess Chandi. He purchased one or two things for the house too. Shorbojoya had asked for a wooden rolling-pin; so he got her one.

He left the train at a little country station a few miles from Nishchindipur and started to walk. It was evening before he reached the village, but he did not meet anybody he knew as he made his way through it. In any case he was too excited to want to stop and talk. He wanted to get home. 'What a mess the place is in!' he thought to himself as he approached the gate. 'That clump of bamboos has fallen right across the wall, and Bhubon hasn't bothered to cut it away.

What a nuisance!' But once in the yard he called out happily as he always did. 'Durga, Opu! Where are you?'

Shorbojoya came up to him quietly and took the heavy bundle from his hands and put it down. 'Come inside,' she said. 'Come in.' Horihor noticed that she was more than usually quiet, but it did not occur to him that anything was wrong. His imagination was carrying him on too quickly to the moment when the children would come in. 'They'll be in presently,' he thought. 'Durga will have a smile all over her face and she'll say, "What's in your bundle, Daddy?" And then I shall open it for them and show them what I've brought, a sari for Durga and some lac for her feet, and the Kalketu story for Opu, and a tin train too. How their eyes will bulge!' He could see it all as if it was already happening. Then he went into the house and said to Shorbojoya, 'I've got you a lovely rolling-pin; it's made of jackfruit wood.' He looked round the house, went from room to room, and then slowly a feeling of disappointment began to creep into his eager and delighted voice. 'Where are the children? Are they both out of the house? They can't be surely!' He sounded impatient.

Shorbojoya could bear it no longer. She burst out crying. 'Durga,' she sobbed. 'My poor, poor Durga! We've lost the poor darling. She's gone and left us. Where have you been all this time?'

By long established custom the Durga festival was celebrated at the Gangulis' house. Everyone in the village was invited, and no one, not even the poorest, was excluded from the banquet. It was an elaborately organized affair. The workmen came at the appointed time and erected the image of the goddess; painters decorated it; gardeners decked it with garlands and men of the bauri caste brought piles of lotuses from the

Modhukhali pond. Dinu, the flute player from Ansmali, came and played as he had done for many years past; and the tune he played was one which expresses the joy of the earth that with the dawn the goddess Durga would come home again. It is a song of loving welcome to autumn, with its new rice and budding shephalika flowers, when the migrating birds come flying in over the Himalayas and the dark goddess's evening lotuses are fragrant and heavy with dew.

Opu was wearing his new clothes. He was going with his father to the banquet. His long untidy hair hung over his face and concealed the eager look in his eyes but he did not say anything; only the breeze through the door murmured his impatience to be gone. In time they set out, but as they walked Horihor's thoughts were not on the festival. 'Run ahead of me,' he said to Opu. 'It's getting late.'

The Gangulis' courtyard, brilliant with its festival decorations, was thronged with children, all of them happy and smiling. Straightaway Opu spotted Shotu and his brother. They were dressed in bright orange clothes. And how attractive Ranu looked with her green sari and pretty hair! Shunoyoni, the daughter of the Ganguli family, had her hair done up, with a night-scented rose in it. She was in the festival room talking and laughing with five or six other girls, whom Opu did not know. They looked like visitors; and their clothes made him think that they had come from Calcutta. He could not take his eyes off them. Then suddenly he heard someone shouting from outside. 'Why isn't the big marquee up yet? Get on with it at once or there'll be trouble. The Brahmins' banquet is due to start at five o'clock. You know that.'

TWENTY SIX

❦

The days passed quickly, and before they realized the cold weather was over. Ever since Durga's death Shorbojoya had been nagging her husband to leave the village, and Horihor for his part had made an occasional enquiry here and there, but nothing that suited them turned up; and Shorbojoya had practically given up hope.

Half way through the cold weather the widow of Horihor's cousin, Nilmoni Ray, had come to live in the village. Her own house, which stood in the next compound to Horihor's, was no more than a heap of rubble completely overgrown with jungle, so she went to live at Bhubon Mukherji's. Horihor wanted her to come and stay with them and did his best to persuade her, but she refused. She had brought her daughter Otoshi and her younger son Shunil with her. Her elder son

300

Shuresh was at school in Calcutta and would not be arriving till the summer vacation. Otoshi was fourteen, and Shunil eight. Shunil was not a particularly handsome child. Otoshi on the other hand was pretty enough though no one could have called her beautiful. Until his death Nilmoni Ray had worked at the commissariat in Lahore, where both children had been born and brought up. Consequently they were strong and healthy, as upcountry children usually are.

When they first arrived Shorbojoya was always in and out to see her rich cousin. She treated her with great respect, especially when she found out that she had inherited ten thousand rupees in cash and government bonds. She deferred to her in everything and did all she could to get on friendly terms; but in the end it penetrated even her dull brain that Shunil's mother did not intend to have anything to do with her. From the beginning she kept the family of her poor cousin Horihor at a distance and ultimately Shorbojoya had to admit defeat. In everything she said and did, however trivial, Shunil's mother made it quite clear that Shorbojoya was not of their class and could not therefore expect to be treated as an equal. Nilmoni Ray had always held a senior post and his family had become used to an entirely different kind of life. They talked like rich people, dressed like rich people and behaved like rich people. The children wore expensive clothes, and were never allowed to get dirty. Their hair was tidy and well combed. Otoshi never went anywhere without a necklace and gold bangles on; and she wore gold rings in her ears. None of them would dream of going out in the morning until they had had a cup of tea and something to eat. Neither did they do any housework: there was an upcountry servant to do all that. Could anything have been more unlike the way Shorbojoya ran her poor household?

Shunil's mother would not allow her son to go out to play with the children in the village, not even with Opu, lest he and his sister should learn unpleasant habits from contact with such rough and badly brought-up youngsters. She had of course no intention of staying in the village permanently. The only reason she had for being there at all was that she had property in the district and wanted to be on the spot while it was being surveyed. Part of her land was leased to Bhubon Mukherji who for that reason put a couple of rooms on the west side of his house at her disposal; but they cooked and ate separately. Bhubon Mukherji was a rich man and his family lived in pretty much the same way as she did; but Shorbojoya she regarded as beneath her notice.

Nilmoni Ray's elder son Shuresh came back from Calcutta for the Swing Festival holidays and stayed with his mother for about ten days. He was about the same age as Opu, and in the fifth class of his English school. He was a dark boy, but because he exercised a lot his skin shone healthily and he was strong and well set-up; so that though he was only a little older than Opu he looked both in appearance and build more like a boy of fifteen or sixteen. His general attitude to the village was the same as his mother's and he kept himself apart from the boys round about, most of whom he looked down on with studied contempt. His only associate was Ramnath Ganguli at whose house he spent practically all of his time. Ramnath, who lived at the other side of the village, was in the same class as Shuresh at school.

The house next door had been derelict and overgrown with weeds and creepers for longer than Opu could remember; but he knew it was his cousins' real home and that made him feel strongly drawn towards them. He knew too that Shuresh was about his own age and that he went to school in Calcutta; and as the days went by he looked forward more and more

302

eagerly to meeting him when he came home for his holidays. Shuresh came, but he took no notice whatsoever of Opu; and, what is more, he indicated quite clearly by his tone of voice and general attitude that he considered himself far superior to village boys. Opu was shy and silent in any case and this treatment dumb-cowed him completely; so that even though Shuresh was very little older than he was he kept away from him as much as he could.

Opu had not been to a proper school, and when Shuresh asked him what school he went to he said he was studying at home with his father. One day during the Swing Festival a number of boys were sitting together under the jolpai tree which grew by the steps which led down to the Gangulis' tank. Shuresh who happened to be there was interrogating them about this and that with an air that could not have been more lordly if he had just won the first prize in a world philosophy debate. To Opu he said, 'Tell me what the boundaries of India are.' (He used the English word 'boundaries'.) 'That's geography, you know,' he continued, using the English word 'geography'. 'Have you done geography?'

Opu did not understand what he was talking about, so he kept quiet. Shuresh pressed him further. 'What about sums? Do you know how to do decimals and fractions?' (Again the English words.)

Opu had never heard of them. But what did it matter? There were lots of books in that tin box of his father's. There was an Everyday Worship, a book called *Prakritik Bhugol*— Opu did not know that bhugol was the Bengali word for geography—an old style arithmetic primer, and a torn copy of *Birangana* and the Mahabharat, which belonged to his mother. All these were there, and what is more Opu had read them, not once but often. Indeed when he had nothing else

to read he read them over again. His father was always on
the look-out for books for him to read. Horihor thirsted, as
a sick man for water, to bring up his son to be a scholar and
a pundit. He was poor and could not afford to send him away
to school; neither was he himself well educated. Nevertheless
whenever he was at home he kept Opu by his side and taught
him what he could. He told him stories, and though he had
forgotten all his arithmetic he went through the old primers
so that he could teach Opu how to do sums. If he found
anything which he thought would increase the boy's knowledge
he either gave it to him to read or read it to him himself.
In the past Horihor had taken the newspaper *Bangabashi*, and
there was a large collection of old copies in his room, carefully
stored in bundles so that Opu could read them when he was
old enough. He could read them now; but there were no new
copies for him because Horihor had not been able to afford
the subscription and the newspaper man had stopped delivering
them. Opu had been most enthusiastic about the *Bangabashi*,
and when the day's games were over he used to sit on Bhubon
Mukherji's verandah and wait breathlessly for the newspaper
man to come with the latest issue. Horihor knew this, and
it cut him to the heart to know that he could not give the
boy what he so longed to have.

Still the old copies were there, and Opu learned a lot
from them. He was especially fond of the stories, which he
used to repeat afterwards to Potu. There were stories about
Liuca and Raphael, about the volcanic eruption on the island
of Martinique, and a thrilling tale about a magician who
could turn anything into gold; to mention only some. Yet for
all this he had never been to school. He had done arithmetic
only as far as simple division. He knew no history, no grammar,
and he had never even heard about geometry; and in English
he had only got to the *Horse* in Book I.

Shorbojoya's ideas about Opu's future were somewhat different. She was only a village girl, and it did not seem to her that going to school was at all a necessary part of a boy's upbringing. Nobody in her family had even so much as seen a school. Her husband was priest to a number of households, and it was her main ambition that in due course her son would be taken on in his father's stead and continue the family tradition. There was another possibility too; or so she hoped. The senior Brahmin priest in the village, Dinu Bhottacharji, was getting on in years now, and none of his sons seemed cut out to follow in their father's footsteps. Ranu's mother, Gokul's wife and the mistress of the Ganguli household had all of them told her that when the old man was no longer with them they would like Opu to help with the Manasa and Lakshmi ceremonies. The women of the village wanted Opu too. He was a simple, handsome and good-looking boy, and they preferred him to that opium-eating son of Dinu Bhottacharji, Bhombol. They told her so whenever she met them in the village. It was only natural therefore that her hopes for the boy should be in this direction. How could it be otherwise? She had been born into one poor family and married into another. How could she possibly conceive of any better future for her son? If only it could come to pass, she told herself, her brightest dream would have come true.

One afternoon a number of women had gathered in Bhubon Mukherji's house to play cards, and Shorbojoya took the opportunity to raise the subject of Opu and what she hoped for him. She began ingratiatingly by addressing all the senior women directly by name, and then went on, 'If you all agree with me and would be so kind as to help me with it, I want Opu to receive the sacred thread this coming February, and then he will be qualified to take part in some of our village ceremonies. If this can be done I shall not have to worry about him any more. There are, as you know, some eight or ten households that my husband goes to; and if in addition to these the lad were taken on by the Gangulis for their religious ceremonies, it would...'

Shunil's mother interrupted her, smiling round the room in her superior way. 'My son,' she said, 'is going to read law when he grows up. His uncle has a big practice in Patna, and he wants to take him into his firm. This uncle, you know, has no children of his own, and he would dearly like to take Shuresh in now and see him through his education. But for a woman like me it would be unthinkable, wouldn't it, to have my son go and live in somebody else's house and at their expense, even though it's his own uncle.' This she said to let them know that she did not go round weeping to other people like that silly woman Shorbojoya.

Later when Shorbojoya got outside, she called Opu and said to him in a whisper, 'Opu, listen to me. Go inside and tell your cousin that you haven't got any shoes, and ask her to buy you a pair.'

'What for, Mummy?'

'Never mind what for. Go and ask her. She's rich enough. If you ask her nicely she'll probably give you a pair. Didn't you notice those red shoes Shuresh was wearing. You'd look very nice in a pair like that.'

Opu looked most embarrassed. 'No, Mummy, I couldn't, I daren't. Besides what would she think if I did?'

'What is there to be frightened about? She's your own kith and kin, isn't she? Go and ask her. What's the harm?'

'No-o-o, Mummy. I won't,' he stammered. 'You know I'm too shy to speak when she's there.'

Shorbojoya was angry. 'Why on earth won't you? You walk about like a lord when you're at home. Yet when you go out, you go in bare feet. You haven't had a pair of shoes for two years. I suppose you think that shoes don't matter. She's a rich woman, I tell you. If you'd asked her she'd have given you a pair. But you're too shy to speak! The king would a-wooing go, but he was too shy to speak!'

It was the day of the full moon and the festival of the god Satyanarayan. The occasion was being celebrated at Ranu's house and Opu had gone there to bring back part of the food offering. While he was waiting for it Ranu saw him and called out to him. 'There was a time when you were always in and out of our house, but you don't come at all nowadays. What's happened? Is anything the matter?'

'No, nothing's happened, Ranudi. Why should it have? Besides, I do come.'

'What nonsense!' said Ranu, and he could tell by the tone of her voice that she was hurt. 'Of course you don't come. You haven't been for a long time. You've forgotten all about us. I think about you lots of times, but you never seem to give a thought to me.'

'No, no! That's not true,' replied Opu. 'I do think about you. Go and ask Mummy if you don't believe me.' How his mother came into it was not clear, but this was the only thing he could think of at the time to mollify her.

Ranu kept him there talking for some time, and then she went off and got the fruit offering and some sweets as well, and gave them to him. 'You can take the plate too,' she said. 'I'll come round and collect it tomorrow.'

She smiled as she spoke, and Opu knew she was a real friend. She had grown so pretty too. He had never seen anyone as pretty as she was. Otoshi might be well-dressed, but she was not nearly as good-looking as Ranu, who was the kindest girl in the village; and he loved her more than anybody he had ever known, except of course Durga.

He took the plate from her but he did not go at once, though it was not obvious what he was waiting for. He shuffled about for a minute or so, and then suddenly out it came. 'Ranu', he said, 'there are some books in that cupboard of yours, but Shotu won't let me look at them. Do you think … you could get me one? I'll return it as soon as I've read it.'

'Which books?' she said. 'I didn't know there were any. But wait a minute and I'll go and see.'

Shotu was there when they arrived, but at first he refused to let Opu have any of them. Then an idea occurred to him. 'All right,' he said. 'I'll let you look at them if you'll do something for me in return. You know that tank of ours out in the fields. Well, somebody's stealing fish from it, and my uncle told me to go and sit there every day and find out who it is. I don't like being there on my own. So if you'll go there for me I'll let you take the books.'

Ranu protested. 'How rotten of you!' she exclaimed, 'He's only a little boy. You're much bigger than he is, and if you daren't go there alone how do you think he can? It's very mean of you. They're not your books anyway. I'll tell Daddy about it when he comes back.'

Opu however had no objection to going into the forest alone, and he longed to get his hands on the books. Besides he knew that Ranu's father was away from home and would not be back for some time. He had often walked up and down near the house eyeing the books longingly from outside. Once or twice he had managed to get inside the room, but Shotu had always caught him. It was not that Shotu wanted to read the books himself. He did not; but he had no intention of letting Opu have them; and just as Opu was getting to an exciting part he rushed in and snatched the book from him. 'Leave these books alone,' he shouted. 'They're my uncle's, and you'll tear them. Leave them alone, I tell you.'

But now heaven was within Opu's grasp.

Every day after this he picked a book, showed it to Shotu and took it off with him into the forest. Once there, he found a shady place, made a comfortable couch of leaves and twigs and lay face-down reading. There were so many books: *The Lotus and the Princess, The Bandit's Daughter, Poisoned Nectar, The Mystery of Gopeshvar*. He could not remember all their names. One by one he read them, and he did not put any of them down till he had finished it, even though his eyes often ached and his temples throbbed. Time stood still for him, and he was not aware how the bamboo shadows were lengthening, even when they had crept right across the tank as far as the weeds on the bank.

What wonderful stories they were! There was one about a Rajput princess named Shorojini. Shoroj, her husband, was taking her by boat to Murshidabad when they were attacked by some of the Nawab's troops and taken prisoner. The Nawab gave orders that Shorojini should be locked up in a room by herself, and that Shoroj should be taken away and shot. At dead of night the door of the princess's room opened, and the Nawab who was quite drunk, came staggering in. 'My beautiful one,' he said, 'my orders have been carried out and Shoroj your husband is dead. So why ... etc?' Shorojini drew herself up proudly and spoke to him as if he were a slave. 'Dost thou not know, base wretch, that I am a Rajput princess? As long as there is breath in this body ... etc.' While she was yet speaking, a foot smote against the window and it burst open. The Nawab with fear in his eyes looked to see who it was. It was a sannyasi. He had a long beard and a powerful body, and with him were four or five men as fierce and strong as the emissaries of Death itself. The sannyasi's eyes flashed with rage. 'Beast of a man!' he thundered. 'Wouldst thou despoil that which thou shouldst protect?' Then turning to

Shorojini, he said, 'Lady, I am your husband's preceptor, Jogananda Swami. He is not dead. The water in my sacred jar availed to restore him to life. Follow me to my ashram where your beloved husband awaits you.' What a genius the author was! He excited the reader's curiosity to know the miracle by which Shoroj had been brought back to life by opening the next chapter with the thrilling words: 'Come, reader, let us see how Shoroj was restored to life after he had been slain in the execution grounds ... etc.'

Each chapter left Opu with a lump in his throat and his eyes wet with tears. He looked up at the sky for a space, reliving in his mind the sensations of pleasure, surprise and excitement he had just experienced. Then, releasing the pent-up flood of his emotions in a long, deep sigh, he set his mind to the next chapter. Evening came. The shadows grew longer and longer, and the birds in the bamboos over his head poured forth the last chorus of the day. He knew he should be going home, but still he lay there, his eyes barely an inch from the page, until not a single letter was visible.

He had never read a book like this before. How could even *Sita's Forest Exile* and *The Story of Duval* be compared with it?

His mother scolded him when he got home. 'What a stupid boy you are! Do you think I don't know what you're up to? All you want is an excuse to go off into the forest by yourself and read a book. That's all this watching of somebody else's fish is. They must think you're crazy; and they're right too.' To her it was stupidity. What was the point of all this reading? What was he going to get out of it anyway?

Next day however Opu went over to Ranu's house, and this time he was allowed to take two books, *Dawn of Life in Maharashtra* and *Evening of Life in Rajputana*. In the silent heat of noon, against a background of ant-hills and thorn bushes, scene followed scene in rapid succession. First the river bank where Jelekha sat tending the wounded Naren. Then the court of Aurangzeb, with Shivaji bursting with rage because he had been given a seat among the regimental commanders. Did they think that Shivaji was only a regimental commander? If they had gone to Poona themselves they would have seen how many regimental commanders he had in his armies.

Opu's days were spent in deserts and mountains, in gay court circles at Delhi and Agra among fashionably dressed Muslim ladies. What a world it was! A world of bright moonlight, of daring feats of arms, of friendship, and of beauty! A world of festival with warriors, spear in hand, galloping across fertile plains and fields of corn after the noble boar! There too was Pratapsingh, the greatest of them all. Whatever a man could do, whatever a hero could do, whatever a Rajput prince could do, Pratapsingh could do all that and much more besides. His story is inscribed on every stone in the mountain tracts of Haldighat, lettered imperishably with the heart's blood of twelve thousand Rajput warriors who fell by his side on the field of Dewar. And on wintry nights, long after it was over, old soldiers sat by the fire and told their children and their children's children tales of matchless valour performed at Haldighat.... A spear was cast by an unknown hand....

Opu had grown up in a countryside where forests were green and shady, thick with leaves and creepers, and heavy with the scent of wet earth—and yet—he knew every inch of the Bhil country of Rajputana, and of Mewar. He loved the wild, unsurpassable loveliness of Nahara and Magro. And what a sight it was to watch Tejsingh, sword in hand, charging down the mountain side to battle!

'For a long time afterwards,' the story ran, 'in the country

of Chappan, there could be heard at midnight in the empty
Bhil valleys and on the mountain peaks a song from the lips
of a girl. Sometimes, in lonely places at dawn, wayfarers
caught a glimpse of her pale face and flashing eyes; and they
said it was the goddess of the forest, alone, restless and sad
....' And the distant echoes of her melancholy song
came floating to Opu's ears from beyond the trees in the
bamboo grove.

Kamalmir, the battle of Suryagar, General Shahbaj Khan,
the beautiful Nurjahan, the flower maiden, the wild country
of the Bhils, the boy hero Chandansingh! How far, how very
far off they were. Yet to Opu they were near and very real.
Then too there was the desert of Rajbara; and on the lofty
peaks of Aravalli the flowers of the chenar trees were in full
bloom and already beginning to fall. Vermilion from the feet
of the goddess Mewarlakshmi stained the boulders that fringed
the rivers Banas and Bir, and the stones by the waterfall; and
in the fields of millet and clover, and in the forest of Mouwol,
her footmarks were deeply imprinted.

Yet alas there was no saving Chittor! Rana Amarsingh
paid homage to the emperor. His father Pratapsingh had
battled at the head of his Bhil armies, in mountain and forest,
for twenty-five years. Where was he now? Did he know that
all was lost? Did he die a second death to see his son's
submission? Tank, ant-hills, thorn bushes, bamboo grove were
all misted over with a veil of tears.

Another day Opu's father came into his room with a
paper packet in his hand. 'See what I've got here,' he said
with a smile. 'Do you know what it is?'

Opu sat up in bed with a jerk. 'It's a newspaper, isn't it,
Daddy?' he said excitedly.

Horihor had written out some texts from the Ramayan
for Behari Ghosh's mother-in-law, and she had given him

three rupees. So without saying a word to his wife he had spent two of them on a subscription for the newspaper. They were in need of so many things just then that Shorbojoya would never let him spend two rupees on a paper had she known anything about it.

Opu took the packet from his father's hand and opened it at once. 'Yes, it's a newspaper,' he exclaimed gleefully when he had torn off the wrapper. He could see the name *Bangabashi* printed there in large type, and the paper smelt new. There too were the long columns, and all those things he had so looked forward to, when a year or two ago he used to go to Bhubon Mukherji's house every Saturday and sit on the verandah watching out for the postman with eyes as thirsty as any dry field could be for water. A newspaper! A newspaper! What fresh news would it have for him, and what new stories would he find printed on its large pages?

Horihor smiled. The delight on the lad's face was ample reward for the two rupees he had spent. It gave him far greater pleasure than he would have had if he had used the money to redeem their pawned earrings.

'Look, Daddy,' said Opu as he turned over the pages, 'Here's a letter signed "English Traveller", and this is the first instalment. We've just got the paper in time, haven't we?' Yet even as he spoke he could not but call to mind the last serial he had read. It was about the Japanese spider; and the paper had stopped coming just before he came to the last instalment. He would never know now what happened to the spider when it got to the king's palace.

One day when he was playing with Ranu, she said to him, 'What is it that you're writing in that exercise book of yours, Opu?'

He looked at her with surprise. 'Exercise book? What exercise book? How on earth ...?'

'I went to your house the other day. Didn't you know? No, of course, you couldn't know. You were out somewhere at the time. I was there for some time talking to your mother. I suppose she forgot to mention it to you. That's when I saw it. We went into your room and I saw that you'd been writing something in a red exercise book. My name's in it, isn't it? and there's somebody called Devi Singh.'

Opu blushed. 'Oh, that!' he said. 'That's only a story.'

'Yes, but what is it about? You must read it to me.'

The next day Ranu brought him a small exercise book with hard covers. 'Here you are,' she said. 'I've brought this for you to write me a story in, a nice one. You will, won't you?'

Opu got down to it with a will. He went on writing so late that the oil in his lamp burned out. 'Please put some more oil in my lamp, Mummy,' he called out. 'I want to finish this tonight. There isn't much left to do.'

'I can't spare you any more. There's very little left in the bottle and I want that for cooking tomorrow. But I'm doing some cooking now, so if you want to go on with your writing, you can come and sit by the fire and do it.'

Opu started to argue and that made his mother cross. 'Yes,' she snapped, 'you work hard enough at night, and you don't care how late it is; but during the day you're nowhere to be seen. Why don't you stay at home and work in the morning? Anyway you're not going to get any more oil tonight, and that's that.'

Opu had no alternative but to bring his book over to the kitchen and write as best he could with the help of the light from the fire. Shorbojoya looked at him lovingly as she stood watching him write. 'Yes, when he grows up we'll arrange a good marriage for him, and then our troubles will be over. We shall be able to pull this house down and build a new one. Next year he'll be old enough to wear the sacred thread; and if after that he gets taken on at the Gangulis' ...!'

Four or five days later he took the book and handed it over to Ranu. She was delighted.

'You've written all this?' she asked excitedly, as she turned over a page or two.

Opu's face was covered with smiles. 'Open it properly and see for yourself.'

Ranu turned over page after page. 'What a lot you've written!' she cried. 'Wait here a minute, I must go and call Otoshi. I want her to have a look at it too.'

All Otoshi said when she arrived was, 'Did Opu write all this? Of course he didn't. He's copied it from a book.'

Opu bridled at once. 'I didn't, I tell you. Copied it from a book to be sure! I made it up myself. Go and ask Potu if you don't believe me. He'll tell you I make up lots of stories, and tell them to him when we're sitting by the river in the afternoon.' Opu was very offended.

'No, Otoshi, you're wrong,' said Ranu. 'He did write it himself. I'm quite sure he did. He writes lots of things. Once he wrote a whole jatra play. I know he did because he read it to me.... But,' she said, turning to Opu, 'you haven't signed it. You will, won't you?'

This request made Opu somewhat uncomfortable. 'The story's not finished yet,' he explained. 'I will sign it for you, but I can't until it's finished.' The truth was that he had modelled the story on a play he had read and he had not yet decided how it was to end. He had been in a dilemma. He wanted to finish the story before giving it to Ranu, but he felt that if he kept her waiting too long she might think that he could not write poetry. Otoshi certainly would. So he had compromised by returning it unfinished.

A requiem celebration was due to be held in a neighbouring village and all the Nishchindipur Brahmins had been invited to it. Horihor was away from home at the time so Opu went as representative of the family. On the morning of the festival he got up early and joined the rest of the Brahmins in the village. Shunil was in the party too. It was to be a large feast, • and Brahmins from as far afield as ten or twelve miles away had been drawn to it; and some of them had brought five or six children with them. To begin with there was some argument about the places the guests were to sit in. That problem was eventually settled and the servants began to serve the food. First of all they put four luchies on the banana leaves before each guest; but when they came round with the fried egg-plants they saw that all the luchies had disappeared. They had not been eaten; the guests had hidden them away in a cloth or duster they kept beside them and which they had obviously brought for that purpose. One small boy, who did not know what the etiquette was on such occasions, had already started to eat one of his luchies, but his father, Bishveshvar Bhottacharji, swooped down on him like a hawk and snatched them away from him. 'You don't eat this helping,' he said, adding the boy's luchies to his own pile which were already wrapped up in his duster. 'These are for you to keep. They'll give you some more presently, and you can eat those.'

There was pandemonium everywhere. They were all shouting at once.

'Bring the luchies down here.'

'Go and get me some vegetables and be quick about it.'

'Look at these luchies you've brought me. They're not cooked properly. They're nothing but raw flour.'

Then a row broke out between the householder and the older Brahmins about the amount of food they were allowed to take home with them. One of the Brahmins, Kondorpo

Mojumdar by name, was particularly irate. 'If that's the way you feel about it,' he yelled, 'you should not invite Brahmins like us to your feast. Each Brahmin is allowed to take two dozen luchies away with him. That's the fixed rate. It's been so ever since the time of Ballal Sen—Ballal Sen in case you don't know was king of Bengal in the twelfth century and he is the infallible arbiter in such matters—and if you are not prepared to accept the rules he laid down, I, Kondorpo Mojumdar, for one, will never again set foot ...' The unhappy householder hurried to placate him.

Opu came away with quite a large bundle as his share. His mother came running out to meet him and said with a smile, 'Goodness me, what a lot you've brought! Let me have a look. Luchies, sweets and all sorts of lovely things. I'll cover them up for you, and you can eat them tomorrow.'

'Yes, Mummy,' Opu replied. 'But you must have some too. I asked for two lots of sweets so that you could have a taste of them too.'

'What!' said Shorbojoya. 'You don't mean to say that you told them you wanted some for your mother? That was a silly thing to do.'

'Oh, no, Mummy,' Opu protested vehemently, shaking his head and waving his hand in violent contradiction. 'You don't think I'd do that? I asked for them in such a way as to make them think I wanted them all for myself.'

Shorbojoya was very pleased, and she took the bundle into the kitchen.

Opu was too excited to stay at home for long. He soon ran off to see how Shunil had fared; but just as he was about to set foot on the steps he heard Shunil's mother's voice raised in anger. 'What did you bring all these things home for?' she barked. 'Who told you to do it?'

Shunil had made up a bundle of food only because he

saw everybody else doing it. 'Why not, Mummy? They were all doing it. Opu brought some away with him too.'

'Of course he would,' she retorted hotly. 'That's because he's the son of one of those food-scrounging Brahmins. Brahmins like him go round to all the feasts there are, talk about Ballal Sen and bring home as much food as they can carry. It's disgusting! His mother's as greedy as they make them too. Now you know why I didn't want to bring you to this village. You've got into bad company already and you're learning bad habits. Go and throw it all away at once. Or you can give it to Opu if you want to.'

Opu was far too scared to go into the house now. He turned back home and tried to puzzle out what it was that made Shunil's mother talk as she had done. His mother had been pleased, genuinely pleased, to get the food. Why then should his aunt be so angry about it? Was the food a lump of earth, fit only to be thrown away? Was it true that his mother was greedy, and that his father was a food-scrounging Brahmin? It can't be, he told himself. Shunil's mother can eat as many sweets as she wants to. His own mother hardly ever did. He had not eaten any himself for many a long day either. No! it might be wrong for Shunil; but how could it possibly be wrong for him?

In the meanwhile, Opu was not making much progress with his lessons. There was so much else to do, such as attending feasts, packing up bundles of food to bring home with him, going with his father to various clients' houses, and, most important of all, fishing. Potu, the same Potu he was playing cowries with on the day they were attacked by the fisher lads, was his constant companion. Potu had grown into a very big boy. He stood at least a head taller than Opu. Day after day he came to meet his elder brother, as he called Opu; and it did not matter to him that he had to come all the way across the village to do so. He could never forget that Opu had come to his rescue and had been beaten himself in doing so.

Opu was passionately fond of fishing. He knew a place where the fish used to rise well. It was near the junction of the little canal, which flowed through the Shonadanga fields, and the river Ichamoti. He went there very often and sat down to fish under a chatim tree which grew out over the river. It was an excellent place. Nobody else ever seemed to go there; and it was very beautiful too. Across the water from where he sat, there was a wide expanse of green thatch grass, broken by a kadamba tree and a silk-cotton tree and both of them were festooned with creepers. There were bushes too, overgrown with a purple-flowering convolvulus; and in the far distance he could just make out the clump of bamboos which concealed the village of Madhobpur. There was not a single discordant note to disturb the harmony of it all, the singing of the birds, the ever-changing light and shade among the trees and the lush green of the thatch grass.

Ever since he was a small boy and had gone for the first time to visit the factory-field, open spaces, forest and river had cast their spell upon him; and now, as he sat there rod in hand, under the branches of the chatim tree, fishing and looking all about him, waves of delight coursed through his heart. When evening came and the shadows crept over the fields, when the air was heavy with the scent of ripening fruit on the date palms, and the note of the sing-my-bride bird came floating down the air, and that of the kokil too, when the god of day before he sank to rest stained the outstretched arms of the banyan tree which stood in the open country near Shonadanga with the crimson hues of sunset, when the river darkened and swarms of little birds twittered as they flew home to their nests, his mind was uplifted by the beauty of it all and his eyes shone bright with joy. 'No,' he said to himself, 'even if I never catch any fish at all, I will come to this place every day and sit under this big chatim tree.'

He very seldom caught a fish. Hour after hour his cane float would lie motionless in the still water, like the unflickering flame of a lamp when there is no breeze. Not that he stayed in the same place all the time. He was too impatient for that. If something caught his attention he would be off to see what it was; but his eyes always kept turning back to his float. Sometimes when he was looking at something which had attracted his interest, it might be a bird's nest in a bush, he would glance at the float and imagine it was bobbing about in the water. Straight away he dashed back and jerked the line out of the water. But no! It was not a fish. There must be swarms of them about, he told himself, but they just will not bite here; so he took his rod and moved along the river to a clump of reeds. The water was dark there, and that could only mean that it was the lurking place of big fish, one of which was bound to bite. But he was wrong again. His float remained as motionless as an ascetic lost in meditation.

Sometimes he took a book with him.

When he did he would set his line first and then settle down to read. This time it was a picture book Shuresh had lent him. It was a lower-school English book, and there was a book of notes to go with it. Opu could not follow the English, so he read the stories in the Bengali notes and looked at the English book for the pictures. Stories about foreign countries, especially when they had heroes in them, had thrilled him ever since he was a little boy; and this book had a number of such stories. One of them was about a traveller who lost his way in a terrible land of snow and ice. He wandered round and round in a circle until he died of cold. Then there was the story of how Christopher Columbus crossed an unknown sea and discovered America. Two English children, a boy and a girl, got themselves into a very dangerous situation while climbing a cliff in search of a seagull's nest. A brave girl named Praskovia Lapulova set out alone across the unending wastes of Siberia to save her father who was in exile there. He knew all these people so well. If he had met any of them he would have recognized them at once.

The story of Sir Philip Sidney brought tears to his eyes. He asked Shuresh about it afterwards. 'You know the story, don't you, Shuresh? Please tell it to me, all of it.'

'Oh, you mean the battle of Zutphen.'

'Zutphen.' Opu gasped. 'What did you say, Shuresh? Did you say Zutphen? What is it? Is it a place?'

But that was all Shuresh could tell him.

It was about a month later. Opu was out fishing again and by some remarkable chance he managed to hook a large shoroputi fish. At last he had found the right place, and after that he never went anywhere else. He made himself a comfortable seat of leaves and twigs, let out his line and then gave himself up to his reading.

Hour after hour passed. Complete silence descended upon the fields by the river, and opposite was the wide stretch of country called Deyar, where the green thatch grass grew; and over the grass and the flowering bushes and on the topmost branches of the kadamba and silk-cotton trees glowed the rays of his old familiar friend, the evening sun, the companion of the happiest moments of his young life. Opu's mind was full of a wonderful story he had read in the *Bangabashi*, in one of the 'English Traveller's' letters. It was about a country called France. He knew where France was. He knew because he had seen it in an English atlas of Shuresh's. It was at one end of a sea called Mediterranean, which meant 'sea-in-the-middle-of-the-land'. For many years the soil of France had been devastated by a foreign army. The people were in dire poverty, the king was powerless and everywhere there was anarchy, looting and terror. In her country's darkest hour, the daughter of a poor shepherd who lived in a tiny village in the province of Lorraine was out in the fields tending her father's sheep. She let the sheep graze where they would and found for herself a seat on a small grass hummock in a corner of that deserted field. She sat there looking at the blue sky, her mind full of the disaster which had befallen her homeland. Every day she thought about it. She could think of nothing else. Then suddenly one day she realized in her innocent young heart that someone was speaking to her. The voice seemed to be saying, 'You are to be the saviour of France. Take to yourself a sword, and go and rally her armies, for the duty of saving the people of your country is yours.' It was a goddess speaking to her from heaven, and the goddess's name was Mary. Day after day the goddess spoke to her, strengthening her. And in the end, the story went on, that loyal-hearted girl took her sword and restored the king to his throne. The French armies found a new courage and drove their enemies out of the land; but the ignorant people accused the girl of being a witch and burned her to death.

In the quiet of the evening Opu sat by the river pondering what he had read, his heart was very full. What remained most vividly in his mind was not the valour of the girl on the battle-field or of the tale of her victory and death which followed, but the picture of her sitting alone with her thoughts in a corner of a field, the green grass under her and the blue sky above, and her sheep grazing around her. On the other side of the picture he could see that invincible enemy, cruel, proud, greedy and questing for blood. It was a picture of opposites; but the side which dwelt with him longest was that of a simple, god-fearing, blue-eyed girl and her sheep. It was she in her youthful innocence who stirred the heart of a boy who was himself just growing out of childhood.

It was time to go home, and at last he wound in his line. Along the bank and on the smooth surface of the dark water lay masses of flowers which had fallen from the low-hanging branches of the acacia trees; and beyond the Shonadanga plain, the huge red ball of the sun was sinking to rest, just as if some heaven-born child playing in the golden sand by Kuvera's city had blown a glowing bubble from the burning foam and was chasing it down the sky. Slowly it slid behind the trees on the western horizon and Opu turned to go home.

A pair of hands closed over his eyes from behind. He threw them off with a violent jerk. It was Potu, and he giggled as he came round to the front of his friend. 'I've been looking for you everywhere; and then at last it occurred to me that you might have gone fishing. So I came here. Have you caught anything? What, not even one? Bad luck! But come on, let's go out in a boat. Wouldn't you like to?'

At this time of the year long-distance cargo boats used to tie up side by side near kadamba tree at a place called Sahebs' Ghat. They carried palm leaves for thatching, rice and shells, especially shells, which fishermen from the south came every year to gather from this part of the river. They gathered them by tying their boats together in pairs out in mid-stream and then letting down a big net. Opu and Potu sat on the bank and watched them at work. A dark-skinned man was diving. He stayed under for quite a while and then came up alongside one of the boats. He took four or five shells out of a bag he held in one hand, shook the sand and mud out of them and threw them on the deck. Opu thought it was great fun. He pointed the man out to Potu and said, 'Look, Potu! See how long he's able to stay under. Let's time him once or twice and see how long it is. I bet you couldn't stay under water as long as that.'

The bank down to the river where the boats were moored was steep and covered with long grass. Opu loved to sit there and listened to the sailors talk about their adventures, the countries they had been to, the different places they had just come from, the many rivers and canals they had sailed, the storms they had encountered, how they coped with the strong tides that ebbed and flowed in the great estuaries, and what they did when they were caught in a cyclone. His one ambition was to sail down many rivers and cross many seas; and the longing had become much more intense since he had read those adventure stories in Shuresh's book. So naturally when he and Potu got near to the boats he went up to the men and began to ask them questions. 'What's the price of those palm leaves? ... Where did you get that rice from? From Jhalkati? Where's that? Is it a long way from here? ...'

Potu interrupted his flow of questions after a while. 'Come on, Opu. Let's go along to the wharf under the tamarind tree. We might find a boat there. If we do we can have a sail.'

There was a boat there. It was a small dinghy. They untied the rope, gave the dinghy a push and jumped aboard as it slid out into the river. The dank smell of water rose about them. River birds were standing among the reeds. They could see peasants working on the sandbanks, some cutting potol beans, others reaping the long grass and tying it in bundles; and at the bend in the river near Chaltepota, sparrows were twittering among the bushes on the bank. And the cloud mountains in the east were changing colour in the sun as it set.

Potu said, 'Opu, sing me a song. What about the one you sang the other day?'

'No, I don't want to sing that one again. Daddy has taught me a new one. It's got a lovely tune. I'll sing that for you; but not just yet. Row on a little further. There are too many people on the bank. They might hear me.'

Potu laughed. 'How shy you are, Opu! What is there to be frightened about? In any case they're a long way from us now. So come on! Sing!'

Opu did sing, but not until they had rowed a little further on. As soon as he started Potu, who was rowing in the stern of the boat, lifted his paddle out of the water so that he could hear properly. There was no need for either of them to row. The stream was doing their work for them, and the boat swung round and round towards a bend in the river which concealed a place local people called Shipwreck Point. Potu took up the singing when Opu stopped, and while he was singing the boat drifted slowly on round the bend until they were within sight of Shipwreck Point. Potu broke off abruptly and pointed towards the northeast. 'Look Opu. There's a storm coming up. don't you think we ought to turn back?'

'No,' replied Opu. 'I love singing in a storm. Let's go on.'

He had barely finished speaking when a black cloud which had risen in the direction of Madhobpur, spread right across the sky, and the water flowed dark beneath it. Potu could not keep his eyes off it. There was a whistling sound in the distance, faint at first, but loud enough to set the birds calling to one another; the wind turned chilly; they got the smell of wet earth from the fields; ripe seeds from an akondo tree were blown in eddies across the water; and the trees began to creak and sway. Then with a roar the black April storm was upon them.

The river was black, the sky was black. Branches from acacia and giant chatim trees on the bank cracked and broke off. Some paddy birds sped in a long line down the wind, their bodies gleaming white against the clouds. Opu was excited. He dropped his paddle in his delight, and his eyes were agog to see what the storm would do next. Potu untied the long end of his dhuti and held it over his head. The wind seized it and carried it out full length like a flag.

'The wind's dead against us, Opu,' he said. 'We can't possibly turn round now though. The boat would capsize. It's a good job we didn't bring Shunil with us.'

Opu did not hear him. He did not even know that he had said anything, even though they were sitting side by side. He could think of nothing but the storm. His body was tense, his eyes staring straight ahead, now at the sky, now at the waves that rushed down upon them. The water danced wildly. The paddy birds were flying. The cloud mountains writhed in convulsions; and on the bank he could see the heaps of shells that the boatmen from the south had piled up. A floating island of water hyacinth swept by, so wide that it hid the water from sight. Suddenly he was voyaging to England like that man in the *Bangabashi*. His ship had sailed from Calcutta. Sagar Island in the mouth of the estuary was behind them, and they were threading their way through a host of little islands in the middle of the sea. The dark green line of coconut palms on the shores of Ceylon was already in sight, and on the far horizon he could make out blue mountains in a strange land, which reddened as he watched them in the light of the setting sun. Everything was different! New lands! New sights! And still he journeyed on, further and further into the unknown.

The unfathomed waters of that distant sea were black and troubled like the waters of the Ichamoti; but the islands in the Arabian Sea were green with trees and bushes. Evening came, and he was ashore at the port of Aden, sitting under a tree; and a beautiful Arab girl brought him a glass of water.

Then he looked towards the bend in the river, and there he saw them, a swarm of sea-birds flying after his boat, just as they did in the newspaper story.

He would go to all these places. He would see all these sights. He would go to England, and to Japan. He would go on trading voyages and become a rich merchant. He would keep moving all the time, from country to country, from sea to sea, no matter how great the danger; and when in the China seas his boat would be on the point of sinking in a storm as violent as this intoxicating April gale, he would take to the jolly boat—he called it 'jali'—and row across the boundless ocean, living on shell fish he would tear from the slopes of a submerged mountain. There was a rift in the mulberry-coloured cloud mountain which hung above the bamboo grove near Madhobpur, and framed in it he saw many things, blue seas, unknown coasts, lines of coconut palms, a volcano, a land covered with snow. There were people too; Jelekha, Sarayu, Grace Darling, Zutphen Sidney, that pretty English boy and his sister collecting sea-birds' eggs, the magician who could turn things into gold, that blue-eyed village girl alone and lost in thought in the fields of Lorraine, and many others, all of them culled from that rich treasure of stories he had found in his three tin boxes, in the books in Ranu's house, in those he had borrowed from Shuresh and in the old copies of the *Bangabashi*. Somewhere in all those lands somebody was waiting to welcome him; and one day the call would come, and he would go.

Not once did it occur to him that all these places were far far away. Nor did he ever stop to think who would take him to them, or how much money he would need to make such journeys possible. Poor, friendless, foolish, undistinguished Opu, whose life would be spent conducting religious ceremonies in other people's houses, though for the time being he had to put up with scoldings from his mother whenever he used up her oil to read with at night! Poor village-born Opu, who had never set foot in a school though he was old enough to go, who did not know what good clothes and good things were! Who was going to invite him to all these gay and happy parties in the big world outside?

If he had ever asked himself such a question, the rushing chariot of his childish fancies and the irresistible fascination which drew him in hope down the avenues of the future would have brushed it aside with all its doubts and fears. If he had asked himself such a question? But he never did. He was sure beyond a doubt that when he grew up all these things would come to pass, and that as he walked the wonderful ways that life held in store for him the fruits of all happiness would be there by the roadside for him to pluck. It only remained for him to grow up. When he did every door would open before him, invitations would come from this country and that, and as he journeyed on in triumph the world and its people would bow themselves to his feet. The hard road from now to then was hidden in the rosy mists of his dreams.

The rain had stopped, the black clouds had blown away with the storm and the sky was clear. He had been oblivious of it all. He did not come back to earth again until he found himself helping Potu to tie up the dinghy under the tamarind tree. Even then he was walking on air as he strode ahead of Potu and whistled with joy along the path through the bamboo grove. Like his mother and Durga, Opu had learned to see visions and dream dreams.

TWENTY SEVEN

It was late and Opu was in bed; but though his eyes were shut he was very wide awake. He was far too interested in what his father and mother were talking about to go to sleep. They were discussing closing down the house at Nishchindipur and going to live in Benares, where, as his father explained, life would be much more comfortable for them. He described his experiences when he lived in the city as a young man. 'People were so kind,' he said, 'and friendly. They were easy to get on with; and they all knew me and respected me. And on top of that, things were cheap too.' Shorbojoya was bubbling over in her enthusiasm to be gone. The picture she had of Benares was of a place in which everything was made of gold, and where no one was poor; so different from Nishchindipur where everything was always so difficult. Once

they went to Benares all their troubles would be at an end;
and all they had to do was to make up their minds when to
go. She would have gone that very day if it had been possible.
She could see no point in putting it off. Horihor was more
cautious, but in the end they decided to leave at the turn of
the year, about mid-April.

Some time previously Shorbojoya had made a vow to go on
a pilgrimage to the shrine of Siddhesvari at Ganganandapur;
but she had kept putting if off. 'It's more than six miles from
here,' she told herself; 'and that's too far for me to walk.'
Now however they were going away, and she felt she ought
to do something about her vow before they left. The trouble
was that she could not find anyone to go with her and she
did not want to go alone. Opu on the other hand was all for
going, and suggested that he should visit the shrine instead
of his mother and save her the trouble, adding at the same
time that it would give him a chance to see his auntie whom
he had never met before. Shorbojoya did not think it a good
idea at all. 'Nonsense!' she said. 'It's nearly eight miles. I
couldn't possibly let you go all that way on your own.'

'Why not?' said Opu. 'I've got legs and eyes and ears,
haven't I? You seem to think I'm not strong enough to go
anywhere outside by myself. Why should you want me to stay
in the house all the time? I'm not a baby.'

'Of course you're not,' his mother replied with a laugh.
'You're quite a man, aren't you?'

Opu however did not let the matter drop. He pestered
so hard that in the end she had to consent.

The road to Ganganandapur ran for part of the way along
an earth track, which being built up a little higher than the
land on either side, cut across the Shonadanga plain like a

low ridge. It ran through a copse of akondophul trees, the long, white branches of which sagged low over the dub grass under the weight of their flowers. There was nobody about. It was very hot and as the hour approached noon the shadows of the trees grew shorter and shorter. The sandy earth under Opu's bare feet was hot, and he liked it. Trees and bushes were in full flower. The newly opened buds of the acacias were tipped up towards the sun, and on one small tree the fruit was already out, full and ripe and as red as the wild dumur; while the sun drew forth from the hot earth a rich aromatic odour, which hung heavy in the air.

Opu strode along happily. From time to time as he walked he bent down, rummaged among the bushes for bitter berries and stuffed them into the pockets of the new red satin shirt his mother had made for him. He could not have described his happiness in words, but the further he went the more thrilled he became with the beauty all around him, the bitter tang from the earth, the way the shadows fell across the dub grass, the wide sweep of the open country burning white in the heat of the sun, the path itself, the trees, the birds, the thickets, the swinging clusters of flowers and fruit, the alkushi plants, the thorn bushes, and the blue creeper which bore the name of the goddess Durga. How could his mother have wanted him to stay indoors when there was a world like this outside? And what fun it would be if his father said to him, 'There's no need for you to stay in any more and do lessons, my lad. The out-of-doors is yours. Go and walk in it.' Yes, what fun it would be! He would walk through shady copses like these, with fruit swinging overhead, his eyes fixed on the distance where a dove was calling from a tree. That was all he asked for, to walk and to walk. He would listen to the rustle and creak of the bamboos; and in the warmth of evening, when the light was gold and red, many birds of many colours would sing to him.

Day by day, as the years of his childhood passed, Opu had walked with Nature. When one season went and another came, the trees, the sky, the wind, the singing of the birds told him about it. His heart leaped within him to behold the seasons touch the changing face of the Ichamoti with new beauties. He knew so well what changes the maturing year would spell out in the trees, on land and water, in the sky, and in the fruit and flowers. He loved them all as if they were his brothers and sisters, and he could not imagine a life without them. Ever since he was born Nature's vast and lovely canvas had been spread before his eyes. The sombre magnificence of the thick black robes which enshrouded the sky as the fierce and airless summer burned to its end; the play of colour in the clouds of the sky as the sun set across the Shonadanga plain; the wide sandbank of Madhobpur at the end of the rains, with its deep carpet of flowering herbs; the enchanting crisscross of light and shade in the bamboo grove on a moonlit night: the incomparable and inexhaustible loveliness of all these had stamped itself indelibly on his keen, ardent, and innocent mind as he journeyed on towards manhood; they had opened his eyes to the quintessense of beauty, and murmured in his ears the words which open the gates to the palace of the gods. Such a lesson Opu was never to forget. There is a vow which leads man to serve at the shrine of beauty for ever; and slowly, without knowing what he was doing, openhearted Nature had led Opu to take that vow.

As he approached Notidanga Opu saw some men fishing in a backwater, and he stood for a while and watched them. Later passing through the village he heard a blind beggar singing and accompanying himself on a one-stringed fiddle. It was a song Opu knew. He had sung it himself many times.

When the moon rises at noonday
It is hard to live through the night...

It was an enthralling song, and his old Vaisnava grandpa used to sing it beautifully.

In Horishpur the road led past a school-house, a small thatched building, and the boys were chanting their tables. Opu stopped to listen. The teacher seemed a young man, not nearly so old as his one-time schoolmaster Proshonno. A thought occurred to him as he stood there, and it kept coming back to him as he continued his walk. 'I'm grown up now. I'm not a little boy any longer. If I were, Mummy wouldn't have let me come all this way by myself. This is to be my life from now on: to keep on moving, moving straight ahead. And next month we're going a long way, to Benares, wherever that is.'

It was late afternoon when Opu reached Ganganandapur; but the moment he set foot in the village he became nervous again, and so uncertain of himself that he did not even dare to look about him to see what sort of a place it was. He kept his eyes fixed on the road in front of him, and had to force himself to continue on his way. All his earlier assurance had vanished. He felt that everybody's eyes were on him, and that people were whispering to one another. 'Here he is! Look, he's coming now!' as if they had all known beforehand that he would be arriving today. He had some coconut sweets tied up in his bundle, and he had the feeling that they knew about them too. The worst part of it was that he was too self-conscious to ask anybody where his uncle Kunjo Chokroborti lived.

At last he saw an old woman standing alone and he plucked up courage to ask her to direct him. There was a wall in front of the house, and when he went through into the courtyard it was quite empty. He cleared his throat, and coughed once or twice. He had not the courage to call out. Nobody heard him, and he might have had to stand there in the hot March sun for a long time, but fortunately for him a young dark-skinned woman some eighteen or nineteen years old, came out to do something on the verandah and caught sight of him. She was surprised to see such a pretty little boy standing shyly just inside the gate with a bundle in his hand, and as she did not know who he was she called out at once. 'Who are you, Khoka? Where have you come from?' The next moments were agony for him. He could neither move nor speak. At last he forced himself to walk towards, her. 'I live ... at Nishchindipur ... and my name's ... Opu,' he stammered.

He began to wish that he had never come. His aunt might be annoyed with him for coming without letting her know, and perhaps she might find him a nuisance. It had never occurred to him—how could it?—that it would be so difficult to go to a strange place, or that when he got there he would be unable to speak. His forehead was bathed in perspiration.

The young woman however quickly relieved him of his embarrassment. She ran down the steps, took him by the hand and led him back up the steps on to the verandah. There she tipped up his face to see what he looked like and spoke to him most affectionately. She asked after his mother and father. She had never met his sister Durga, but she was very sympathetic when he told her that she was dead. Noticing how hot he was, she undid his shirt and took it off for him. Then she washed his hands and face and dried them with a clean towel. That done she hurried inside the house and got him a glass of sweet sherbet. Opu could hardly believe that she was his aunt: she seemed so young. She looked very little older than Raji's sister.

His aunt now was able to take a good look at him. She had not realized until she saw him that her cousin's son would be so young, neither had she expected him to be so good-looking. When one of her neighbours came in and asked who he was, there was a note of pride in her voice as she told her, 'He's my nephew. He lives in Nishchindipur. His father's a cousin of my father's. They're our own family, but we don't see very much of them; in fact this is the first time I've seen my nephew.' Then she looked at Opu once more, and there was pride in her eyes too. 'Yes,' she seemed to say, 'he's my nephew. He's got the face of a prince, hasn't he? You've only to look at him to know what a noble and distinguished family ours is.'

That evening after it was dark, Kunjo Chokroborti came home. His face was deeply wrinkled and his general appearance was forbidding. He looked an old man, but it was hard to be sure whether he was or not. If Opu had been very shy when he first me his aunt, he was positively scared when he saw his uncle, who reminded him of Proshonno, his schoolmaster; and it would not have surprised him if his uncle had roared at him as Proshonno used to, 'I can see that you're a very naughty little boy'.

Early next morning Opu got up and went for a walk round the village. It was an island in the middle of the jungle. There was no open country to be seen, and scarcely any grass land, only jungle. His aunt's house stood by itself, and to get to the next one he had to walk a long way down a path that was narrowly hemmed in by wild bushes. Further on the path ran through the compounds of some of the houses. There were few people about, but here and there he did come across some boys of his own age, who gaped at him so rudely that he made no attempt to get to know them. Indeed he hurried past without looking at them a second time.

When he had walked as far as he wanted to he was in something of a dilemma about going back. At home he usually had a meal about this time, baked rice, coconut, sweets, or perhaps some boiled rice that had been left over from the day before; but he did not know what the routine was in his aunt's house. Last night he had had some rice, and his aunt had given him sweets to eat with his milk. If he went back now he was afraid that she might think that he was greedy and had come back only because he wanted something more to eat. Surely, she might think, he can't expect to have sweets every day! So he decided that it would be better not to return just yet, but to stroll round some more and go back in time for the midday meal. But he did not know the place, and it was difficult to put in time by wandering round or just standing about; and in the end he had not alternative but to go back, though he walked as slowly as he could.

There was a little girl in the yard when he got there. She was six or seven years old. In her hand she carried a metal jar, and she called to his aunt from outside. 'Auntie, have you been cooking jackfruit? If you have can you let me have a little?' Opu's aunt shouted back from inside the house, 'Oh, it's you, Gulki! No, I'm not cooking any now, but I shall be this evening. Come and get some then.' Gulki put her jar down, but she did not make any move to go away from near the verandah where she was standing. Her hair was short like a boy's but it was very untidy and looked as if it was never oiled. Her clothes were dirty too; and she had a dark skin. She was not at all abashed to see Opu. In fact she stared hard at him for some time; then with a little giggle she picked up her jar and ran out of the yard.

'Whose little girl is that, Auntie?' Opu asked when he got inside.

'Who? Oh, you mean Gulki! Her real home's not in this

336

village. Both her father and mother are dead and she has no
near relatives to look after her. At present she's living in the
house next door with Nibaron Mukherji's wife, who's a sort
of distant relative of hers.'

Next day a boy from the village came to the house
asking for Opu, and the two of them made friends and went
for a walk round the village. After their walk, when Opu
was going back to the house, he caught sight of the little
orphan girl Gulki squatting by the side of the path. She was
eating something, though Opu could not see what it was.
As soon as she saw him she bundled up whatever it was in
her sari. It turned out to be some half-ripe bokul fruit. After
he had seen her the day before, Opu heard her whole story
from his aunt. She told him that Nibaron Mukherji's wife
was not kind to Gulki and gave her very little to eat. 'In
fact,' said his aunt, 'she's a very cruel woman. Many a day
she gives the child nothing to eat at all, and she has to go
round the village begging from other people ... I suppose,
though, it's difficult for her,' his aunt went on after a pause.
'She's got seven children of her own and there's not always
enough food to go round. And Gulki's not a particularly
close relative.'

Opu was not in the least shy of Gulki. For one thing she
was such a very little girl, and for another she was on her
own. Now that he had seen her again he wanted to make
friends with her. So he went up to her and asked her what
it was she was hiding in her sari. She looked at him and
giggled; then holding on the her sari with both hands she
darted away. It struck Opu as being very funny, especially as
the bokul fruit, which was what she was trying to hide from
him, began to fall along the path as she ran. He picked them
up with a laugh and called after her. 'You're dropping them,
Khuki. Look, they're all falling out. Here they are. I've got

them now. Come and get them. I shan't tell anybody.' But Gulki was out of sight by then.

Opu was sitting in the house just after returning from his bath in the tank, when he saw Gulki standing behind the back gate. She kept poking her head round the corner and then pulling it back again. When at last their eyes met she giggled at him. Opu stood up at once and shouted to her. 'All right, I'm coming. Wait there for me.' But she did not, so he shouted again. 'What's the use of running away? I can catch you very easily.' Gulki did not so much as look behind; she made a bee-line for the tank as fast as her legs could carry her, but as soon as she realized that she could not possibly outpace Opu, she stopped and waited for him to catch her up. When he did he grabbed hold of her by her bedraggled hair. Her first reaction was of fear: she thought he was going to beat her; but when he let go of her hair and laughed, she knew he was only playing and she laughed too.

Opu felt very sorry for her. He could tell by the way she laughed that she wanted to make friends and play with him, but she was only a little girl and did not know how to tell him so; she could only suggest it by hiding and peeping, by giggling and running away from him. She reminded him of Durga, who used to behave in just the same way when she was Gulki's age. Durga also used to wander round by herself collecting things and tying them up in her sari. Why she did it nobody knew; nor did they bother to find out. Durga was always on the lookout for things to eat too, just like this simple little girl. 'She's nobody to play with,' Opu thought to himself, 'so she wants to play with me. How sad it must be for her! She's lonely. She has no father or mother; and she has no one to play with either.'

He let go her hair and took her by the hand. 'What shall we play, Khuki? Oh, I know! Let's have a race. You run and

I'll catch you. Let's see who can get to that jackfruit tree first.'

She pulled her hand away and darted off. Opu shouted after her, 'You'll have to run faster than that, or I shall catch you easily.' When he thought she had a long enough start he drew a deep breath and pounded after her. 'Hu-u-u-u! I'm coming.' Gulki saw he was gaining on her, and ran with all her might; but it was no good. He caught her easily. 'You'll have to run faster than that, Khuki. You're not nearly good enough to get away from me,' he said. 'What shall we play now? Oh, yes, let's play thieves and policemen. You be the thief, and come and steal these jackfruit leaves. And I'll be the policeman and come after you.'

Gulki's face was covered with smiles. Ever since she had first seen this good-looking little boy she had wanted to make friends with him. So she nodded at once, and then as if to cement their friendship by making some gesture of her own, she said, 'What about gathering tamarind seeds?' She used rather a vulgar word for them, and Opu thought that she must have learned to use such words through living in a farmers' village. The milkmen's children, and other low-caste children in his own village, talked just like that.

At midday his aunt came to the gate and called out to him. Gulki followed him into the house. Opu sat down to his meal at once and when he had finished his aunt asked Gulki if she would like something to eat. 'Sit down in Opu's place,' she said. 'This is banana curry, and I'll give you some daal to have with it.' Opu felt a pang of regret that he had not been more thoughtful. 'What a pity!' he thought. 'If I had known she was going to stay I would have left her some of the fish.' Gulki sat down at once without waiting for a second invitation, and helped herself generously to the rice, and took some daal which she mixed with it. But though she sat there eating for a long time she could not get through all she had taken. She had to leave a lot on the edge of the leaf she had been eating from. Opu's aunt laughed. 'Your eyes were bigger than your stomach, weren't they, Gulki? See what a lot you've left. But you mustn't eat any more now. You're quite out of breath.'

When Gulki had gone, Opu's aunt said to him, 'How cruel it is of her auntie! She's only a little girl. It's very late now and they still haven't called her in for her meal. I know she's not really one of the family; but she's such a little thing.'

On Saturday Opu went to the temple of Siddhesvari. The priest was a handsome old man, with a long white patriarchal beard. He was assisted by his widowed daughter, who made the arrangements for the various ceremonies. It was she who attended to Opu. He gave her four pice for the ritual offering. 'This isn't enough,' she said. 'The prescribed offering for this rite is two annas.' 'Four pice was all my mother gave me,' he replied. 'I've no more money on me.' 'All right,' said the young woman: and she took some bananas and radishes and wrapped them up in a leaf for him. 'This is the gift of the goddess. I'll give you a bel leaf from the shrine and some vermilion too. They are for the womenfolk in your house.'

'What kind people they are!' Opu said to himself. 'If I'd got it I'd give them two more pice.'

When he got back to the house the moon was up, and he sat on the verandah and told his aunt all about his visit to the temple. Suddenly his tale was interrupted by a shrill scream from the house next door. It was Gulki. 'Oh, Auntie! Don't beat me any more. You've cut my back and it's bleeding. Don't, Auntie, don't! I can't bear it.' A harsh voice shouted through the child's screams. 'You shameless creature! You good-for-nothing wretch! You went to the Chokrobortis' house again today scrounging for food. I'll burn your tongue with a hot ladle and that'll take the edge off your appetite.

340

Going round begging at other people's houses indeed! That's why they say I never give you anything to eat. Little do they know that you're eating us out of house and home, you little devil! I'll show you!'

'That's the sort of thing that goes on,' Opu's aunt said to him. 'She's shouting as loud as that on purpose, to make sure that we can hear. And there's nothing we can do about it. If I were to speak to her, as I should like to, she'd only say that it was my fault for feeding the child. To tell her the truth would only lead to a quarrel.' Opu did not reply. He was very upset; his throat was so dry that he could not say a word.

Opu had to leave for home the next day. He had his meal in the late afternoon and then walked to the part of the village where the milkmen lived. His uncle had arranged a lift for him in a tobacco cart that was going as far as Nawabganj. It would put him down on the road to Nishchindipur early the following morning.

He set out before it was dark and just as he was rounding a bend in the path through the Brahmins' sector of the village he ran into Gulki. She had been out playing somewhere and was now on her way home. 'Why didn't you come and play with me this morning, Khuki?' he asked. 'I've got to go home today.' Gulki just laughed as if she did not believe him. 'It's true, I tell you. It is really,' he said. 'Look, here's my bundle all tied up. I'm going on Kartik Goyala's cart. Why don't you walk part of the way with me?'

Gulki did. She followed him quite a long way. Beyond the Brahmins' houses there was a small stretch of open country, and after that came the milkmen's sector. Gulki walked with him as far as the edge of the open country. There she stopped. 'How much did that red shirt of yours cost?' she asked, pointing to it.

Opu laughed. 'Two rupees,' he said. 'Why? Would you like it?'

Gulki giggled in a way that seemed to convey that if he offered it to her she would not say no.

Suddenly Opu turned away from her, and scanned the road ahead. At the far side of the open field, through a gap in the trees, he could see a patch of bright sky; and the thought flashed across his mind that next month about this time there would be another day like this. They would be going away, and it would be a very long way. In a moment or so he turned back to Gulki. 'Don't come any further, Khuki. You're come a long way as it is, you ought to be going back now. You might get into trouble at home. I'll come and see you if I come here again, that's if you want me to. But perhaps, you know, I may not come here any more. We're going to Benares in April, to live there.'

Gulki giggled once more.

It was the fourteenth day of the month, and the moon was full. That was a very special conjunction. Opu never came that way again, but the picture of his first journey away from home by himself remained clear in his mind for many a long day. Straight down the road, over the distant trees, the full moon was already rising, though he did not realize that it was a full moon of the fourteenth day; and following him down the road to see him off was his little friend, a simple, tousle-headed orphan girl.

TWENTY EIGHT

❧◈❧

By the middle of April Horihor had completed all his arrangements for leaving Nishchindipur. Whatever he did not want to take with him he sold, and used the money to pay off various small debts. Their old bed, a good one made of jackfruit wood, the chest and a large number of lesser items were laid out in the verandah room, and as the news of their departure got about, people from all over village came flocking in, hoping to pick up a bargain.

The older men of the village came to see Horihor and did their best to persuade him to change his mind. They argued the many advantages of staying. Living in Nishchindipur they said was cheap; fish and milk for example cost far less than they did elsewhere, etc. Only Rajkrishna Bhottacharji's wife took the contrary view. She had come to invite Shorbojoya to her house for the Savitri Festival, and she discussed the question of their departure at great length. 'What is there in Nishchindipur to stay for?' she asked. 'I certainly would not advise you to stay. Besides, it's not a good thing to let yourself get bogged down in one place. It makes you so narrow, doesn't it? And it prevents your mind from developing. I've promised myself to go away and do a pilgrimage one day, if God lets me live long enough.'

When Ranu heard the news she came to see Opu. 'What's this story I hear, Opu, about your going away from here. It isn't true, is it?'

'Yes, it's true all right,' he replied. 'Ask Mummy if you don't believe me.'

Ranu did not believe him. The very idea seemed incredible; so she took him at his word and went into the house to ask Shorbojoya. When she heard that it was true and that they really were going, she was stunned. She called to Opu to come out into the yard. 'When are you going?' she asked him.

'The Wednesday after next Wednesday.'

'And won't you ever come back again?' Her eyes were now full of tears. 'You've always said that our Nishchindipur is a lovely little village, and that no other place has a river or open country as beautiful as ours. How can you go away and leave it?'

'It's not my fault,' replied Opu. 'I never said I wanted to go. It's Daddy who's so set on going. He says we can't afford to live here. But I'll give you all my copy books before I go, Ranu. And perhaps when we're grown up we shall see one another again.'

'You never finished that story in my exercise book; and you didn't sign it either. I think you're horrid.'

She brushed the tears away from her eyes, and ran out of the yard as fast as she could. Opu felt that it was unreasonable of her to be cross with him like this; and he could not understand why she should be. Surely she did not think it was his idea that they should go away!

A little later he went down to the tank for his bath, and there he met Potu and told him the news. Potu had not heard it, and he was very distressed when Opu told him. His face dropped, and he said with bitter disappointment in his voice, 'I've been to such a lot of trouble to get a place ready for us to fish in. I actually climbed down into the water to clear the weeds away. It wasn't an easy job, and I wouldn't have done it for anybody else but you. And now I don't suppose you'll ever go fishing there, will you?'

This year the Swing Festival in honour of Ram, the Chorok Puja to Shiva and the Krishna ceremonies were more than usually close together, following one after the other at intervals of only a few days. It had always been a season of inexpressible delight for Opu. He and his sister never had time even to eat or sleep. Now it had come round again, and as far as Opu was concerned it was not going to be any less wonderful than it had always been.

Aturi, the old witch, died on Chorok Puja day. Near her double-thatched cottage was that part of the open country they called the New Field, where the fair was to be held as it had been for a number of years past. Crowds of people were going in that direction and Opu joined them. He was the same Opu who had crashed through the bamboo grove in his terror to get away from the old witch; but he was only a little boy then, and as he thought of the incident now he laughed. He knew that Aturi was not a witch, and never had been. She was just a poor, friendless old woman, who had to live quite alone beyond the limits of the village. There was no one to look after her, for she had neither son nor daughter. If there had been a single soul she could call her own, she would never have been reduced to such a miserable solitary existence, living day in and day out, as she had to do, in that desolate house; nor would she have been left to die such a lonely death, without anyone to do anything for her, even to perform the last rites. And now she was gone. Panchu, the son of one of the fishermen, went into her house and dragged out her precious jar. It was still full of slices of dried mango. The old woman used to collect windfalls, and when she had dried the fruit and sliced it she wandered round from market to market trying to sell it. Opu knew that she did because only the year before, during the Chariot Festival, he had seen her at the fair with her wares.

It was the Chorok Puja, but somehow this year it proved to be a hollow thing to Opu. Last year his sister had bought herself a new picture at the fair and she was so happy. Opu remembered it well. They had quarrelled that morning, and in the afternoon Durga had said to him, 'Opu, I'll give you some money. See if you can find me a picture of Sita's Abduction at the fair.' Opu scoffed at the idea. 'You and your stupid pictures;' he said. 'I refuse to buy you anything so silly. Why don't you get a picture of the battle between Ram and Ravan?' 'How like a boy!' Durga had replied. 'All you can think about is war and battles. What's wrong with a picture about a goddess anyway?' Opu had never had any respect for his sister's taste in pictures.

Yet how he missed her now! The red flowers in the hedge reminded him of her; as did the singing of the birds and the swinging clusters of flowers on the orkolmi bushes; and he felt very lonely. The only living creature to whom he could run and share his pleasures had gone away and left him. So far away too! And she would never, never come back and play with him again.

Above the confused noise and general hubbub of the fair Opu heard the sound of a flute. Somebody was playing a beautiful tune he had never heard before and he went at once to see who it was. It was Haran Mal. He had a stack of bamboo flutes on the ground by his side, and he was playing a tune on one of them to advertise them. Opu asked him how much they cost. Haran Mal knew Opu very well. He had often been called in to repair the thatched roof over the kitchen. 'What's this I hear about you going away, Khoka?' he asked. 'Where are you going to?' Opu bought one of his flutes for a pice and a half. 'Show me how it works, Uncle Haran,' he said. 'Which hole do you put your finger on?'

His mind went back to a tune he had heard a few months ago. Something had woken him up and for a while he had not been able to get to sleep again. It was a black night, and as he lay there in the darkness he could hear away in the distance the monotonous, regular thump-thump of the fishermen's nets and baskets as they worked by the river in the light of their lamps. Suddenly he heard another sound, from much further away. It seemed to be coming from the path, singing a full-throated song. Very few people walked across the factory-field late at night; but occasionally someone did; and often Opu lying between sleeping and waking was able to recognize what it was that the unknown wayfarer was singing as he made his way home by the light of the moon. Usually it was one of Modhu Kan's songs, which Opu knew very well; and he would lie listening to the sound of it as it faded slowly into the distance. That night however the song he heard was a new one. He did not recognize it then, and he had not been able to recapture the melody of it since. It seemed not of this earth, but as if some beautiful goddess of music herself had walked singing down the road which leads from a sleep to a sleep and disappeared before he was fully awake. He did not hear her sing again, yet he never forgot the sound of her voice as he heard it that night.

Peasant children from the villages round about were trooping home in small groups after the Chorok Festival, the boys wearing brightly coloured shirts and the girls new, unbleached saris; and some of the boys were playing flutes as they walked along. Many of them came from as far away as eight or ten miles, but they all had something to take home with them, cork birds, wooden dolls, fans made of coloured paper, painted jars and curd pots. Chinibas the sweet-seller had opened a vegetable and confectionery stall at the fair, and Opu had bought two pice worth of fried vegetables from him, though he did not eat them until he got home. As he walked away he wondered whether there would be a fair like this in the place they were going to. Would he ever see a Chorok or a Krishna festival again? They might not have fairs in Benares, he thought to himself; and he made up his mind there and then, if they did not have them, he would ask his father to let him come back to Nishchindipur at fair time. He could always stay with his aunt for a few days.

The day after the festival season ended, the packing began in earnest, for they were due to leave at about noon the next day, as soon as they had had their meal.

It was evening, and Opu's mother was in the kitchen frying some pancakes for him to eat while they were hot. Outside, in his Uncle Nilmoni's compound next door, the leaves of the coconut trees were sparkling in the moonlight. Opu's heart was very heavy. Though for a long time he had been very excited about going to a new place, now, as the day drew nearer, the song in his soul became sadder and sadder and he knew that it was going to hurt to say goodbye.

Here was the house that had always been his home; there the bamboo grove, the mango orchard, the river bank, and the place where he used to go for picnics with his sister. How dear they all were to him! Would there be a coconut tree like this one in the place they were going to? As long as he could remember he had known that coconut tree. How lovely its leaves looked in the moonlight! He remembered how he often used to watch the light glinting on them when he sat on the verandah playing cowries with Durga, and how he used to tell himself what a lovely place Nishchindipur was. This coconut tree, which stood near the edge of the forest not far from their kitchen steps, how could there be another one like it in the place they were going to? Would he be able to go fishing there? Would he be able to sail boats? Would he be able to play trains? Would there be steps down to the water like those under the kadamba tree? And what about his friend Ranu; and the Shonadanga plain? There were such wonderful things in Nishchindipur. Why had they to go away and leave them? It seemed so unnecessary.

Next day a curious thing happened.

Shorbojoya was out. She had gone to see celebration of the Savitri rite to which she had been invited. Horihor had finished his meal and was having a nap in the next room. Opu was sorting through some things on the shelf in his room to see whether he wanted to take any of them with him. While he was moving an earthenware vessel at the back of the shelf something rolled out of it and fell on to the floor. He picked it up and examined it with care. Inspite of the dust and the spiders' webs which covered it, he had no difficulty in recognizing what it was or recalling how it came to be there.

It was a small gold jar, the one which had been stolen from Shejbou's house last year.

It was noon and Opu was alone. He stood there for a long time, the jar in his hand, his mind far away; and in the stillness of that hot summer day the bamboo grove creaked, and whispered a tale from the past. 'Poor little Durga!' he thought to himself. 'She must have stolen it and hidden it in that pot on the shelf.'

For a while he was lost in thought, and then, very slowly, he went out of the house and stood by the back gate. As far as his eyes could see, the bamboo grove was shimmering in the heat of the sun; and a fish hawk called its shrill cry from the top of a tree. It was the same sad hour of the day when that unhappy defeated prince of a bygone age had crept into hiding by the Dvaipayan Lake. For a moment Opu pondered, and then abruptly he hurled the jar into the heart of the grove where the bushes grew thickest. It fell among the dry leaves that lay in heaps near that very thorn bush through which the dog Bhulo crawled panting when Durga called him.

'There let it lie!' he said to himself. 'Nobody will ever know about it now, because nobody ever goes there.'

Opu did not tell a soul about the gold jar; he never spoke of it at all, not even to his mother.

Afternoon came, and the three of them climbed aboard Hiru's cart and found seats for themselves among their luggage under the awning which covered the cart. Hiru goaded the bullocks into motion; the heavy wheels creaked and their journey had begun. In the early morning there had been a few clouds in the sky but before ten o'clock they had disappeared, and by midday the vast orb of the summer sun was pouring its fire like burning rain upon the trees, roads and fields. Potu walked behind the cart for a long way before he turned to go back. 'Opu,' he said, 'a wonderful theatre party had been booked for our village festival this year; but you won't be here to hear them.'

'Yes, I know,' Opu replied. 'But you can get an extra programme and send it to me.'

The road ran alongside the Chorok field. The ground was littered with sliced coconut husks and they reminded Opu of the fair. Someone had cooked a meal not far from the road, for the earth was still charred from the fire, and there was a cooking vessel blackened with smoke lying close by. It was a new one too.

Horihor did not say a word. He was very uneasy. Was he doing the right thing? His ancestors had lived on that piece of land. He thought of the deserted compound next door, and how its glory had departed. Would the jungle swallow his house too? The evening lamp had burned there for years; but tonight no one would light it and all the rooms would be dark. What would his father Ramchand Tarkabagish think as he looked down from heaven?

The last house in the village was old Aturi's double-thatched cottage, and Opu kept his eyes fixed on it as long as it was in sight. The next landmark was a large orchard of date-palms, beyond which the cart came out on to the main road to Asharhu. As soon as the village finally receded from view Shorbojoya felt that all their poverty, all their sordid deprivation and the contempt they had had to suffer were now left behind. Ahead lay a new world, a new way of life, and a new prosperity.

The sun was setting as the cart rolled slowly across the Shonadanga plain. Horihor pointed out a large banyan tree which stood a short distance from the road. 'Look,' he said. 'That's the tree and there's the Thakurjhi Lake where the dacoits had their den.' Shorbojoya quickly leaned outside the

351

awning to have a look. What she saw was a stretch of marshy land and a vast banyan tree with a forest of hanging roots. She had often heard the story of the old Brahmin and his son. Fifty years or more ago, at about this time of the day and under that same banyan tree, her husband's ancestor had cruelly murdered that helpless old man and his innocent child, just for the sake of money. And that marshy land was all that remained of the Thakurjhi Lake where they had buried their bodies. How many months, how many years perhaps, had that poor mother waited in vain for her son to come! He never came. Shorbojoya's eyes suddenly misted over, and there was a catch in her voice.

The Shonadanga plain was the largest expanse of open country in that part of Bengal; and dotted about, here and there, were clumps of trees and bushes, silk-cotton trees, thorn trees, date palms with clusters of fruit hanging from them, shondali trees with their swinging flowers; and over them all, in the evening air, thrilled the piercing cry of the sing-my-bride bird. The plain went on for mile after mile, and above it stretched the blue sky, blue as a linseed flower. There was nothing to impede the view. The slightly undulating land was covered with coarse green grass, for there was no cultivation, only the occasional clump of trees and tangled thickets to break the unending plain. Ahead the earth track, as it led on from distance to distance, bent and swayed like a Baul singer, homeless and free. Some way on they came to the old bed of the Modhukhali. Long ago the river flowed there, but in time it dried up, leaving behind only sunken swamps to mark its course, like footprints on the road of life; and what had once been the wide channel of a living stream was now a field of lotuses. Opu's eyes, as he journeyed on, were taking in all the colours of the landscape and the beauty of the over-spreading sky; but on the canvas of his mind appeared and faded many a dream picture of the childhood which this day had brought to an end. He had left his village. It was now a thing of the past. He was on his way to places distant and unknown, perhaps to those many lands and that wonderful life he had seen in his dreams.

Horihor pointed out a village in the distance. 'That's Dhanche Palashgachi,' he told them. 'Just beyond it, is Natabere. Every year in August they hold a big fair there, outside the temple of Bonobibi. I've never seen such cheap pumpkins as you can get there.'

The moon had risen by the time they got to the Betravati River, and the water gleamed white as they ferried across. Asharhu bazar was on the other side. Today had been market day, and on the other ferry, which passed theirs in midstream, were several vendors talking at the top of their voices. Opu's cart had been taken on to the ferry with them, and when it was off-loaded on the other side, he asked his father to let him go and have a look round the market. It was not a large market, just a few stalls set in rows and divided from one another by matting partitions. He stopped for a while by a goldsmith's stall, fascinated by the click-clack of his hammer, and then he moved along to where a number of bullock carts were standing outside a shed, which turned out to be a storehouse for date molasses. They were now only eight miles from Majherpara station. The road there was broad, but not metalled. On either side were trees, banyan, pepal, and mulberry, all of them planted years ago by the old indigo sahibs; and the bright moonlight gleamed on the new leaves and filtered through the curtains of roots which hung down from the branches of the banyans.

It was Bengal and early summer, when field, grove and orchard ring with the kokil's gushing song, when the rose chestnuts bow their leafy branches under the weight of countless blossoms, and the south wind, drenched with moonlight and heavy with the scent of forest flowers, fans the ecstatic dance of summer. Here was all the season's magic, and Opu saw it with new eyes. Bengal! The unearthly beauty, which its fields and rivers, its untrodden forests and the changing glory of its moonlit face painted for him then, young though he was, became part of his life for ever, filling the pensive moments of his later working days with sweetness and inspiration.

It was about ten o'clock when they drew up outside the station. For the last hour or so Opu had been sitting impatiently wondering when they would get there; so the instant the cart stopped, he sprang down and bounded on to the platform. The half-past-eight train had been gone a long time, and when Horihor asked he was told that there would not be another train that night. It was all the fault of Hiru's two bullocks. If they had hurried Opu could have seen a train by now. He saw some bales of tobacco stacked together on the platform, and two porters were loading them into a contraption which was fitted with long bars. It looked like an iron box. The railway lines gleamed in the moonlight. At one end of the station near the lines were two red lights at the top of a pole; and at the other end there were two more red lights, also at the top of a pole. On a table in the station room there was a lamp on a four-legged stool and nearby lay a pile of exercise books with stiff covers. Opu stood at the door for a while looking in. The station clerk was pressing something which looked like the peg on a wooden sandal, and as he pressed it it made a clattering noise.

A station! A station! It would not be long now, only tomorrow morning. He was not just going to see a train, he was going to ride in one.

Opu was very reluctant to leave the platform, but his father himself came to call him. Horihor told him that the thing which looked like the peg on wooden sandal was telegraph instrument.

When Opu got back he saw that his mother had started cooking near a tank just outside the station. Nearby was another cart. He had noticed it before. Its passengers included a young married woman, some eighteen-or nineteen-years-old, and a youth. Opu was told that the young woman was married into a family named Bisvas, who lived at Hobibpur, and that she was going with the youth, who was her brother, on a visit to her parents' home. She and Shorbojoya were already on friendly terms, and were preparing the meal together: one was washing the daal and rice, and the other peeling the potatoes.

The train came in at half past seven next morning, though Opu had been out on the platform long before that, leaning over the edge and gazing open-mouthed down the line. 'Khoka, don't stand so near the edge,' his father shouted out to him as the train approached. 'Stand further back.' One of the porters too was asking people to stand back.

What a huge train it was! And what a terrible noise it was making! That thing in front was what they called an engine, wasn't it? How wonderful.

The young woman from Hobibpur also was curious to see the train as it approached the platform and she drew aside her veil to have a look.

When it stopped there was pandemonium. Everybody shouted at once; and bundles and packages were seized and dumped in the compartments. Opu's compartment looked just like a big room. It had wooden benches facing one another down either side; and the floor seemed to be made of cement. There were doors and windows too, real ones.

The train was big and heavy, and now that it had stopped Opu wondered whether it would ever be able to get going again. Perhaps it would not! He would not have been surprised to hear the station men shouting out, 'All of you get out. The train won't be going today.' Then he caught sight of a man with a bale of thatch grass on his head standing outside the fence, waiting for the train to go so that he could get across the line; and he felt sorry for him; for he must surely be disappointed that he was not going to have a ride in a train. Hiru the cartman was there too, standing near the gate watching the train.

The train started. It had a curious swaying, jerking movement. Opu had never felt anything like that before. In no time they had left the station behind, and all the people in it, the bales of tobacco on the platform and Hiru the cartman standing gaping after them; and soon they were running through fields of thatch grass. The trees on either side were running past the windows. And how fast they were going! This really was a train! It was making the countryside whirl round and round; and trees, bushes, long grass and thatched cottages were being hurled together so that he could hardly tell one from another. From under the train came a long grating sound, as if someone was turning a millstone; and what an astonishing noise the engine was making in front!

The signal outside Majherpara station got further and further away.

Opu's mind went back to another day a long time ago. He and his sister were out looking for the calf, and they went to look at the railway line. They ran so fast that they were both out of breath. How different it was then from now!

The trees that lined the metalled road from Asharhu to Durgapur receded slowly until in time they merged into the horizon; and he saw the earth track from the village winding its way towards them across the Shonadanga plain. Near the bend in the track where it turned in the direction of Nishchindipur he could see the rose-apple tree he knew so well, and standing under it, staring after the train, was his sister, pale-faced and sad.

They had not brought her with them; they had all come away and left her behind. Though she had been dead for a long time now, he always felt her near him when he was in any of the places where the two of them used to lay together, by the river, in the bamboo grove, or under the mango tree. Every corner in their dilapidated old house in Nishchindipur still spoke to him of her loving though invisible presence; and now he was being parted from her for ever.

He knew that no one else had ever really loved Durga, no one, not even his mother. No one else was sorry that she was being left behind.

Suddenly Opu's heart was filled with a curious emotion. It was not grief, nor was it loneliness. He did not know what it was. It was compounded of so many feelings, so many memories, that flashed across his mind in a single moment of time: Aturi the witch, the steps down to the river, the path under the chalta tree, Ranu, the games he played in the afternoon, the games he played at midday, Potu, Durga's face, and all the things she longed for and never got.

And there she was, still watching.

Then the words of his heart found expression in tears, as time and time again he struggled to send her a message: 'I'm not really going away, Didi ... I haven't forgotten ... it's not that I want to leave you ... they're taking me away!'

It was true. He had not forgotten, and he did not forget.

Later in his life when he became so well acquainted with the earth and its girdle of ocean and tresses of blue; when his whole body thrilled to the speed of movement; when from moment to moment, as he stood on the deck of a ship at sea, the unearthly beauties of the blue sky flashed new on his sight; when the blue slopes of a mountain wreathed with vineyards faded from distance to distance and vanished beyond the dim bounds of the ocean's horizon; when the sweet siren melody from some far-off shore, faintly discerned through a concealing haze, came to his ears like the voice of the lord; then, and at all times like them, his memory took him back to a stormy monsoon night, to a dark room in an old house and the ceaseless noise of the rain, when the daughter of a poor village family spoke to him from her bed of sickness, and said, 'Opu, when I get better will you take me to see a train?'

The distant signals at Majherpara station became fainter and fainter; and then finally he could see them no more.

Glossary

alta	red lac, used by women to dye the edges of their feet
Bagdi	a low caste
Bauri	a low caste
beel	a strech of flood water
boudi	short form of *bou didi,* literally elder brother's wife
bouma	a term of address and reference to one's son's wife or a woman treated as having similar status
Chorok	name of an annual festival in honour of Lord Shiva held in the last few days of the Bengali year

Glossary

daal	a generic name for nine different species of pulse grown in Bengal
dhuti	loin cloth
Goyala	of a low caste, whose occupation is that of a milkman
Gajon	name of a particular form of singing and dancing in honour of Lord Shiva, performed on the occasion of Chorok by mendicant devotees of Shiva known as sannyasis
holud	turmeric
Imon	a raga in Indian classical music
jatra	a stage entertainment which has been popular in Bengal for centuries. The play is accompanied by instrumental music and permits of interludes of singing dancing and improvised buffoonery. The female parts were played by boys.
khoyer	name of an astringent bark eaten with betel nut
kirtan	a song festival in honour of Krishna with whom are usually associated his consort Radha and saint Chaitanya.
luchi	puri, a light puffed pancake
sannyasis	ordinarily, the name given to a Hindu ascetic who has renounced the world.